Sean Padraic was born in country New South Wales. His grandfather ran a pub and during the beer shortage of the 1930s brought in beer from South Australia on a truck accompanied by the local police sergeant. This was the start of a long association with New South Wales Police. Padraic currently lives in Chicago and this is his first published book.

CONFESSIONS OF A CROOKED COP

Sean Padraic as told by
Trevor Haken

ABC
Books

The ABC 'Wave' device is a trademark of the Australian Broadcasting Corporation and is used under licence by HarperCollins*Publishers* Australia.

First published as *Sympathy for the Devil* in 2005 by ABC Books
for the Australian Broadcasting Corporation.
This edition published in 2010 by HarperCollins*Publishers* Australia Pty Limited
ABN 36 009 913 517
harpercollins.com.au

HarperCollins*Publishers*
Level 13, 201 Elizabeth Street, Sydney, NSW 2000, Australia
31 View Road, Glenfield, Auckland 0627, New Zealand
A 53, Sector 57, Noida, UP, India
77–85 Fulham Palace Road, London, W6 8JB, United Kingdom
2 Bloor Street East, 20th floor, Toronto, Ontario M4W 1A8, Canada
10 East 53rd Street, New York NY 10022, USA

National Library of Australia Cataloguing-in-Publication data

Padraic, Sean.
   Confessions of a crooked cop / Sean Padraic.
   ISBN 978 0 7333 2817 6 (pbk.)
   Includes index.
   Haken, Trevor.
   New South Wales. Royal Commission into the New South Wales Police Service.
   Police corruption - New South Wales.
   Police misconduct - New South Wales.
   Ex-police officers.
   Australian Broadcasting Corporation.
364.132309944

Cover design by Darren Holt, HarperCollins Design Studio
Cover images: image of surveillance video tape by NSW Police/Newspix;
   money by Shutterstock.com
Typeset in 10.5/16pt Minion by Kirby Jones

CONTENTS

'A FAIR DINKUM ROYAL COMMISSION'

As an independent politician, John Hatton spoke out about police corruption in New South Wales. He had a reputation for honesty, and people with stories to tell knew that he would hear them out. He would act on information and it seemed the more hopeless the case, the more passionate he became. While Hatton had the protection of parliament to help expose the truth, there was still danger in what he did.

Senator Don Chipp, the founding leader of the Democrats, had raised questions in Federal Parliament about the need for an inquiry into the administration of law in New South Wales. In State Parliament, John Hatton said what many feared: that the police force was out of control. Hatton faced a largely uninterested press, a hostile police force and a weary public. Yet his ripples of activism and growing public awareness eventually forged into the tide that brought about the Royal Commission into the New South Wales Police Service.

John Hatton has an intensity and passion common to people with a mission. He is a man who is never short of words or an opinion. He believes in the truth and speaks as if every word can make a difference. In recent years, Australians voted for John

Hatton as a National Treasure so it is clear that people valued what he said and did. This acknowledgment by the public is something that still moves him.

Journalist Frank Walker wrote at the time 'Whatever judge's name ends up on this inquiry, it will always be the Hatton Royal Commission into Police Corruption'.

While history has not recorded it this way, Hatton and many others know the truth. When pressed for a summary of his contribution to the establishment of the Royal Commission, John Hatton told me: 'It would appear to be immodest if you quote me directly, but the truth is that it would not have happened without me'.

There are few who would disagree with Hatton, and, although he qualifies his remarks, these include the former police minister, Paul Whelan.

Whelan spoke to me about John Hatton, whom he called a hero:

> He was very anti-corruption and had his teething in the mid 1980s with the disappearance of the Griffith fellow — Don Mackay. With that Hatton learnt a lot about the Police Service and the way it worked, and the way it should not have worked. He had a lot of issues; he got a lot of informal information from people within the Service. Some were disillusioned, some were not the right informants for him, but some were. And to a certain extent, I have to say he was quite brave — he just ploughed on and if you don't worry about the cause of it but worry about the justifications and effect of it, then Hatton would have to be up there as a political hero. He did a great job. No one can deny that. But having said that, I think the merit of the argument he put in the Parliament about formation of his Royal Commission

wasn't new stuff, but there was a new regime in the opposition, a new political will in the Labor opposition to do something about it.

In Hatton's view, there were many forces that led to the Royal Commission. There had been a long history of exposure of actual police corruption, which, over a period of time, created a climate of opinion that police corruption remained rife. Then there were some specific events that set the stage for a Royal Commission, such as the Rigg Inquiry. The Rigg Inquiry had looked into the attempt of Angus Alexander Rigg to kill himself in the cells of Milton police station in 1991. The police response in that case had been one of paper shuffling and obfuscation.

The Rigg Inquiry described the reaction to the television program *A Current Affair* as 'touching off a terminal rupture in relations between the then minister and the Commissioner of Police' since Mr Pickering was not appropriately advised of the incident by the police service.[1]

Hatton sees the Rigg Inquiry as a pivotal point in the minds of many who sat in parliament. First, parliamentarians were directly involved through the committee that consisted of members of both sides of parliament. It became clear to these members that police were prepared to lie under oath. John Hatton told me: 'To a lot of thinking people in parliament, this was a gross distortion of the Westminster system'.

In the inquiry into the relationship between Police Commissioner Lauer and Police Minister Pickering, it was accepted that Lauer warned Pickering with the words, 'If you put shit on me, I'll put shit on you'. Hatton made a key speech in parliament pointing out that it was an extraordinary situation where the police commissioner could threaten a minister. A parliamentary committee had found that Lauer did threaten a minister of the

Crown and yet the Minister resigned and the Police Commissioner had his time extended. The words Hatton used in Parliament were that this 'stood the Westminster system on its head'.

It is John Hatton's view that there has always been a group of MPs within both the Liberal and Labor Parties that knew there was corruption within the police force but thought that it was benign. Suddenly, some of the more conservative members of the committee such as Liberal Andrew Tink and National Party member Don Page were stunned by the behaviour of the police at the inquiry.

Hatton claims that it had a dramatic effect on people such as Bruce Baird and the Speaker of the parliament, Kevin Rizzoli, even though they voted with their party against the establishment of the Royal Commission into the NSW Police Service. It is also Hatton's view that the inquiry changed the view of a lot of conservatives who would traditionally have supported the activities of the police without question.

It's conventional wisdom in State politics that governments take on the police force at their peril. Hatton pointed out in his August 1996 submission to the NSW Police Royal Commission document 'Police and the Community — The Necessity for Change' that 'It is an undeniable fact that governments are afraid of the perceived political power of the police force'. This view was already developed in Hatton's Churchill Report on accountability: 'The significant political clout of police and particularly police unions will continue to be skillfully used to manipulate divisions between governments and oppositions to slow down the introduction of mechanisms of external scrutiny and accountability.'[2]

John Hatton also points out that police are able to attack sensitive electorates through suggestions that crime is on the rise or that a politician or party is soft on crime and does not support the police on the front line. One only needs to have witnessed the competition to see who is 'toughest on crime' in the last state elections in NSW to know that Hatton's view is vindicated.

Hatton feels that the Wood Royal Commission broke, at least for a limited time, the spell that the police had on parliament. The members of parliament believed that the police had very important political influence. Not only because there are over 12,000 police, as well as their families and friends; but because they can make life hard for local Members who fail to support police by simply manufacturing or highlighting crime in the Member's constituency.

At one point, the Police Public Relations Media Branch had over twenty-six members. Hatton explains: 'It was an enormous PR machine. Local cameramen and news reporters in country towns and major radio and television stations depend directly on the police for scoops. It is no coincidence to find yourself left out of the picture if you are seen as a consistent critic of the police.'

When John Hatton stood to deliver his speech in parliament calling for a Royal Commission, amazing scenes ensued. Hatton's secretary had to come up from Nowra for the delivery and things were running late.

'It was a very nerve-wracking time because we had a computer problem. The time had been booked and advertised, and people were waiting for Hatton to detonate a big charge on the floor of parliament, and we couldn't get the bloody speech out of the computer.'

Journalist Frank Walker reported that Premier John Fahey let Hatton talk on despite the embarrassing pauses and shuffling. His speech against the NSW Police Force lasted 80 minutes.[3]

Hatton's secretary was feeding material to him while he was speaking. She was going back and forth and got lost wandering in the corridors of parliament. She ended up wandering into the private Member's area. According to Hatton, 'There she heard Police Minister Griffith on the phone saying "Tony, Hatton's on his feet, lying his head off. You'd better get some troops over here, straight away. I need some people in the Gallery".' Hatton's secretary gave evidence at the Royal Commission into the New South Wales Police Service about this matter.

The public galleries soon filled up with uniformed police officers 'all glaring down on the parliament'. They came from all over the place — the 'police radio and phone network ran hot'. Officers ranging from Inspector right through to Assistant Commissioners were sitting there in full uniform. As Hatton recalls, 'Griffith, a Minister of the Crown, directly organised the intimidation of parliament.'

It is no wonder senior police felt threatened by the speech. Hatton, sounding like John Steinbeck's Tom Joad, declared that his motion 'speaks out for those who have spoken out, who have been ostracised, who have been vilified, who have been set up, who have been threatened, sometimes assaulted and, in two cases, shot at'.

It was reported that in parliament Police Minister Griffiths attacked Hatton as 'paranoia personified', 'a poor man's Sherlock Holmes' indulging in 'fantasy not fact', 'a liar' and 'a disgrace to parliament'.[4]

Hatton says that the Labor Party showed some courage in supporting his call for a Royal Commission into the NSW Police Service. 'I remember negotiating with the Labor Party and they knew my reputation. It was really my reputation over a long period of time; it's the force of integrity. Carr was prepared to go with me, but it took courage, especially coming up to an election …' Hatton said to Carr, in words that probably still ring in his ears, 'You will not be disappointed'. Hatton says now, 'It must have been the understatement of the year'.

When Opposition Leader Bob Carr supported John Hatton's call for a Royal Commission into the Police Service, he did so in the knowledge that he could well be creating political problems for himself down the track. Immediately, the Commissioned Officers' Association, which represented senior police officers, wrote to Carr to complain about his support, saying that he was using the Police Service as a tool and a medium to gain political advantage. The Police Association also condemned the Labor Party.

The Liberal Premier John Fahey had been quoted in the *Sydney Morning Herald* as saying that he supported the Independent Commission Against Corruption (ICAC), and that instead of a Royal Commission the allegations of police corruption should be investigated by ICAC. ICAC had had some success with reports, such as 'the climate conducive to corruption' it found surrounding land deals on the New South Wales north coast. In February 1994, Ian Temby released findings on ICAC's first major inquiry into the NSW police. There were ten people named as corrupt, including Gaming Squad officer Bradley Conner who was alleged to have tipped off an illegal gaming house about raids. The perception was that ICAC had failed to properly deal with this issue.[5]

Not surprisingly, the former Police Minister Paul Whelan told me that the state Labor Party played a large role in the establishment of the Royal Commission:

In percentage terms 94 per cent. Because there were 47–50 voted for it and with the three independents — Hatton, Moore and McDonald — we were able to win the argument here in the Lower House and therefore, ultimately, the Royal Commission had ... to be created. But having done that, then it was up to the Government to try and denude the effect of resolution, and we were able to defeat them on that as well. It was both a matter of courage and also a matter of conviction that there had been a long period over decades of reports about police and bribery and corruption, let alone inefficiency, and one begets the other actually.

It was propitious for us as an opposition to seize that opportunity. We were reasonably confident ... that we were showing up really to be a viable alternate government. We wanted to have a Royal Commission. It was time to give leave to a Royal Commission to find what it could and Judge Wood did that.

John Hatton feels that the Liberal Government still did the right thing and highlights the honesty of John Fahey in choosing James Wood as the Royal Commissioner. Fahey picked Justice Wood because he knew him personally to be an honest and capable man. It is suggested by sources that were very close to Justice Wood that, prior to his appointment as Royal Commissioner, John Fahey offered Justice Wood the position of Commissioner of ICAC. Wood had declined.

Hatton's view of ICAC was very clear. He felt that ICAC had failed to properly investigate the information it had at hand. It lost the opportunity to properly investigate allegations of corruption within the Police Service. Quoted at the time the police whistleblower Kim Cook said, 'They've been an abysmal failure'.[6] In the parlance, ICAC was said to have leaked like a sieve. It was an organisation that had used NSW Police as investigators, and this is the reason put forward for its leaking of information. The Wood Royal Commission would not suffer from the same problems that had plagued earlier inquiries. The then Acting Head of ICAC, John May, could not see the problem and told a parliamentary committee that he was bewildered that parliament had decided to set up a separate body to look at police corruption. Hatton comments:

The thing that parliament couldn't do was choose the Royal Commissioner, but what they did, based on previous experience of Royal Commissions, was to ensure that no serving or past NSW police would be a part of the Royal Commission.

Paul Whelan agrees with Hatton:

Yes, it was a very important point. We couldn't run the risk of NSW Police Officers either directly or indirectly providing information and, to use a sporting analogy, they had to be sin-binned for a while until we could get the reserve players on who came from interstate and who were not part of the cops' milieu in NSW. Now that's a bit unfair, and having said that, you either make this break or you don't, and there's no half measures.

According to John Hatton, you 'fix' a Royal Commission by doing the following things: First, you narrow the terms of reference as much as you possibly can; second, you choose the chief investigator who in turn chooses the investigation team; third, you choose the counsel who in turn chooses the legal team; and finally, you choose the judge. Having done all this, you know what the answers are going to be.

In this case, such a 'fix' was headed off by the wording of the motion stating that the Royal Commission would not have restricted terms of reference, and that the Royal Commissioner would decide who the chief investigators would be, ensuring that they would not be from the NSW Police Service. The Royal Commissioner would also choose the legal team. In Hatton's words: 'That set the stage for an absolutely fair dinkum Royal Commission.'

And so the Royal Commission issued by the Governor, by letters patent under the public seal on 13 May 1994, appointed the Honourable James Roland Tomson Wood sole commissioner to make inquiry into, and report on, the operation of the NSW Police Service. Wood appointed as his senior legal counsel Gary Crooke QC who had vast experience at the Fitzgerald Inquiry (which investigated police corruption in Queensland). Although New South Wales was a very different situation, there would obviously be some lessons — both good and bad — from the Fitzgerald Inquiry that could be put to use in New South Wales.

The Director of Operations — who controlled the hands-on task of investigations in the field — was Nigel Hadgkiss, a commander from the Federal Police. Hadgkiss was also very experienced, after a career that included a previous Royal Commission, and work with the Hong Kong Police, Scotland Yard, and the National Crime Authority. He brought with him a seasoned crime fighter from the Federal Police, Bruce Onley, to assist with the investigators. Counsel assisting the Commission included John Agius, Virginia Bell, James Black and Paddy Bergin. Police from every state, except New South Wales, were hand-picked by Hadgkiss and Onley. These police and analysts were relocated to Sydney to start the long process of targeting areas of inquiry and specific squads and individuals.

For all involved it would be stressed that they were dealing with people for whom the element of surprise was non-existent, who were well-versed in surveillance and investigative procedures, and who were determined not to break the code of silence. This Royal Commission would have to do things differently and use different technologies and approaches if it was to succeed.

Such a fresh approach was key to the Commission's success. The way things were to be done in the field, in the office and in the hearing room were meticulously planned in the very early stages.

Its careful approach lulled those who were not in the loop into a false sense of security and a smug belief that this would be another inquiry that went nowhere. (A *Daily Telegraph–Mirror* cartoon of the time depicted a be-wigged judge holding an antique gun atop an elephant with a sign on its hide saying 'White Elephant Hunting Safari'. Justice Wood had a copy of this cartoon framed and hung in his office, which was both a sign of his self-deprecating humour and a motivation to prove the cynics wrong.)

The announcement of the Royal Commission into the NSW Police Service was a worthy news item, even overseas. The *Gulf News* wryly suggested that it was perhaps two centuries too late. Although late in coming, Wood wanted this inquiry to have some teeth, and so asked the State government for increased powers even before it had begun investigations. These included the full range of telephone tapping powers as well as powers of arrest and the powers to seize documents.

Wood also headed off the potential non-cooperation of whistle-blowers when it was proposed by Tony Lauer that Ian Temby be appointed as representative of the police. Temby had only left his position at ICAC four months earlier and whistleblowers feared a very real conflict of interest. Wood argued that it would be unacceptable if witnesses felt they could not assist the Commission for any reason, Premier Fahey intervened and ordered the NSW Police Commissioner to withdraw the brief given to Ian Temby. Temby would not represent the police service and Wood had passed his first test in the eyes of many who hoped this Royal Commission would indeed be 'fair dinkum' — and that included a jaded press.

Temby called the intervention of John Fahey an 'unnecessary political act', but others thought differently. The *Sydney Morning Herald* said, 'Witnesses' fears became a practical threat to the success of the Royal Commission'.[7] The *Canberra Times* editorialised that 'Mr Temby, in such circumstances, should have had more sense than accept the brief and Mr Lauer should have had more sense than to hire him. The whole episode reflects rather more on their judgement, and perhaps their arrogance in not recognising the problems, than it does on Mr Fahey'.[8] Mark Coulton wrote that 'Ian Temby does not have a political brain'. In the same article he went on to say that Fahey had ridden right over the top of his Police Minister Mr West, who a day earlier had refused to dump Temby.[9]

Wood then stopped Lauer creating an internal police unit; the fear was that this unit might have had the effect of controlling information between the police service and the Royal Commission. The then Minister for Police, Mr West, acceded to a request from Wood that the more serious complaints of misconduct against officers of the NSW Police Service be referred to the Royal Commission. Wood was confronting many seasoned headkickers and he did not blink.

John Hatton applauded Wood's actions but not everyone shared Hatton's enthusiasm for the Royal Commission or the Commissioner. Former Premier of NSW Nick Greiner was quoted in the *Sydney Morning Herald* at the time as saying that the Royal Commission would be an 'exercise in self-indulgence' and that it would waste 'wads of money'. Hatton and the two independents in parliament, Clover Moore and Peter MacDonald, had earlier forced Greiner to resign as Premier over the Metherell affair. (ICAC's Ian Temby had found that Greiner and a senior minister had acted corruptly in appointing Terry Metherell to a senior public service position. They both later successfully appealed but their political careers were over).

Others joined in the chorus. Prominent Sydney criminal lawyer Chris Murphy claimed that 'Lawyers are laughing at Justice Wood's Royal Commission into corruption in the police force before the paint dries on the door'.[10] Sydney solicitor John Marsden complained about Wood to the *Sydney Morning Herald*:

'Unfortunately, he's gone through private schools, lives on the North Shore and has no touch with reality. He probably doesn't know if his children have ever smoked a joint or not.'

The headquarters branch of the NSW Police Union called on the Premier to rescind the order for the Commission. Over 100 branch members of the Police Association pledged support for Commissioner Lauer and deplored the actions of the Independent MP John Hatton. Police Minister Griffiths predicted that 'silly' allegations would surface. Mr Lauer had spoken at the Police Associations conference earlier in the year and was quoted as saying, 'We have been regaled with … the same litany of allegations of police corruption which properly belong in history books. There is no entrenched police corruption in the police service today and I stand by that statement.' He added later in the speech that since Ian Temby had taken a somewhat positive spin in his Miloo Inquiry, Wood would come to similar conclusions.

Commissioner Lauer accused MP John Hatton of conducting a personal vendetta against his leadership of the police force.[11] Police Minister Terry Griffiths maintained that entrenched corruption did not exist in the force and that any criminal activity was confined to 'a few rotten apples'. He told the *Sunday Telegraph* that he feared the commission would become a 'warehouse' for the vaguest rumours of corruption. The attack on Hatton continued with Griffiths telling the *Telegraph* that 'Hatton has been looking for the Royal Commission for twenty years. This is his reason for living. I think it is to a point of almost obsession. I feel sorry for him I really do.' At the opening of a new police station in Wellington NSW, Griffiths was quoted as saying 'I don't want to give any credence to the Commission'.

And so pressure was on to get results. The critics were already on the attack and a strong leader was needed, someone with intelligence, skill, experience and stamina. Justice Wood was that man.

Justice James Wood is a trim, athletic man. Quietly spoken, he possesses a gentle manner that charms most who meet him. He is publicly guarded but warm with those working with him. Despite having achieved so much in his legal career his manner remains humble.

Wood was appointed a Supreme Court Judge at the age of forty-two. Although he has a traditional conservative background, he is not afraid to go against the tide of popular opinion. When powerful Sydney radio announcers were supporting the principle of mandatory sentencing, Wood spoke out against it as a threat to the freedoms that we cherish. He passionately believes in the law and has a vocation in working within the system. There are some judges who 'retire to the bench', Justice Wood was not one of those. He also has a reputation for hard work. In his spare time away from the bench he is a triathlete. His physical fitness was an asset, for it was said at the time that he would need all his skills of strength, endurance and cunning in the years facing him at the inquiry.

Justice Wood was well known in court for his efforts to cut the time people spent waiting for trials and cases to come up. In criminal cases, he had shown compassion in sentencing those who were themselves sometimes victims, and was able to deal severely with those whose crimes were heinous. These included John Wayne Glover, the infamous 'Granny Killer', who was sentenced to life imprisonment.

As a duty judge he would see many different cases in one morning. Says one former employee, 'He had an amazing ability to quickly read and understand various documents about a matter that lawyers had been working on for months'.

Wood had experience in all areas of law, from commercial matters to personal injury claims. The majority of his time on the bench, however, was spent dealing with criminal trials. This practical experience, particularly in criminal matters, would prove to be invaluable. Hatton comments, 'It is absolutely true to say that if you did not have Jim Wood in that chair, [the Royal Commission] would never have happened in the way it did.' As Bob Carr once put it, 'James Wood ... brought his years of experience as a judge to bear in exposing corruption and systemic weaknesses.'[12]

Most police and commentators saw the Royal Commission as yet another inquiry that would run dead. They opined that the code of silence within the police brotherhood and the criminal milieu would not be broken and that there was a lack of will to get to the truth. They would be proved wrong.

Sometimes the right circumstances can create opportunities. The right people were now in place. The final ingredient needed to make the Commission a success would be a high profile 'roll over'. Trevor David Haken was to be that element.

CHAPTER 1

DEAD MAN TALKING

'Better to die once, than to suffer torment all my living days'

AESCHYLUS, *PROMETHEUS BOUND*

Trevor Haken lives and breathes somewhere in hiding. But he is also dead and living in hell, a hell of his creation. All as a result of his decision, after a career as a corrupt police officer, to become an undercover informant for the Royal Commission into the New South Wales Police Service and expose the truth.

His police badge sits mute on my desk, inscribed *Detective Sergeant Trevor Haken*. It is one of the few relics of a tumultuous life. Born in 1950, for a short time Haken lived a normal suburban life, and then the world seemed to turn on him. As a young boy scout, Trevor suffered at the hands of his scoutmaster who molested him. While still a teenager, his father died. As a result, he felt that he was different from those around him, that he was an outsider, and it was a sensation he never liked. And so Haken joined the brotherhood of police and joined a way of life. When he broke the solidarity of his group, that life came to a bitter end. Oscar Wilde once said that the truth is rarely pure and never simple. It is a thought worth considering when looking at the life of Detective Sergeant Trevor Haken.

Over twenty-five years in the 'police force' (as it was known through that period), Haken progressed through the ranks. From the humble beginnings of the North Sydney traffic branch, he learnt about the kickbacks and perks that could come from associating with tow truck drivers and undertakers. Police would receive a 'spotter's fee' for work that was sent their way. This was his 'blooding' into the realities of policing following his initial training. Right from the start, it seemed that the police were open for business with everyone.

Haken then became one of the elite, a detective. Once you were a part of an elite squad, you were 'playing A grade'. As part of the Criminal Investigation Branch (CIB), he joined a power base that could move in on any investigation and take it over. In many ways, the CIB were a law unto themselves. This was particularly the case with the notorious 21 Division. Located in the training academy in Bourke Street, Surry Hills, 21 Division was the training ground for plainclothes officers; it was a subdivision of the CIB and controlled by it.

21 Division was a troubleshooting squad, which primarily dealt with prostitution and gambling. If there was a problem, then 21 Division would solve it very quickly, using whatever means deemed necessary. It was said that 'you didn't fuck with 21 Division, they fucked with you'. Haken would move on to Chatswood Detectives, to Phillip Street Detectives, and was a part of the Joint Federal and State Drugs Task Force. From Central Detectives and Chinatown, he then moved to Kings Cross as head of the Drug Squad and eventually ended up in charge of detectives.

Haken was not the most corrupt police officer in the force. There have been many who were more forceful and dangerous. There are detectives who have killed in order to protect their corrupt interests, some have even tried to kill other police officers to this end. Haken did nothing like this, but his crimes were significant. He became the bagman for corrupt payments in Kings Cross and then the middleman between the crooks and the system. The four main drug suppliers to Kings Cross pumped their stock through eight main outlets under the paid protection of police. In the year before he turned informant, Haken received about $68,000 from those who ran the clubs in which drug business took place in Kings Cross, individuals such as Bill Bayeh, 'Fat George' Pandelis Karepis (a known receiver of stolen goods, former operator of drug sale fronts the Pink Flamingo brothel and the Battlers Inn and 'the shooting gallery' 48A Darlinghurst Road); Robert Daher, 'Skinny Steve' Stavrou (part-owner of Porky's Stripperama and Love Machine) and others.

Most times, Haken's work with other detectives and his meetings with the criminal fraternity were opened and closed with long drinking sessions. Drunkenness has been described as nothing but voluntary madness; Bertrand Russell called it temporary suicide. The detective lifestyle was one of continual drinking of alcohol and illegal money. Alcohol has had a significant detrimental effect on policing in New South Wales. The mantra of Sydney detectives was that 'you never trust a man that doesn't drink'. The police culture absolutely embraced drunkenness. It was supposed to bond a group and nullify any feelings that came from dealing with the ugliness of the job and the people they dealt with. And so it was accepted that while on the job, many detectives would regularly drink themselves into oblivion, largely because they could. Proper management of detectives was almost nonexistent.

For those involved in taking illegal payment, 'the drink' as it was known, things were just as indulgent. Ironically, these detectives would have never described themselves as being corrupt. Their view was that they worked hard, played hard, and deserved whatever came their way for 'putting themselves on the line'. Haken explains, 'Everybody was doing it. It is just business, and that is what it was; everybody was out to make a dollar.' When corrupt detective Neville Scullion gave evidence to the Royal Commission, he was asked if entrenched police corruption extended back to the days when he was in Darlinghurst in the 1970s. He answered simply, 'I think it probably went back to the First Fleet.'

Detectives today are taught that good habits are developed by watching and imitating others. It is now an accepted policing premise that you need to practise at behaving well. It seems that in Haken's time as a detective, there was little in the way of good behaviour to follow. As a detective, time in between 'the drink' was spent making arrests. Yet again, this was a corrupt system. Haken explains, 'There were no rules, the only rule was to get a conviction.' Detectives saw themselves as the good guys, and if they believed someone was guilty then they would do whatever was needed to put the crook away. They saw the only issue as being law versus order, and they chose order and ignored the law. These arrests and convictions were made by illegal methods and were a part of everyday life for a detective.

Haken was an active part of a system that would 'verbal' witnesses (creating false statements and attributing them to the accused). These 'verbals' were mostly used in unsigned records of interviews and notebook confessions. Detectives would fabricate and 'load up' or plant evidence to incriminate a suspect. If a crook didn't have a gun present at a crime scene then a detective could easily provide one. It followed that by the time the matter came to court, he would conspire with other detectives and perjure himself to secure a conviction. If they chose to help a crook, detectives would 'gut a brief'. This is where documents or evidence were removed so that the charges would be dropped or a case would be weakened. On the other hand they could also 'salt' exhibits, which meant tampering with evidence to assist the prosecution. These methods were taught to detectives the way an apprentice would learn a trade. Ironically, detectives did not trust the justice system they were supposed to support.

Policing in Sydney followed similar patterns to police behaviour overseas. For example, the New York Police Department in Brooklyn was home to the infamous 'buddy boys'. These were police who had served properly for a long time but grew disillusioned when they saw drug dealers seemingly acting with impunity and making huge amounts of money. Initially, the 'buddy boys' arrested dealers to steal their money. Eventually they became involved in the protection and distribution of drugs themselves. Once a line is crossed, it is hard to know when to stop. In Sydney, it was hard to know if that line ever existed.

Haken and his fellow detectives would drop charges in return for payments (that is, accept bribes), prosecute 'on-the-spot fines' to save going to court (a form of extortion), steal money from drug dealers and other criminals (which they saw as just rewards for a job well done), and in various ways protect the interests of other criminals. The rationale was that there would always be crooks and dealers, so they could only really control and restrict it so that it was manageable. In short, Haken was a very active player in a perverted game of justice. He worked in an era when it was possible for criminals to be given the 'green light' by the CIB. The 'green light' meant that select crooks were allowed to rob banks and jewellery stores, deal drugs, hold up payrolls and the like with the protection of those charged with prosecuting them. Heads was tails and Sydney was 'open for business'.

All of these corrupt activities were a part of a system that was well established before Haken joined the force.

There were rules for police to follow, but detectives saw these as anachronistic. If the crooks were not using a rule book, then why should police? And so, many detectives would fabricate evidence to obtain convictions. If a case required a little extra evidence, then they were happy to supply the missing piece of the puzzle. Conversely, if someone was in need of a favour or was able to pay for the privilege, then the same piece of the puzzle could go missing. Although procedures were clearly stated, no one seemed to be following them and the hierarchy did not seem to be enforcing them. To many police, it seemed that much of the court's time was spent arguing the admissibility of evidence and it was a type of game. Many police therefore sought to subvert the court process to get the desired result.

The man convicted of the backpacker murders, serial killer Ivan Milat, had been previously tried for raping two women who he allegedly picked up while driving along the highway (the way he would later target the victims he murdered). Milat was found not guilty. Haken sees this as a classic example of someone who was obviously dangerous and should have been convicted no matter what the technicalities. Milat was represented by solicitor John Marsden who has stated that he 'got Ivan Milat off the rape of two girls in 1974. ... I had a job to do and I did it'[1]. In Haken's eyes, the legal games were played, Milat walked free and his violence escalated. A detective should have done whatever he had to do to prevent Milat from walking free. Haken still holds this view.

Trevor Haken first did the detectives course in 1977. He was taught to prepare records of interview and learnt what was legally admissible. He was then lectured by a number of legendary and 'successful' detectives. Joe Coco was one such person.

Coco was always around the squads in Darlinghurst, and at the time he was lecturing was the officer in charge of the Consorting Squad. Coco's lecture to aspiring detectives consisted of, 'Look, you're the goodies, they're the baddies. You've got a job to do on them and if you're not prepared to do a job on them ... well pack your bags and piss off out of this course.' (Coco later hanged himself in Surfers Paradise well before the Royal Commission into the NSW Police Service began hearings. It was said that he had tax problems as well as a serious illness.)

Haken was taught from day one at the academy that if you wanted to get things done or if you got into trouble, you battened down and stuck together and then you'd have no problems. This was emphasised even more during the detectives course. It seemed to Haken that everybody accepted this view of the way things were done. 'Crooks were crooks, and there was never any suggestion that we were crooks.'

Haken's approach was simple: the compilation of the record of interview was dependent on the attitude of the person he was interviewing. If they were compliant, then it may well be that the record of interview would be conducted in the correct manner. He states, 'but if they were a difficult person and they were to be convicted, then of course the record of interview was conducted in any manner that one thought proper to attain that conviction.'

The detectives course covered law and criminal investigation techniques. It also looked at how to ensure convictions. Haken comments: 'That's what's been so widely criticised, you know, the fabrication of evidence. Well, not so much the fabrication of evidence but the glossing of evidence to ensure that matters aren't going to be dismissed. Or, that there is sufficient evidence to ensure that there will be a conviction — that's probably a proper way of putting it.' In David Hickie's book *Chow Hayes-Gunman*, it was reported that in the 1950s when Detective Ray Kelly arrested the murderer Chow Hayes he told him, 'I'll tell as many lies as I can to convict you and you can tell as many lies as you can to beat it. Is that fair enough?'

How detectives wrote up their records of interviews was a matter of personal choice. Haken comments:

> I personally believed that unsigned records of interview were as believable as unicorns, you know. The Hold-up Squad used to use them time and time again and I thought it was just so pathetic. You'd get to a trial and they'd stand up and say, 'I did this record of interview and he was completely honest with me but then at the end of the interview he wouldn't sign it'. And you'd think, how can you? It was much better to put a verbal confession together in your notebook as an unsigned interview — that spontaneous, 'I'm sorry, you've got me copper' confession — and note a reluctance by the suspect to go into a signed record of interview.[2]

Although they had been used successfully for many years, Haken saw unsigned confessions as a poor option. There were a lot of other methods that could be used. The 'Bumper Farrell' school of bashing a suspect to obtain an interview was also used by some 'old school' police.[3] 'I personally thought it was stupid and futile,' says Haken. 'You take a bloke into a room and then bring him out and he needs bloody surgery. But some police were used to that way of doing things and they never changed.'

There were other forms of guile. 'If a crook gets into court and says, "look, this interview is all bullshit. I was in the room and they typed it out, but I didn't answer any questions. This bloke here didn't type it, he was sitting on top of the locker with no clothes on, or strumming a guitar" and of course the jury would say, "Hang on a bit, this bloke is a rabbit", but it did happen. You created a scenario that no jury would believe.'

Strange things went on in interview rooms — far stranger than the writers of a television series might think of. Any methods of interrogation that were available were used. Police were only limited by their imagination. For tough nuts they would argue they needed some heavy alternatives. Naked detectives or phone books wouldn't be enough for some.

> If you could threaten to lock up the girlfriend, wife, sister, brother or anyone else to get somebody on side, then you would. That's the thing, there were no rules. The only rule was to get a conviction. The means were not so important. What was important was putting the person in jail. And for the most part, the crooks were the crooks. We weren't putting people away who were not guilty!

Haken agrees these practices opened a gate to further abuse.

> They could jam an innocent person if someone was of the mind for that, and that could happen still. There is nothing that prohibits that at any stage when someone is in a position of authority and if you have that frame of mind. That's why I qualified it to myself that you jammed people that deserved it. There were people who locked away druggies that were not at the house at the time but they had been at the house before or were on their way. So it was just a case of moving it all around a little bit. It wasn't the case of them being innocent.

The Police Board annual report in 1985 conceded that during the 1960s and 1970s corruption was rife. Corruption in those years was blatant and led from the top. Police Commissioner Norm Allen (1962–72) falsified crime statistics and admitted that he could not stop corruption. Fred Hanson (1972–77) had gone hunting with drugs boss Robert Trimbole. His successor, Merv Wood (1977–79) was even charged with perverting the course of justice. And so as soon as he joined, Haken became a part of it all. You were either in the game or a 'squarehead', an outsider. Once it was known that you accepted the way things were, then you too would be accepted and allowed to participate.

Haken was an ordinary man who was now a part of an extraordinary world. With little or no management, this corrupt behaviour was allowed to explode. It was not a matter of 'a few bad apples' in the force; corruption was widespread and institutionalised, yet there was very little chance of Internal Affairs exposing this. At best, it concerned itself with occasional individual targets and was largely hampered by the code of silence among the brotherhood. Haken recalls:

> I was a regular at what turned out to be Internal Affairs in Hurstville. Any time you arrested somebody in the later years they would make a complaint, so it was no big deal. It got to the stage with investigators over there that they would sit you down, three in a room and say, 'We'll just do a report, see you later'.

For many years, the police force, the legal profession and politicians within New South Wales were able to act with little accountability. In trying to capture corrupt police, the Royal Commission eventually came across a number of solicitors who acted questionably. The criminal lawyer Maggie Sten was heard in a covertly recorded phone call telling drug dealer Bill Bayeh about a Royal Commission informer. 'He's [KX6] definitely doing us and they've [the Commission] booked him for about three days'. Caught on tape by the Royal Commission, she admitted that she had committed 'a complete dereliction of duty' and acted totally unprofessionally.[4] Haken informed the Royal Commission that Bill Bayeh was covertly recorded talking to Haken about information he was receiving about the Commission's activities.[5] He stated a certain solicitor at the Commission would tell Stan 'everything' and 'Maggie would tell Bayeh'.

Haken was to give evidence to the Royal Commission that the solicitor Val Bellamy met with him to discuss a way of letting his drug-dealing client off an assault charge. Bellamy suggested that he could get $5000 from his client for the charges to go away. When Haken explained that the victim had disappeared anyway, Bellamy still stung the client for $5000 which he and Haken split.

As E.J. Delattre points out, 'Few have ever maintained that human beings can be trusted to behave well unless they are held accountable'.[6] It is certain that many of the corrupt practices of police would not have been possible without the cooperation of the legal fraternity.

The public image of the police department was paramount. If police were actually caught acting corruptly, the department preferred to see the matter quietly disposed of and kept out of the public eye and press. The police hierarchy would often temporarily transfer a corrupt officer and later return the officer to the same posting.

There were attempts in the 1980s to reform the force by Commissioner Avery, who received death threats for his efforts. He set up inquiries into allegations of corruption by officers. He moved quickly in the early '80s and broke up the CIB. He decentralised the agencies and squads into four different regions, but unfortunately this only spread the corruption around.

The problems of promotion within the force had been going on for decades. Selection of candidates for senior positions was based on seniority not capability. Some very good street police made dreadful managers. The Royal Commission found that misleading information was often provided to committees assessing candidates. Many involved in the selection process failed to declare conflicts of interest and many decisions defied logic. Senior police would receive promotion towards the end of their careers, which left them little time or incentive to change anything. By that stage, their main interest seemed to be keeping their jobs and protecting their entitlements. Police opposed Avery's attempts to change the make-up of the force, as Haken testifies:

> The promoting of academia by Avery closed the door on a lot of experienced police and opened it to a wide-ranging group of incompetent but qualified people, who went up and just made a botch of it. This was when the police force stopped being a force and became a service, which is striving for a utopian society, something that will never happen ... If he had existed in a little English country town, he would have been fine, but in a city like Sydney it was a joke.

Many police saw it as unfair and became cynical and distrustful of the whole process. Disillusioned officers spoke about the only means of advancement as 'promotion by suction'. Morale was low and many police eventually lost faith in what they were doing. Their language reflected this disillusionment. There were many famous police expressions that reflected these feelings such as 'TJF' (The Jobs Fucked), 'NRMA' (Nothing Really Matters Anymore), 'POPO' (Passed Over and Pissed Off) and 'WOFTAM' (Waste Of Fucking Time and Money). Haken explains:

> When everything goes rotten, you say TJF. Where a senior constable was promoted to some sort of rank and bypassed a lot with more experience and who were a lot

better, it was POPO. And people who are not going anywhere are people who are not interested anymore. This would compound the view that well, if I'm not going anywhere and I can't make any more money, then NRMA.

Haken had reached the stage where he had become totally disillusioned with the brotherhood he had once enjoyed. His family life was in turmoil. His wife and children were precious to him but his life as a detective had taken its toll on his marriage. The long hours and the hard drinking were a lethal combination, and he could see that he either did something about his drinking or it would ruin him and his family life. Long before the Royal Commission, Haken sought to change his life. He says, 'The last drink I had was on the 30th of September 1990. I just realised I was just being "played off the break" and being done by other people because I was drinking too much. You become terribly blasé when you're half stung all the time.'

Haken has never done things in half measures. Going sober while working among Kings Cross detectives shows a certain strength of character. They would continually goad him about being on the wagon and try to tempt him to return to his old habits, but he stood firm. 'It was an extraordinarily hard change because your whole work and social life revolved around it. Remember, "never trust a man that doesn't drink". It was the first thing I was told as a policeman.'

There is nothing quite like the experience of staying sober whilst those around you get drunk. It does provide insight. His relationship with his wife had deteriorated and he was devastated to find that she was having an affair with another detective. His respect for the brotherhood was finally gone.

* * *

When the Royal Commission into the New South Wales Police Service was announced on 13 May 1994, most detectives thought it would be like so many inquiries before it. All agreed that if they 'held the line' and did not cooperate there would be nothing to worry about. The Royal Commission decided to approach most of the key players in Kings Cross. At the very least, it would let them know that something was happening.

Graham 'Chook' Fowler was driving to work at City of Sydney Police Station one morning when his car started playing up. When it stalled he pulled into a nearby service station, and as soon as his car was stationary two Royal Commission vehicles pulled alongside his vehicle. The investigators introduced themselves and announced their intention to investigate corruption at Fowler's station. While he was taken aback that these guys had seemingly appeared out of nowhere, he was unmoved by what they had to say. He had met plenty of 'toe-cutters' before. However, these investigators were different from any he had previously encountered. Most importantly, they were not from the New South Wales police. The Chief Investigator, Nigel Hadgkiss, was present. Hadgkiss was a Federal Police commander. Hadgkiss was accompanied by a number of other investigators and a barrister, John Agius, who was familiar to local police as a successful prosecutor. Their approach was business-like and discreet. Fowler predictably refused to cooperate and reported his encounter to Haken.

Haken too was approached by investigators from the Royal Commission. In Haken's case, the timing was perfect. His life was a mess, he was already under investigation and he was totally disillusioned. This perhaps was an opportunity to get out of the game once and for all. Haken thus had a dramatic opportunity presented to him. He wanted to make an impact.

On 2 September 1994, Trevor Haken decided to assist the Royal Commission into the NSW Police Service. In the parlance, he 'rolled'. Haken decided that if he were to assist the Royal Commission, he would have to do more than simply tell his story. He agreed to work as an undercover informant. He would be wired to record every meeting he had with other corrupt police and criminals.

In true Haken fashion, his reason for accepting this dangerous brief was simple commonsense. 'No one would have believed me without proof. They [other corrupt police] would have just said nothing or lied to the Commission and that would be it.' It is worthwhile noting that for all the venom directed towards Haken since, all his assertions to the Royal Commission have been corroborated. It is a matter of disgust to Haken that not all have been acted upon.

It is wrong to assume that Haken thought he was facing a jail term for his corruption. Historically, very few investigations into corruption ever went further than allowing an officer to resign or, at worst, be dismissed. Two officers had been convicted as a result of Operation Raindrop (which looked at the corrupt dealings between a criminal and police) in 1985 but were later freed on appeal and the convictions quashed. Prior to the Royal Commission there had been many inquiries into corruption, such as operations Casper, Casper 2, Seca and Asset.

John Hatton told parliament of former police minister Ted Pickering's comments in reference to Operation Asset, 'Their operation was compromised from the word go'. It was simply blown straight out of the water almost overnight and the whole thing was a joke. Hatton concluded that the 'New South Wales police could not be trusted to investigate serious organised crime activities within the ranks of the police service'. It was unbelievably compromised. He went on to say, 'You can trust the officers concerned but there are senior police who compromise those operations'. In 1993, the Independent Commission against

Corruption (ICAC) conducted the Milloo Inquiry looking into the relationship between police and criminals. While some disciplinary proceedings took place, there were very few prosecutions.

Among the many meetings later recorded between Trevor Haken and Graham 'Chook' Fowler, one recorded by Haken at the Berowra Cellars and played at the Royal Commission confirmed this.

> Fowler gave me the undertaking that had been given to him by two senior police officers. And that was that they had to look after the integrity of the police force above all matters and that they guaranteed that anyone who maintained their silence would be given whatever job they wanted after the Commission folded. Or at worst they would be given a pension and that was an open slather offer ... and it's there on tape, it happened but people don't refer to it! They were obviously terrified at that stage that I was going to roll. They didn't believe that I'd rolled but they were terrified that I might.
>
> A lawyer said to me that if you hadn't gone on side with the Commission that you would have had all your assets seized and you would have been in prison and the like. And I said that it also might well have been that I became a superintendent with a position in the CIB.
>
> The suggestion that John [legal counsel for the Royal Commission] and Nigel [Chief Investigator at the Royal Commission] told me what they had on me is simply not true because I purposely never asked. I didn't ask and I made sure that it was recorded that I didn't ask. Because if you did ask and you found out that they did have a lot, then that is different.

Working undercover meant that he would continue to talk the talk of a corrupt policeman, meeting contacts and accepting corrupt payments. However, he and his vehicle would be wired with electronic devices to record months of meetings with fellow corrupt police officers and criminals. In some cases the meetings would even be filmed via cameras secreted in his vehicle and other places. It was a momentous decision for both Haken and the police force he was a part of. Before the Royal Commission into the NSW Police Service there had never been concrete proof of endemic corruption in the force.

Haken provided irrefutable evidence of police corruption, as captured on audio and video. There had never been a witness like Trevor Haken, and Commission investigators were ecstatic to have such a key player operating for them. It was a coup on a grand scale which then led other witnesses to 'roll'. Haken's involvement and cooperation proved the integrity and credentials of that inquiry. Haken was certainly a key factor in the success of the Wood Royal Commission.

As the months progressed so did the danger to Haken and his family. They parted the day he was revealed as an undercover informant. His barrister, Eric Kelly, succinctly told a newspaper, 'When it's over, he won't be Trevor Haken anymore'.

Prominent Sydney lawyer Chris Murphy suggested during the Royal Commission hearings that once the hearings were over, Haken 'should be able to elect to live in supported obscurity, watering grape vines in the south of France'. As to Haken's actual, post-Commission life, nothing could be further from the truth but Haken has become used to living double lives. He was an effective police officer who acted corruptly. He was a loving family man who associated with drug dealers. He dealt with hardened criminals and yet, looked wholesome enough to appear as the typical family man in a fast food commercial.

Haken's fear is that one day he will wake and find that he is on his own, like so many informants who have gone before him. It is now dangerous for Haken to keep anything that might identify his past life. There are people who are in jail as a result of his evidence and actions and the inquiries that followed. Some of his former associates would like to see him dead. And so, he has changed his name and has relocated to whereabouts unknown.

To track the path of Trevor Haken from innocent schoolboy to corrupt police officer, then Royal Commission informant, and tell the story of how this particular life went off the rails, is also to track to some considerable degree the nature and extent of police corruption in New South Wales over the past twenty and more years. And to do that requires going back to Trevor Haken's own unique and early days.

CHAPTER 2

YOUR SINS WILL ALWAYS FIND YOU

As has always been her way, Betty Haken lives quietly. She is in her kitchen arranging flowers when I visit. While her voice falters with age, she is an intelligent woman who chooses her words carefully and is never far away from making a joke. Betty has had three knee reconstructions as well as pins inserted in her ankles and so it is an effort for her to move around. Although she uses a walking stick, she does without this for most of the time. She apologises to me when she finally uses it.

The house is simply decorated with a number of framed photographs including those of her husband Ernest and her children and grandchildren. There are many special objects accrued over a lifetime that decorate the lounge room and dining room of Betty's house. Her dining room has some traditional Wedgewood blue plates, one celebrating the wedding of Prince Charles and Lady Diana and a collection of seventy-two spoons mounted on three wooden frames.

There are small flowers on the windowsill that overlooks her backyard. The yard is a source of pleasure for Betty and the plants are always well-maintained.

Ernest Haken and Betty were both raised in Sydney. Ernest had three brothers and three sisters and grew up in Hurstville while

Betty grew up in Sydney's northern suburbs with two brothers and two sisters. As the youngest, she 'was very much at the bottom of the family pecking order', she says with a laugh. Her brother is ninety-two, her sister is ninety and her other siblings died at eighty-three and eighty-seven. She says with another chuckle, 'They don't get rid of us easily!'

Betty was born in Sydney's Blue Mountains in 1918 and her father died the same year: 'It must have been the shock of seeing me!' she jokes. Her mother sold the family property in the mountains and bought some land in Chatswood. The family were very close and her mother had to work hard to support and raise her family. 'There was no pension in those days, no child endowment. The first government pension she ever got was when she was eighty-two years old! Up till then it was a case of you nearly had to swear your life away to get ninepence ha'penny.'

When Ernest and Betty met, they were interested in similar things. 'We weren't socialites in any manner.' Instead, they liked to go walking or fishing. They would hire a boat up on Roseville Chase or Salt Pan Creek and spend hours together talking and fishing. Having fallen off a ladder while working, Ernest had spinal problems and in 1940 was operated on and subsequently spent six months in plaster. For that reason he was not accepted into the army. 'He was put into an engineering workshop, which wasn't his trade and they didn't release him until the end of the war,' Betty says. Ernest returned to the building industry. They were married in 1944 and lived in a flat in Naremburn until building their house in Chatswood.

Their first child, Andrew, was born in 1946. On 21 October 1950, Betty Haken gave birth to a baby boy at the Mater Hospital in Crows Nest. They named him Trevor David Haken.

Children born that year were born in the Chinese Year of the Tiger. Trevor recalls, 'All the Chinese crooks want to know when you're born. It's almost mandatory. If you form an association with these people, they'll slip it in and ask, "What year were you born?" I'm meant to be a strong personality, no dramas.' But while Trevor has a strong personality his life has seen plenty of drama, with him too often in the lead role.

The Australia that Trevor Haken was born into had seen the trauma of the Great Depression and two world wars. Australians sought comfort in simple pleasures and the familiar. It was the time before television, when the radio was the centrepiece of every household. Prime Minister Menzies tried to outlaw the Communist Party. Teachers used the cane to enforce discipline in what were fast-growing classrooms. The Pill wasn't yet a part of society, and only 'tough girls' smoked or drank. Fewer families owned cars. Society found comfort and direction in the known: the Christian faith, the royal family, the law and especially sport. The legacy of conservatism would remain for many years.

In 1950s Australia, crime and corruption existed but in the public mind these things were largely confined to certain areas such as Darlinghurst and Kings Cross. Drugs had not yet infiltrated the mainstream population. Marijuana, cocaine and heroin were far removed from a society that had not yet really even begun to drink wine in any quantities. People had faith in the system that had seen them through the wars. Those who were a part of the underbelly of society were dealt with by police when they stepped out of line. Newspapers would occasionally run stories of criminals and their reckless lives. These stories, while titillating to the general public, seemed to support the view that those who broke the moral and social code would end up paying the price. Although the law spoke of the presumption of innocence, there were few juries that ever doubted the word of a police officer given under oath.

The Hakens moved into their house in Chatswood in 1954. Ernest was a quiet and even-tempered man, but Betty recalls that on occasion he could chase Trevor with a stick calling out 'I'll catch you' when young Trevor had done something wrong. Ernest and Betty did everything together. He loved the garden and planted vegetables. It was a comfortable life with the most important asset of the time, as Betty recounts: 'Good neighbours on either side!'

Ernest was in partnership as a builder, mainly constructing cottages. Trevor says of his dad, 'He was one of those dads who went to work all the time. There was never an abundance of money. Times were pretty tight for everybody we knew.'

Trevor was born into the Methodist faith but his family were not strict adherents. He enjoyed going to Sunday school but at one point his father suddenly stopped the children from attending. The church had sent a circular around stating that they had decided that the tithe would be reintroduced. This was a system whereby members of a church would give a weekly percentage of their income to support the church. The circular stated that if you were sending your children to Sunday school and were not paying the tithe, then that meant that somebody else was subsidising your child's education. Ernest was a fairly blunt sort of a man and in response simply said, 'That's it, you're not going back'. That was the end of Trevor's church attendance.

While Trevor stopped going to church at age thirteen, he was already spending time at cubs and then the scouts. His parents thought that this was a good organisation for a young boy to be involved in. Having started with the cubs at age eight, Haken went right through the scouts until after his father died. At his troop he met a certain scoutmaster, a thirty-six-year-old single man who lived with his mother. He was a police officer of rank, and he was a child molester. He retired as a Superintendent. In what is now recognised as a common pattern of behaviour of paedophiles, this person gained the trust of the parents of the victim. Ernest and Betty innocently thought that it was good for Haken to be going on outings with him. He was a trusted member of society and included Trevor in activities that the Hakens couldn't afford. He had a boat and took Trevor fishing with him.

When interviewed on this subject, Haken's eyes turn red and he is visibly upset and angry as he recalls:

I got to the stage where I didn't want to go but couldn't say why when my parents were pushing me to go. And it's a sick bloody society because nobody realised what was going on and they never do. I'll be frank with you, this is the first time I've ever mentioned it. There's a lot of talk about these things now ... it's sexual abuse! I'm not talking about penetration, but it was sexual abuse by a sick bastard. He was a policeman. It's a sick bloody thing with a bloke that's over six foot coming on to you all the time. And ... if there's one bloke that deserves to rot in hell, then he does! Somebody else coined the phrase that there should be a special place in hell for them. Even Jesus said that if you touch the little ones then there should be a millstone around your neck.

It's the sort of thing that you bottle up because you sort of think to yourself that in some way did you promote it? It was an area that was completely taboo. Nobody ever gave me an opening. And going back as far as I'm going back, it was just totally in the hands of the perpetrator because if a kid had ever said anything they would have got belted for lying.

You don't understand that it is not your fault ... you just bottle it up and live in fear of being left alone with the bloke, because you know what's going to happen again and again and again and again. The problem is that the more attractive the proposition he puts forward such as going away, the more your parents push you to go. It's a scary hell. You're trying to say no, I don't want to go … In hindsight perhaps I could have said something. With the Royal Commission revelations [the Royal Commission inquiring into paedophilia and police corruption] it was like a floodgate where people came forward who hadn't for so long.

Such is the power of the abuser that many years later Haken would occasionally encounter this person but never raised the subject. The perceived shame of such an experience as a child remained with him. It is something that he has never raised specifically with his mother.

All I've ever said to her was whenever his name is mentioned I say that he was a low bastard. I said that one day you'll see, but they never did and couldn't. Because you never expand on these things and it was probably a matter that was closeted by others as well.

I should have said something to Paddy Bergin [the legal counsel in charge of the Royal Commission into paedophilia and police corruption] and said cop this one and have a go. But there are some things you just can't and you don't. Maybe I'll regret saying anything now. My mother is eighty-four and her expectations in those days were that school teachers were totally believable, police were totally believable, and lawyers were nearly God.

In those days, that's why these things could flourish because nobody would believe that these things took place. The most I ever heard about homosexuality was that they were strange old men who lived together.

The scoutmaster's abuse of Haken continued for nearly two years and stopped when Trevor moved up to the senior scouts and away from him. Haken heard some talk that a neighbouring scout troop had made a complaint about the same sort of behaviour regarding the same person, but nothing came of it.

It's a long time ago and it was very unpleasant and very real. People talk now about being abused as children and how it can have an effect on your life and you sort of think to yourself that you're probably overreacting and then you think, hang on, that maybe it does have an effect on your life. Maybe it really is what causes you problems in life. Maybe if it hadn't happened things would have gone differently and you just don't know ... whether you might have gone down a different track in your relationships with other people. I worked in one of the most sordid areas of Sydney and we as police just didn't do anything about it. And that wasn't just child abuse, that was young boys who prostituted themselves. We had too much to do anyway but there were no complainants and there were no victims. The victims were there, they were there by the bucketful! But we didn't do anything about it because we weren't looking to isolate and identify the victims. As far as we were concerned they were just the rubbish who lived in their own world ... they were just trash and that's the way it was. That's a sad indictment on the cops because we weren't looking and nobody was.

And so you've got to ask, well, who were the people driving the Mercedes and Rolls Royces picking these kids up every night? We used to go into Greens Park in Darlinghurst opposite St Vincent's and you'd be doing a job and you'd see them picking the boys up. And more than that, you'd get a person making a complaint about being robbed in one of the better hotels in Sydney and of course the perpetrator was one of the boys from The Wall. And these guys would actually come in and complain about being robbed by a person they'd picked up from The Wall. We'd do the job and find some of these guys ... it was their specialty. There was a kid named Aaron who would call up his mates and they would meet in the hotel room and take a guy for what he had.

The only thing I do regret is not hammering him [the scoutmaster] at some stage down the track. The other thing I regret is not raising the issue before. I feel sorry for people involved in this type of thing because the ramifications of it are so wide-ranging. To expose yourself to being the complainant, exposes everybody that you know, puts a hell of a load on your kids and you wouldn't want anyone to suffer from what to all intents and purposes is buried. But it's not buried, it stays with you, like all things I suppose. It's a trauma in your life that never leaves you and never goes away. I'm worried about how it has affected me. I got tied up with this scoutmaster and one wonders what would have happened if he hadn't. I've never talked to anyone about this. And it's funny that even at this age, with all the things I've been through, I've never ever discussed things, but they stick with you.

Ernest Haken became ill in February 1967 with prostate problems. He had it attended to and was assured there was no sign of cancer. The family booked their annual January camping holiday. Then Ernest complained about pain in the lung area and went to the Mater Hospital. The initial inspection was inconclusive and so the Hakens were told that an operation was needed to find out what was wrong. Betty recalls: 'They just operated and closed him up and said that he's got three months to live, and that was that. Almost to the day he died it was three months.'

Despite the prognosis, Ernest continued to work from home, checking house plans until it became too difficult to concentrate. He dissolved his partnership and waited to die. Betty would drive Ernest in the family Holden nearly every day to St Vincent's Hospital for radiation therapy, which made him sick for a few hours afterwards. One day Ernest got out of bed and fell to the floor. He returned to St Vincent's and Betty was told by a doctor that they would have to operate in order to save his life. Ernest had told Betty that there was to be no more surgery and so Betty refused to sign the papers. 'If it [the surgery] extended his life, it would only have been for a couple of weeks. They would give him a needle occasionally, but they didn't have the palliative care they've got nowadays. Nor did they have the knowledge with treatment that they've got now.' Trevor recalls: 'Although it is not a long time ago, there was no real treatment in those days. You were given a sentence, a painful one at that.'

Ernest Haken died on 7 February 1968, but the boys were not able to say goodbye to him. Haken's older brother Andrew was twenty years old and had joined the ABC by this time, where he worked until his retirement in 2000. Trevor was sixteen years old when his father died. Betty's recollection of this time is very painful, but she bore things as stoically as she could.

Trevor went to Chatswood Public School and then on to Chatswood High. His memories of school are not happy. Betty confirms that Trevor was not a keen student and looks back with regret on what happened after Ernest died: 'That's where I made my first mistake, because when his father died, he was so upset and he left school and went and got a job in a nursery and that's where I should have left him because he enjoyed that and he enjoyed the garden the same as his father.'

Trevor had taken the job in the nursery but Betty thought that he should go on to do the Higher School Certificate. Trevor had only been working in the nursery for a week when Betty called the nursery owner on the telephone. She was told that the owner took young Trevor on because 'he was a much better type of boy than he normally got applying for jobs'. Betty replied, 'Well I'm sorry, but I'm going to have to insist that he goes back to school.' Today she pauses then adds, '… and I should *not* have done that.' Although Trevor returned to school, he did not apply himself: he was simply marking time.

After his father died, Trevor spent the rest of his time trying to work out how not to go to school. Trevor attained his HSC and left school in 1968. The way he handled his education is now a disappointment to him, as he had aspirations in the early part of high school that later disappeared. Haken now reflects, 'That's why you hope your kids will go to better levels and have better opportunities.'

As a teenager, Trevor tended to hang about the beaches. 'We were beach people and did all the things that hoodlum boys did. Surfing at Freshwater and Harbord. Freshwater to Bungen; Palm Beach was too flash for us.' But after his father died, 'You didn't do anything anymore. Other people did family sort of things, we didn't … everything stopped after my father died.' The effect on Trevor at the time was that he began to feel like an outsider.

After the death of his father there were also the issues of survival that directly affected his family.

Nineteen sixty-seven was before social welfare or any sort of social reform. People in my mother's position stayed at home and looked after the house and the kids. She was the usual sort of housewife in those days. I don't think I knew anybody's mother who went to work. It was basically taboo. When my father died my mother had no choice but to go to work as there was no sort of assistance given. There may have been a widow's pension provided but it was very basic. My older brother was doing an apprenticeship at this stage but I was a shit of a kid. I expect it did add to my behavioural problems because there was a lack of supervision. My mother was a very caring and close person but how much can you keep your eye on a seventeen-year-old kid?

Betty Haken was also dealing with the loss of her husband. Says Trevor, 'She was a mess for a long time after my father died.' The support of her wider family enabled her to find her feet again. Trevor's aunt found a position for Betty in the accounts department of Grace Bros Chatswood. While working there Betty saw too many people who knew her husband and this was far too painful for her. And so when a position became available with a local doctor over at Northbridge, she took it. Although geographically close to where she lived there was little public transport to the area and so it was only the locals who attended the surgery; she could thus be left in private while keeping active. She stayed there for seventeen years until she retired.

When Trevor left school he travelled to Guyra, in the New England area of New South Wales, where he had some friends. There he worked as a station hand, from December 1968 to the following October. Betty had not had a letter from him in a long time and so sent him a telegram saying: 'Please advise the condition of right arm!' At the time Trevor had a car and had rolled it in an accident. He thought someone must have told his mother about it. He called and said, 'Mum, I don't know who told you but I didn't hurt myself.' Betty's response was, 'You can be sure your sins will always find you!'

For a wild young boy in the rapidly changing 1960s, the young Trevor made a conservative career choice in joining the police force. The outdoor aspect of police work appealed to him, rather more than being stuck in an office. As Betty recalls, 'It was the only thing he was interested in at the time.' Trevor wanted to be '... out and about and doing something different'. So while Trevor Haken joined the police force, he also says, 'I still haven't fathomed the absolute reason why'.

CHAPTER 3

I'M STANDING ON YOUR BLOODY HAIR

'A "them and us" siege mentality with the associated police culture is the enemy of effective policing and acceptance of support for police.'

JOHN HATTON, CHURCHILL REPORT

'What would people say if I became a policeman and took an oath to arrest my brothers and sisters and relations and convict them by fair and foul means? It takes eight or eleven of the biggest mud crushers in Melbourne to take one poor little half starved larrikin to a watch house.'

NED KELLY, *NED KELLY MAN AND MYTH*, CASSELL, 1968

The police have always suffered bad press in Australia. Even if the critic happened to be Ned Kelly, it's been hard to avoid the 'us versus them' view of law enforcement. In Kelly's day, the police were seen as operating in the interests of the squatters, who were mainly of English Protestant descent, while many of the small landholders were of Irish Catholic descent. This reinforced the notion that there was one law for the rich and one law for the poor. The notion of the underdog has existed ever since, nurturing our anti-authoritarian tendencies even though the vast majority of Australians are now middle class in socio-economic terms. The view that there were two tribes eroded slowly, but the suspicion of police remained.

For a young boy growing up in the suburbs, police life may have seemed exciting. Like many teenage boys, Trevor Haken didn't think too deeply about his career choices. He thought the police force had 'a certain amount of flashiness' to it, but the main appeal was that the job was outside and he wouldn't be stuck inside an office. Alluding to his current situation he says, 'You don't really know where you're heading until you give it a try'. He adds dryly, 'Isn't that the truth?'

Trevor Haken gave the police service a try. Like so many others over the years, he made his way down to 'the depot', the old Police Academy located in Bourke Street, Sydney. The depot is a large three-storey brick building with arches. In Haken's day it had a grass quadrangle, which has since been tarred over for vehicles to park on. Everyone who joined the police force passed through these arches. Trevor began his initial police training in October 1969.

The process was fairly simple. Haken walked in and asked for an application. Every applicant would be measured and weighed, and if you were of suitable stature and dimension and could pass a spelling test you would be included in a take-up. Haken continues:

> You would go in for an initial interview and then be brought back to Bourke Street for a second interview in front of senior police who ran you through the hoops. They asked questions like, 'Who are you? What do you do? Why do you want to join the police service?' If they liked the cut of your jib you were called up to the next class. The only things that

prevented people from being accepted into the service were if they had a police record or if they weren't tall or heavy enough. I only scraped in on both of those requirements. The joke of the day was that if you had a pound note under each foot you were tall enough! I was only just tall enough. Apparently I was one of the smallest to join.

Haken found the six-week training course fairly intensive. There were class lectures and exams. There was a lot of physical training and a lot of discipline. If you couldn't handle the verbal assault of your instructors then you were marched out the door. It was a military-style approach to training. Trainees would start the day marching around a quadrangle. The drill instructors were often ex-army and they would yell in the faces of the trainees:

He would come up behind you and scream, 'Am I hurting you, son?' and you would say, 'No sergeant'. He would then say, 'Well I should be because I'm standing on your bloody hair. Get over there and get a hair cut!' The training course had a purpose. I suppose it wasn't a bad way of operating because people either toed the line or they were out and, trust me, it really did weed a lot of people out. After this sort of intense training, once you got out on the streets it didn't matter what people said to you, you would just grin and bear it.

Haken went through a crash course in basic law so that he knew what was required when he was sent to work on the streets. At first he went out as a probationary constable to a station. He would be required to go back to the station every quarter during the year of training and a report would be compiled on him and sent back to the academy. At the end of the training year he did seven weeks at the academy, as 'polishing off'. If you got through the exams (police procedural exams sufficient to make you operational), you would return to your station and get sworn in. And so Trevor Haken was sworn in as a probationary constable on 8 December 1969 and stationed at North Sydney.

> The first years I was working as a constable was during the time of the anti-Vietnam rallies and the Springboks tour. I had friends who were in the marches yelling out and calling us pigs. I would say, hang on, these are my mates, what's going on here? One girl I used to go out with was in the demonstration and it became decidedly unpleasant. It became a 'them' and 'us' situation. I lost friends very quickly. Some never spoke to me again.

If ever there was a time when Haken was seen as an outsider, it was during his early years in the police force. It was a time of passionate political feelings and there was no middle ground. At first, middle Australia reacted badly to the anti-Vietnam protesters and their image. The long hair and different clothes made them stand out as targets. 'It was very difficult because you had a view on protesters rather than what they were protesting about,' Haken says. There was also the view that people shouldn't be protesting, which was one commonly held among police. Haken's attitude was that if the country was at war, Australians should be there. 'The other side of it was that all my friends were protesting and they didn't share my view.'

> Apart from the Depression era, I don't think there was such a public division as in that time; it was tremendously violent. It was eye-opening for me to see people in a peace demonstration like that carrying clubs with nails through them like a mace, which they were swinging at cops. That

was during my first year in the job. It was pretty full-on. I was working with guys who had been around a while and they were picking people up and throwing them through the windows of David Jones. I was thinking, what's going on? The cops were pretty pissed off about the whole thing because they were getting walloped and belted. There were no special units in those days. There was no protection for police, just batons in the long baton pocket of your trousers. Police got hurt.

Police did not receive any training for these extraordinary events and many, like Haken, were young constables straight out of the academy. It is little wonder that things got out of hand.

The South African Springboks Rugby tour of Australia of 1971 was another dramatic event that divided the community. These were the early days of the anti-apartheid movement that sought to bring internal change in South Africa through external pressure such as banning sporting interaction. Despite opposition, the Liberal-Country Party government of the time allowed the tour to go ahead. State police forces were used as a means of enforcing the political will. It was a confrontational approach that pitted the police against demonstrators and was instrumental in showing the police in a negative light on the front pages of newspapers for a number of weeks.

The tour started in Perth and the protests and incidents that took place were to be repeated to varying degrees throughout the country. One Sydney newspaper reported, 'Police did little or nothing to interfere as anti-apartheid demonstrators were punched and roughed up and had their signs torn up [by anti protest demonstrators].'[1] In Adelaide the first smoke bombs appeared, as well as firecrackers, whistles and chanting. At the same time, the union movement joined the protest with the Amalgamated Postal

Workers Union stopping deliveries of South African mail. In the ACT, police replaced unionists who refused to build an eight-foot fence around the ground. Melbourne saw some heated demonstrations reported as 'what happens when the rule of law breaks down'. There were an estimated 5000 demonstrators who tried to invade the pitch and were dealt with quite severely, the paper continued: '... senior police officers present made no apparent effort to stop policemen striking people unnecessarily, and many police apparently did not care who saw them doing this'.[2]

It appeared to many journalists observing the confrontations that arrests were being made for little identifiable reason. Police were accused of overstepping the mark as they flailed the crowd with their batons and did 'knee-drops' on those they arrested. Mounted police appeared to be deliberately running down demonstrators. Of course this inflamed the protestors, who reacted violently. Journalists were taken aback by the violence that ensued and warned police in other states to be ready.

In Sydney, the police were prepared for the violence and searches of the crowd took place on entry to the ground. Police confiscated a large number of smoke bombs, flares, firecrackers and weapons. They formed a ring around the Sydney Cricket Ground, and in some sections they were two and three deep. Four strands of barbed wire were placed around the ground above the white picket fence, making it a ten-foot fence. There were 700 police on duty in and around the ground. The press coverage of the tour showed very clearly the passions involved. The headlines ran: '140 Arrests in Day of Wild Scenes', 'Smoke Bombs, Mass Arrests' and 'Police Win Out in Fiery Clashes at SCG'.

A photograph of the time shows a linesman dressed in his white starched jersey and shorts. He is holding up the flag while there are thirty police in the same picture either tackling demonstrators or wrestling others or directly facing the crowd waiting for something to happen.[3] The demonstrators blew whistles and jeered throughout the match. They also threw oranges onto the pitch as well as orange smoke bombs. Paddy wagons were actually placed on the oval and as strands of barbed wire were cut, demonstrators would attempt to run onto the field. Only one made it as there were plenty of police on hand. There were fights between demonstrators and those who favoured the tour, and these clashes would also be broken up.

The *Sydney Morning Herald* editorialised, 'Among the demonstrators, the larrikin minority ... were not without vicious weapons and instruments of disruption.' It was an emotional time: 'behind this rowdiness run the passions of a nation divided'.

The police knew the protesters were going to be throwing smoke bombs. Sergeant Bill Fahey of the Police Rescue Squad described balloons and plastic toys filled with tacks, attached to bungers and thrown at police. There were also phosphorous and arsenic flares. Fahey claimed that the fumes from the arsenic flares could have been potentially fatal. Haken remembers:

> You couldn't pick up the smoke bombs because they would burn your hands, they were covered in sulphur. The senior police told us, 'Don't worry if they throw them. The rescue squad will be coming.' However, the rescue squad merely dug holes all over the cricket ground and simply popped these canisters down the holes. There were about five rows of barbed wire stretched all around the fences. It was like a war zone. Not too many of the nail bombs went off but they were four inch nails wrapped around some type of explosive. The tension between young people and authority in those times was full-on. There was a definite hatred between both sides.

For a young constable in his first year of service, this was a violent introduction to the job he had chosen. It highlighted that it wasn't just a job that you left behind at the end of the shift. 'I suppose this sort of experience was what formed a closer community among police and explains how they came to associate mainly with each other. Nobody your own age, outside the police service, wanted to be associated with you. Nobody else had a look in. There was a wall up and anybody on the outside just didn't belong. It was a complete division.' By joining the police force, Haken had picked a side, whether he liked it or not.

Haken spent his first year in general duties as a traffic policeman at North Sydney. Directing traffic wasn't a bad job. Your shift was from 7am to 3.30pm, but the unwritten rule was that you had to be there early. Police controlled the big intersection on the Pacific Highway at North Sydney, the Crows Nest intersection, where there were no lights, and Christie Street near the Royal North Shore Hospital.

Haken worked at a traffic point for about an hour and a half and then would work on accidents or whatever needed to be done. The second shift was from 3 pm until 11.30 pm. North Sydney had one of the highest accident rates in Australia back then. You had to be fast on your feet otherwise you may have been knocked over. It was at North Sydney that Haken had his first personal exposure to corrupt activities and the drinking culture within the New South Wales Police Force.

The police drove Mini Minors at that time. After Haken did the afternoon point, a Mini Minor would take him and others straight down to the Platypus Naval base. They would 'get on the turps' in the Chief Petty Officers' mess.

It didn't have to be after hours for us to hit the grog. After your traffic point, you'd go and get some dinner or go down to the sailors' mess. Everybody would be there. Some of the officers would work their shift from the mess. This behaviour opens your eyes fairly quickly, or closes them, one of the two.

If an accident came in via the radio they would go out to the scene and take details and hope that the driver wasn't as drunk as they were. Alcohol was an inseparable part of police life and it would be a long time before Haken would kick the habit. In those early days, he didn't see it as a problem. 'You drink, you got drunk, you fall down, not a problem! Back then, in a lot of industries, people used to drink during the day.'

Joining the police force was a lifestyle change for Haken. He had a new set of friends and these were the people he looked up to. Unfortunately, the people he looked up to drank heavily and he followed suit. He acknowledges that this lifestyle was a recipe for disaster. 'There were occasional officers who stood alone. They were quite happy to be there for their shift and quite happy to go home at knock-off time. I think they didn't really want to be there anyway — that's probably closer to the mark.'

People who didn't adopt this lifestyle were regarded as being 'squareheads'. Like a square peg in a round whole, they didn't fit in with the others. 'Squareheads' was a term used by both criminals and the cops. 'If you were talking to a crook and you were talking about a particular bloke, he'd say, "Oh, he's a squarehead, he won't take a quid you know", and he was the abnormal not the normal, they were on their own. Usually that was the type of bloke who would go off and become a lecturer at the academy or something.'

At that stage it appeared to Haken that the 'in' crowd to belong to were called 'The Group' (those who drank and would take a quid). That's the way it continued, even through to various detectives' offices.

Each shift at each station had its own particular station sergeant and Haken remembers one who one day booked a greengrocer's truck. By the time he got back to the station, the sergeant was waiting for him on the footpath. He asked Haken if he had booked the grocer's truck and Haken replied, 'Yes, he was parked on the footpath. I told him to move, he wouldn't move and so I booked him.' The sergeant bellowed at Haken, 'I've been getting my fruit and veggies from him for twenty-five years, you can't book him!' To emphasise his point, he added, 'so and so gets his fruit and veggies from him. Go back and get the ticket and get rid of it.' There was no pretence about it. This sergeant had an arrangement and it was not to be disturbed by young constables.

Another sergeant would bring three quarts of beer for himself to the nightshift. He'd come along with a bundle of food ready for 'work'. Haken recalls:

He was a giant bloke, one of those sergeants that you were frightened of. He was six foot four inches and looked to be about twenty stone! This sergeant would cook up a big meal in the frying pan for himself, drink three quarts of beer and then go to sleep in the passenger side of the vehicle. So you'd be like the Holden precision team, leaning to one side!

Being on general duties means you do anything from deceased persons to accidents [when traffic police weren't working]. This particular sergeant's main objective was to sleep the night away. Three quarts of beer wasn't a big issue for him. He got three quarts from the pub in resealable bottles. I thought it was disgraceful. We should have been out there doing something, but this was acceptable behaviour. The station sergeant had done his whole service at North Sydney. He lived in Cammeray and used to be picked up by the shift before and dropped home at the end of the shift. He'd been there for twenty or thirty years. He wasn't an isolated case. They'd get dropped off and picked up like they were the managing director of a company.

There were some police who stayed as uniformed constables. There were, however, opportunities that presented themselves for those who wanted to progress. Not everybody on traffic had a radio, but if you took a car radio out and responded to all the calls, then you would get the arrests. Eventually, if you were keen enough, you would apply to get on what was called the ungraded list of applicants for plainclothes.

After traffic, I then worked with motorbikes, which was sort of a progression. At one stage I was even going to do an instructor's course on motorbikes. While on bikes I did a lot of mundane things like serving summonses. No summonses could be posted, they all had to be hand-delivered by police. It was like being a mailman in some respects. There were all sorts of side issues. For example, if a break and enter occurred and you were out and about then you could go along. That's how you progressed in the police force then. You just had to show you were interested and on top of everything. If there was a description given for someone who did a robbery and you managed to 'do the pinch' then you'd get a few brownie points with the detective inspector and your name would be mentioned.'

In Haken's first year, North Sydney covered two major hospitals, the Mater and the Royal North Shore. North Sydney had an older population and so elderly deaths were common. Haken soon found out that there was a business relationship between the police and local undertakers. He claims that this was never a matter of secrecy and even doctors were involved. He explains the process:

> People would have a tragedy — for example, it might be that an aged relative has died and the relatives who were maybe from out of the area and unfamiliar with the local scene would be there. Police would give the relatives of the deceased person a card or the name of an undertaker. They would tell the grieving relatives that the undertaker was a good person and could be trusted to look after them properly and that they should call him. They were very grateful for the contact. Just to be steered on to somebody and to have the weight of the problems taken off their shoulders. This sounds like a sales pitch, doesn't it? It'll only cost you three times what you make in a year! We've all been ripped off by them, haven't we? It didn't seem to be to the detriment of anyone really. It may well have been that it was. It was just the way it was, just the way it happened.

If a policeman recommended somebody to an undertaker, they would receive a kickback. However, police involvement with the dead sometimes went well beyond recommending a preferred funeral business. Some police would steal from the deceased.

> The first time I saw an officer rip a deceased person's house apart, when they were found dead in the house, I thought, this is not kosher, you know, but you couldn't say anything. Like, the senior officer you're working with says, 'Son, this is terrible, you don't want to be in here, and so you sit in the car.' The next thing you hear are floorboards being ripped up and cupboard doors being ripped open and you think,

Jesus, this is crook. It was common knowledge. People would come to granny's house and say, 'Oh I thought she had a box full of money, you know'. And there's an empty box with a screwdriver mark on it!

I found it to be completely distasteful. The very thought of taking things from dead people irked me completely. I suppose it comes back to the different styles of people that were involved. Some of the people that I worked with I didn't like and I wouldn't have had anything to do with them if I wasn't working with them.

Seeing dead bodies made you grow up quickly. The first dead body I saw was on the third night we went to North Sydney out of the academy. I was taken to the old morgue in North George Street. It was probably some sort of ghoulish pleasure for an old sergeant to watch a group of young constables puke all over the place. It was an unpleasant place at the best of times. All the bodies were out on the tables. The sergeant took us very late one night and said, 'This is where they do post-mortems'. We walked into a semi-dark place with all these bodies.

Haken got to see a lot of bodies over the years and developed the common police way of dealing with most things — drinking.

I've been at a murder scene and seen an old lady with a mattock through her head. I don't know how it affects you. You just go and get pissed. It's a case of mutual propping up really. Who knows what other people are thinking, because you are all putting on some sort of bravado act. You become blasé about it all but I don't know that it ever loses its sting.

While at the North Sydney traffic branch, Haken became involved with the tow truck operators of the area. As Haken told the Royal Commission, it was an arrangement that was already in place when he started working at North Sydney.[4] He saw the association as just another facet of his job. While carrying out their duties there were certain premises where food and drink were laid on for police. Then there were the kickbacks in the form of cash. 'It's hard to recall how I first became involved in it. I suspect that it was through the drinking. You would be with the boys [other police] and they'd say, 'We've got a friend who runs tow trucks and he needs a little help.' So you would ring him.'

If Haken heard of an accident and he was the first person to ring a towie, he'd get a kickback and the towie would write his name or initials in a little book. Whenever he next saw the driver he would tally up how many tows he got off him and Haken would get a few extra dollars. It was six dollars for the tow and ten dollars if the repair job was done at one of the towie's shops. The tow truck racket was something that everybody seemed to be involved in. 'At the time it didn't seem to be grossly wrong, although you always knew it was. I mean let's face it, you were helping a bloke, he was a good bloke, he was probably even a friend and it wasn't like you were overtly hurting anybody.'

Haken and other police would drink with the towies at the end of the afternoon shift. The towies always had a fridge full of alcohol and a police radio, so the police didn't have to worry about being 'off the air'.

At this stage, Internal Affairs was a very small operation. They rarely investigated towies. Haken recalls, 'It was going on every day. It wasn't as if it was clandestine. Anybody could have sniffed it out if they were interested, but nobody cared because everybody was in the same boat. Everybody was aware of it. The whole attitude was, hold the line, don't say a word and you'll be okay.' There was never the suggestion that tow trucks were a real problem to anyone. The system worked as long as no one got too greedy.

'Well it goes to the old saying, 'Better the devil you know, than the devil you don't'. I think that's the way it works, and they did toe the line. If they didn't, it only took a phone call to the towie's boss and they were carpeted.'

There were methods of behaving to limit exposure to trouble. 'That was common from day one, and in fact, was taught at the academy. You batten down and stick together and you've got no problems. It was emphasised even more so when you did the detective's course.'

There were some at North Sydney who weren't involved in the tow truck business. At 3pm, 'the outcasts' as Haken called them, would pack their bags and go home and the others would go and have a drink.

It's just the way it was. It struck me as being no different to the highway patrol, or as they were referred to then 'the special traffic patrol cyclists'. They put radios on their bikes so they didn't have to stay on the road. They just got extension speakers and ran them into their homes and just went home. Like it is currently — the best police have portables and sit at the back of movie houses with their earpieces on. I mean, what's the difference? Where there's a will, there's a way of getting around it.

It was a funny lifestyle, because, like the prostitutes later, you became fairly used to the towies. You were there at accidents and so were they, and they'd help you out. There were some towies that were 'off-side' and you made sure they didn't get any business. Generally, however, the towies were there for a purpose, you were there for a purpose and we formed a close association.

Occasionally, there were fights between towies. Haken assisted the ones who were on-side. Some towies stood over motorists. For example, a woman might have had a broken headlight and the towie would have signed her up. She would then be told that she couldn't drive the car home. If the towie was off-side, the police would get the towie to drop the car and let her drive home. With someone 'on-side', on the other hand, police would have suggested to the woman that it would be safer for her to go in the truck.

Haken's time with the towies came to an end when he left traffic and joined plainclothes.

CHAPTER 4

ONE STEP ABOVE GOD — DETECTIVES AND 21 DIVISION

'Law-abiding citizens sleep peacefully in their beds, solely because dedicated men and women stand ready to do violence on their behalf.'

POLICE ADAGE

'You learnt quickly not to say anything. Whatever you saw you just shut up about it.'

TREVOR HAKEN

While there were clear divisions between the police and the rest of the community in the 1970s, there were also divisions within the police themselves. The CIB had GT Falcons, which said it all. As Haken recalls, 'they were regarded as one step above God and ordinary police didn't really talk to the guys from CIB'.

Haken's aim was to become a detective. He had come to this decision around 1972 when, in the traffic police at North Sydney, he became more impressed with the idea of doing active things such as going out and looking for crooks. The detectives there circulated a list of a number of people and Haken went out looking for them. He also started finding them. He had a feeling that because he had made those arrests, they were more inclined to say, 'Why don't you come upstairs' (detectives were always upstairs). And it certainly beat pulling up motorists for a career. To do so he would have to spend time in 21 Division Special Squad.

A plainclothes police officer could be assigned to 21 Division and eventually become a detective. The CIB used 21 Division as a troubleshooting squad to support the work of detectives. It was an effective and powerful squad full of young and enthusiastic trainees keen to prove their worth. They had cars that were used in the first response to armed hold-ups, the night patrols sorted out hoodlums and, if you were a cop in trouble, 21 were a dependable backup. There was a police adage: 'You don't fuck with 21 Division, they fuck with you'.

As Haken puts it: 'You had a group of people to fall back on when things got out of control and they did as they were told. The flying squad [a special group of troubleshooters in the UK police force] is probably the nearest equivalent. When the CIB had a problem, 21 would go and fix it. It worked brilliantly.'

Haken maintains that 21 Division also had an unwritten charter as a collection agency of sorts for money going from gaming and prostitution to the CIB hierarchy. As to being accepted into 21 Division Haken recalls:

> You purposely tried to grab a few people doing daylight house busts or whatever it may be, and that wasn't hard to do, especially if you were on bikes or cars around North Sydney. So with a bit of interest and hard work you could move into 21 Division. Being a detective was the most prestigious position in the general run of police, and from there you could climb the ladder.

To get onto the 21 Division ungraded list of applicants, you were then assessed by your local detective sergeant at the division where you worked. If he thought you were acceptable you would be given a stint at the plainclothes office as a trainee. A trainee would make coffee, answer the phone, observe everything and be attached to another police officer. 21 Division was an unusual division because you would work with someone of equal rank. It was said that you were put in twos to see 'who could catch and kill their own'.

A trainee would then be assessed by a panel and accepted if they 'behaved themselves'.

Behaving yourself was based on the statement 'never trust a man that doesn't drink'. To be trusted didn't necessarily mean to be trusted to do the right thing. This is how I was accepted and transferred to the 21 Division.

On Thursdays and Fridays, they'd lend half a dozen blokes from 21 Division to the armed hold-up squad and they'd be the response cars. If there was a hold-up, a 21 Division car would respond quickly because CIB would probably be busy at lunch.

Haken arrived at 21 Division Special Squad as a plainclothes police officer on 1 May 1974. The division was situated in the Police Academy building in Bourke Street, Surry Hills. There were two arms, the permanent staff and the training detectives who came through, staying a year and then moving on. There were around thirty to forty permanent people and sixty detectives working seven days a week, three shifts per day. There was a very tight clique at 21 Division. Detectives were given a car that they could call their own and Haken felt that he had made it. He was part of an elite squad admired by his peers and it was a clear sign that he was on his way up.

The view of police in earlier times was that it was better to let something exist (that is, gambling and prostitution) and to have some control over it rather than to drive it into the hands of people they could not control. By the time Trevor Haken came into contact with detectives, the habit of association between detectives and criminals had been longstanding.

While at 21 Division Haken would be told to go into premises with a specific direction, such as, 'Go inside and arrest the SP better. He's wearing a red shirt and blue jeans.' Haken takes up the story:

> You'd be given the knockdown. You'd walk inside and see the bloke in the red shirt and blue jeans waiting for you and there in the corner going hammer and tongs would be the SP better who'd wink at you as you walked past. He [the man in the red shirt] was the fall guy who got his fine paid and a bit of extra money, provided the police had their result for the day. That was the whole purpose of this charade. We just wanted to look like we were arresting people.
>
> There was the Sameras Club and the Forbes Club. We also went to Brownies at Ryde. You'd go there three nights in a row with your mates and on a Friday night when you were working they'd say, 'Listen, we'd like you to try and get into the Forbes Club'. You'd say 'righto' and they'd check what colour coat you were wearing. The bloke who had let you in for the past three nights would say, 'Sorry boys, this is a closed club'. So then you'd go back to the station, type your log up and say, 'Tried to get into the Forbes Club, not successful'. Nobody was really serious about doing it.

On the inside of the Forbes Club there were cards, roulette, all sorts of games being played, and food and grog was laid on. It was a decent joint, well run, well policed and everybody was happy. From time to time these clubs were genuinely turned over [raided], with all the occupants taken out and arrested. The ethnic gaming clubs were only raided from time to time as well.

21 Division was also practically the only group outside the vice squad that had a charter to look into prostitution. A car was assigned to patrol the streets, with officers looking into the premises of prostitutes. The lanes had mainly closed at this stage but there were still some girls working in cars. East Sydney was an active area and that was how Haken got to know quite a few of 'the girls', because they used to drink at The Lord Roberts, a pub in East Sydney, then a seedy part of town.

Haken would accompany his sergeant in the police car to a brothel. He would be told to wait in the car and the sergeant would go inside and emerge a few minutes later. No arrests were made and no explanations given for being at the premises. Haken quickly deduced that they were picking up payments. 'They'd go in, come out and you'd be gone and that was it.' While Haken did not receive any money himself, he would receive free drinks from the sergeant he worked with on the night. He says, 'The girls were practically given a free rein to do whatever they wanted to do. They were arrested on a rostered basis, if at all. The specifics of the arrests were organised by a sergeant who was in plainclothes.'

'The girls' would eventually be lined up across the back of the court. Phil Roach was a successful lawyer who represented most of the prostitutes in court. Roach had a rapport with the girls he represented, as he did with the cops, and an easy familiarity with the court system. They would be straight in and out of court. The system seemed to work for everyone. The women were able to ply their trade, police were seen to be making arrests, lawyers made money and the public felt something was being done. Things were in equilibrium, or as the saying goes, 'everything was everything'.

To Haken, the whole process was as much of a joke as anything else that happened in those days. Prostitutes would be presented before the magistrate, who would then announce the accused's name, 'Jane Doe'. Roach would then say, 'The usual facts, Your Worship.' The judge would hand down a fine and that was the end. In a few minutes, 'Jane Doe' was out of court and back on the street.

Roach had seen it all before, he had his role to play and he did it well. If he represented somebody for possession of an unlicensed pistol, he would stand up and say to the police witness, 'You say you found this gun in my client's possession?' The police witness would reply, 'Yes, we found it in his pocket.' The magistrate would ask, 'Would you like to look at the gun, Mr Roach?' And Roach would reply, 'No, I've seen it twelve times before.' And so the magistrate would chuckle and Roach would chuckle and even the police would chuckle. It was all a bit of a laugh for everyone except the prisoner in the dock.

The sergeant giving out the day's jobs would be instructed by the boss of 21 Division on how many arrests were to be made that shift, to make sure they arrested the 'right' number of prostitutes and so on. 'This was just so that we could justify the existence of the unit. In parliament, if somebody asked about 21 Division, they would be able to proudly quote numbers of arrests and so on, giving the impression that 21 Division was an effective crime-fighting team.'

A further function of 21 Division was what was commonly referred to as 'the warb patrol'. At least one 21 Division 'truck' each afternoon shift had the duty to drive to a number of locations and pick up the city's homeless and drunken men. It seemed that they would gather, as if by instinct, at one of these points in Hyde Park or the Haymarket, or the park near Central Railway, and wait for the truck to take them to Central cells at the old Central Police Station. These men were housed overnight in the 'drunks' tank'. The tank was a large open cell with mattresses on the floor. 'They just flopped on the floor, and when it was cold there were big gas heaters to keep them warm.'

The next morning the men would be fed breakfast and then appear before the court. The court would generally admonish the men and allow them to go. Haken comments: 'Nowdays these people are left to freeze to death because the do-gooders say that you can choose to live whatever lifestyle you want. More importantly, no one wants to take care of them. It was an old style of policing, but it worked.' Payments to the CIB were made on a regular organised basis, and that's where Frank Hakim came in.

Haken told the Royal Commission that Hakim, a well known gambling figure in the Lebanese community, was referred to by Police as 'Mr Fix-it'.[1] When Louis Bayeh gave evidence to the Royal Commission, he was quoted as saying that Hakim introduced him to the then head of 21 Division Reg Edwards, and that Hakim had told Bayeh that he 'looked after his policemen'.[2] Bayeh stated to the Commission that he believed Hakim had bribed police for years and that he had kept company with Pat Watson, a superintendent, and Merv Wood when he was police commissioner. Bayeh said that they had been to see Hakim at his flat in Kensington. Bayeh described Hakim to the Royal Commission as 'a very strong powerful man with the NSW police'. Frank Hakim was the middleman between the police and most of the ethnic gaming clubs.

Louis Bayeh told the Royal Commission that Hakim looked after two dozen clubs. Hakim was 'known in the 1980s as Mister Fix It' according to newspaper reports.[3] Bayeh told how his brother Fred had his nose broken by a bouncer up at Abe Saffron's Palace

Nightclub. Louis returned to the club and broke the butt of a rifle attacking the bouncer. He visited Hakim the next morning, told him the story and was told that Hakim would fix things and would speak to the police commissioner and Saffron. Bayeh told the Commission that after paying $1,500 to Hakim and $6,000 to Roger Rogerson, Louis was given a good behaviour bond.

Hakim shared an office with the solicitor Howard Hilton (who was later disbarred) in Redfern. Howard Hilton was reported to be one of the 'all-star underworld cast' referred to in evidence given by Louis Bayeh.[4] Hilton was the preferred solicitor for what Haken remembers as a mostly Lebanese clientele. No one is quite sure what Hakim professed to do as a legitimate job but he listed his occupation as businessman.

Trevor Haken referred to Frank Hakim as 'Cousin Frank'. Hakim would call Haken his cousin because of their similar surnames. Haken says Frank was always on the boil. 'He'd say, "Hello cousin, how are you?" Then be telling you about his connections. My friend is this, my friend is that. He was always looking for an opportunity.'

Haken worked the ethnic clubs on Friday nights with one particular sergeant, and the SP bookmakers on Saturdays. Haken did what was required and said nothing. As a consequence, he got a smooth run through 21 Division.

On Friday nights, Haken would go to work around 6pm. He would be at dinner until 10pm and then they would turn over some ethnic gaming clubs. There were a number of ethnic clubs in the inner western suburbs of Leichhardt, Annandale and Marrickville.

A number of shops had an upstairs section. There was often a gate over a doorway in between shops, and upstairs there were bars around the windows and the lights were on all night ... it's a pretty safe bet that you've come across a club. Back in those days it was mainly the Lebanese, the Maltese and the Greeks, all with their own clubs.

The clubs were forewarned and so by the time the police arrived the inhabitants would be playing canasta. 'Any other night of the week there'd be forty blokes playing fan-tan or baccarat,' says Haken. Police would make a detailed log of the premises that they visited and turned over. They might only turn over a place three times a year. There were some places that were not touched. If clubs were part of 'the system', they were looked after. The clubs on the outside did not stay that way for very long because it was the case that everybody was looking for 'assistance'. People like Frank Hakim helped to find it.

As Haken explained to the Royal Commission, Frank Hakim's 'morning teas' represented a rather quaint ceremony. He would arrive every Saturday morning at 21 Division with a bag of cakes and a bag of money. He would set up the morning tea for everybody and would then go into a 'conference' with Haken's bosses, deciding where the money would be divided. Haken explains, 'What is very plain is that when people rotated from power positions in the CIB they came for a little rest [meaning a choice job, collecting money for no effort] down there at 21 Division. They either went to Darlinghurst or 21 Division. It was great place for them to be.'

For Trevor Haken it was different. '21 Division was just a constant drink, you know. We would go to work and unless we were called out we'd go out and have lunch or dinner and just go on the drink. That's the way it was.' While it was a huge freedom, it also became tedious. 'That in itself was a difficulty because you would be just not going anywhere.'

The strangest of all Haken's gambling raids took place over a number of days in towns across the state. Haken was told that they would be going to Nimmitabell, a small town at the top of the Snowy Mountains. There were three carloads of men from 21 Division.

According to Haken, the group left Sydney and travelled down the Hume Highway to a pub in Collector, just outside Canberra. Someone then suggested that they should all start drinking rum and milk because it was cold, while repeating the saying in 21 Division: 'Share the wealth'. Haken says: 'This guy had a roll of bills that would choke ten horses. After we finished drinking we went to one of the flashest restaurants we'd ever been to in Canberra and we almost took it over. He paid for everything!'

The group had lunch and moved on to Cooma to stay at a motel. By this stage, 'everyone was quite pissed'. Being drunk, members of 21 Division and in a country town, Haken and his mates did what drunken cops could do then: they got into their cars and chased each other through the streets of Cooma with sirens wailing.

After the night in Cooma they travelled across to Wollongong, ignoring the job they were supposed to do at Nimmitabel. The trip was an excuse for some of the squad to meet those who were paying their dues across the state. The arms of 21 Division were long.

Life was full of ironies, or as Haken saw it, 'talk about fuckin' Jekyll and Hyde'. The usual routine was that on Friday nights the constables would attend 21 Division dinners before going out to turn over the ethnic card clubs. Often times they were instructed to meet the sergeants at the Athena nightclub in Cleveland Street, Surry Hills. One Friday night, Haken reports, a senior officer was so drunk that he was unable to drive his Holden police car out of his parking spot. Like some Looney Tunes cartoon sequence, the constables watched as he crashed into the car in the back of his parking spot and then drove forward into the car in front. He was apparently making a lot of noise but not a lot of progress.

Haken and other constables ran over to help him out of the car and to take him home as he was obviously too drunk to drive. Although drunk, he had one thing on his mind, to protect his briefcase. The constables found him seated at the wheel of his car clutching his briefcase tightly to his chest. No matter how hard the constables tried, they could not remove the briefcase from him. 'It was like a mother holding onto her newborn baby. You can only wonder what was in it!' Haken says.

One senior officer was well liked by constables because he lived up to the 'share the wealth' adage. But when he was drunk, he sometimes went too far. He was well known as someone who would buy local prostitutes bottles of Chivas Regal. 'Share the wealth, boys, share the wealth!' he was apparently fond of repeating.

21 Division could be fun for a young constable but it also had serious business to attend to. Fairfield is a working-class suburb on the outskirts of Sydney. One of the main roads is called Cow Pasture Road, and in those days it did have cow pastures surrounding the area. Being a tough suburb, there had been reports of problems caused by hoodlums. Standover men were hanging in doorways of shops intimidating businesses and stopping people from coming in unless the owners made a payment. Simply put, 21 Division hit town, hit the crooks and the harassment immediately stopped. 'Fairfield really was a place where you could take guys out into the paddocks, give them 'a towelling' and leave them there. There was no one around.' Haken looks upon this example as an effective way of policing:

That was in the old days. If a guy was given a belting out back it worked. We kept a check on the gangs. Today they'd say that was bad, but things like the gangs are out of control. Many of us don't see the necessity for change. I have one of those attitudes but it seems that the rest of the population thinks that it is necessary to change those methods.

If you went out on a gaming raid on the weekend and made arrests, then you would be required to attend court on the Monday. 21 Division would send a car to the court to ensure everything went well. Haken told the Royal Commission of an instance when he was with a young constable and they raided a gambling club. When Haken and the young constable attended Fairfield court regarding this matter, the constable saw some of the men who had been arrested and told Haken that the matter was being stood over until after lunch.

The constable in question shared the same Greek background as the accused and also spoke the same language. He told Haken that they would go for a coffee. During this time the conversation between the young constable and the others continued in Greek and at times became animated. They had lunch, coffee and quite a few drinks. Haken and the constable were late getting back to 21 Division. Normally the place was deserted by 3pm, but when they returned 'all the bosses were there and asking where we had been'.

Haken was taken into one room and the young constable was taken into another for questioning. Haken was asked what the conversation with the accused was about, but he had no idea as it had all been in Greek. He was asked if he had any money he should not have and was searched. In a matter of hours, Haken was moved to Chatswood station and the young constable was back in uniform. Haken had been 'rorted' but it turned out well for him. Although he left under a cloud, he was sent to a good posting. He had done the right thing at 21 Division and so was being looked after.

The young Greek constable had played double jeopardy. The gamblers had rung 21 Division from Fairfield complaining about some officer putting the bite on them when they were already paying. The main players in 21 Division would have to show that ethnic group and others that if anyone stepped out of line, they would be dealt with. So both the young constable and Haken were dealt with, and quickly. Haken had been at 21 for a year and had not stepped out of line with the gaming and betting people. They realised Haken wasn't involved, but ironically, they had to show the crooks 'that justice was seen to be done'. To all appearances, he was dealt with, but internally he was looked after (in as much as he didn't end up back in uniform). 'In some ways I was the bunny that went along to the slaughter,' says Haken. And that was how Trevor Haken left 21 Division.

CHAPTER 5

CHATSWOOD — CLERKING FOR THIEVES

'I could see that a divisional detective was really … a burglar's clerk, not able, because of the antiquated procedures involved in the recording of crime, and the sheer volume of it, to properly or thoroughly investigate any of it.'

PHILIP ARANTZ, *A COLLUSION OF POWERS*

'Once you become involved in these things, that's it, you're in. And once you're in there's no way out.'

TREVOR HAKEN

From 4 May 1975 until September 1979, Haken was stationed at Metropolitan No. 25 Division, Criminal Investigation Duty, Chatswood Detectives. He attended his detectives course from January until April 1977. Chatswood station was in an old brick house in a prosperous 'old money' suburb of Sydney. There were fifteen detectives in three rooms, while the uniformed police had the station front. 25 Division covered many of the most desirable suburbs in Sydney. Accordingly, daylight 'break and enters' formed a large part of the work. Haken recalls, 'If you started on the afternoon shift you'd just be virtually run off your feet running from house to house taking record of what went missing.' Police work at Chatswood was clerking for thieves.

Most work was reactive policing — break and enters, business fraud and shoplifting. After working in Darlinghurst, Haken found Chatswood 'was like kindergarten. It's almost civilised, people wear suits and they are nice to one another. It was a respectable area, not like 21 Division, which was just the gutter.' Haken's partner at Chatswood was Alan West. West was later promoted to be Superintendent in charge of what was then the Internal Security Unit. At the time he transferred, West asked Haken to go with him. 'I should have gone, shouldn't I? I would have been good there,' he now says.

During this period Haken was taking money from offenders, seeing it as a reward for hard work.

Well, if there was a bonus at the end of the day then that was fine. The harder you worked, the more you stood to gain. What did Alan Jones say? "The only result of laziness is failure". Once you become involved in these things, that's it, you're in. And once you're in there's no way out.' You had a few options if you were a crook. You get busted, you get hit with the full amount of what you could have been charged with, or you could make an arrangement. If you've got a suitcase of money in your hand you might say, 'I never saw the suitcase if I walk'. I mean, the options are limitless. And that's still going on, make no bones about it.

Haken told the Royal Commission that while there was no organised system of corruption at this posting, there were certainly isolated incidents. For instance Chatswood Detectives at one time had information that someone was selling heroin from a room in the Artarmon Motel. After learning that David Pearce, a junkie known to them, had rented a room in the motel to set up as a base to supply heroin, they decided to turn him over (search his room). Haken remembers Pearce as 'an insipid-looking person, whining all the time'. In those days there were people involved in the supply of heroin on the north side but not many users in the area, comparatively speaking.

In evidence to the Royal Commission Haken said that on 8 August 1977, he was working a shift this particular day with Ian Donald (who Haken had originally trained with), and was accompanied by Detective Senior Constable Peter Symonds and Detective Constable Paul Morgan to the Artarmon Motel.[1] Symonds had been doing drug and vice work and since he had been at Chatswood longer, was senior to Haken. When Pearce opened the door to them, they informed him that they were from Chatswood Police Station and that they believed the room was being used as a heroin distribution point. Pearce was cuffed and they then searched the room. They found heroin cut up ready for selling. In addition, Haken went into the bathroom, removed the tissue box holder and the tissues. On the bottom of the box was a plastic bag containing an ounce of heroin.

Heroin wasn't as widespread as it is now and when Haken went to the drug squad in 1979, they could mount a major operation on a five gram bag. 'You know, kilos weren't even heard of. You talk kilos and you were talking about people like Smith [Neddy Smith] and those two guys that ended up in Thailand forever and ever [Haywood and Fellows].'

The Federal Police had a system where if something was found on a raid, it would be declared to an exhibits officer. The officer would have non-resealable bags in which the evidence would be placed. The bags would have to be destroyed to open them. If the officer took five bags to the search then they would all have to be accounted for. More importantly, everybody would have to be a party to something being found and not put in the bag. No such system existed in Haken's time. On a raid such as the Artarmon Motel, you put the heroin in your pocket. 'And if you took it out of your pocket again, well that's all well and good.'

Haken recounted to the Royal Commission how he then passed the heroin to Symonds.[2] The two detective cars then went back to Chatswood station with Pearce in Symonds' vehicle.

As Haken was the junior man in plainclothes, Symonds and Donald made the decisions regarding Pearce's charges. The critical time was when it came to writing up the event and formally charging the accused. Decisions were made between the location and the charging about what would happen.

According to Haken's evidence to the Commission, the following day Haken was approached by Donald who pressed an envelope into Haken's hand containing about $300 and was told that Symonds had received the money from a friend for the sale of heroin.[3]

But this matter did not go smoothly. A complaint had been made and it was looked into by the local region detective inspector. Haken reported to the Royal Commission that although Internal Affairs did not investigate the matter, Detective Sergeant Shields, Officer in Charge (OIC) of Chatswood Detectives spoke to Haken and asked if the assistant to the detective inspector of the district had spoken to him about Symonds and missing drugs.

Haken told the Royal Commission that Detective Inspector Doug Knight, OIC District Detectives, prepared a resignation for Symonds and Morgan to sign and that it was his belief that this resulted directly from this incident.

Haken recalls, 'It was all kept "in house" and Symonds and Morgan were given the option to either resign or have the matter publicly aired; they chose to resign.' Haken still wonders why they took the option offered to them. 'I still think even now that if they'd just stuck to their guns they probably would have been sweet, you know.'

As Haken reported to the Royal Commission, he executed a search warrant for a drug matter in Wahroonga with Alan West, Detective Peter Repaja and Robert Hall.[4] During the search, detectives found $1500. When they returned to the station, Hall and Repaja had the money and the detectives agreed that the money had come from the sale of drugs, although the resident had claimed that it was from the sale of a motor vehicle. After a discussion with the resident, Repaja then told West that things had been worked out and that the detectives could keep the money. Haken told the Commission that the money was then divided among the detectives and Alan West spoke to the resident saying, 'Are you happy with that little arrangement?'[5]

Unfortunately for the detectives, the resident was not really happy and later that same night made a complaint at Hornsby Police Station. The Royal Commission was told by Haken that he was telephoned at his home by Kevin Lancett from Chatswood Station and warned of the complaint and so he went outside and buried the money in a pile of sand underneath his home.

Haken told the Royal Commission that the complaint was eventually investigated by Detective Sergeant John Burke, who was the ex-principal of the detectives course.[6] All four officers involved got together (a 'scrum down') and pieced together a version of events and explanation with the knowledge that they would be interviewed by Internal Affairs. In evidence to the Royal Commission, Haken reported that the detectives were interviewed and all denied the charge and maintained the fabricated story.[7] As a result, the charge was not sustained.

While at Chatswood, Haken would often go with his work mates to a steakhouse on the Lane Cove River for dinner. The place was called Willy Fennell's and then the Double Bay Steak House. It was cheap and in the area. Haken's future wife Jane was then a waitress living in a flat underneath the steakhouse, with one of the other girls who worked there, and that was where Haken met her. Haken now suggests 'it was probably the worst steak I ever had'.

When asked to describe her he says, 'She looked like a Barbie doll'. They met around 1975. Jane was only twenty years old and Trevor was twenty-five. He saw her at the steakhouse a number of times. 'She was a very nice person and she was a good sort, a very good sort!' They got on very well and soon graduated from having a steak to having a few drinks after work to having lots of drinks in her flat after work.

The steakhouse was 'a boozy sort of a place', a place for long lunches and lots of drinks. It was a lifestyle they both enjoyed. 'I think she was enthralled with the idea of the cops coming down and eating at her steakhouse and showing her a lot of attention, and so that's the way it developed from there.' Trevor and Jane lived together for a time and married in 1977.

By now Haken was Detective Constable (first class) based at Chatswood; he was later promoted to Detective Senior Constable while still at Chatswood. He was moved to Pymble at one point during this time. He and Jane bought a caravan and intended to live on a property on the Hawkesbury River owned by work mate Michael Stevens. They wanted to try what Trevor now describes as 'a hippie lifestyle'.

After nearly four months they found the river location too remote. It was then that they bought a small two bedroom fibro house in Mount Kuring-gai, for $38,950. At the time, the northern suburbs was thought to be a bit far from the city but it was a nice area for kids to grow up in. There was a railway station within close walking distance and so initially Haken would take the train to work. Not long after he bought the house, his boss, George Sheill, bought the house opposite. As Sheill was a detective sergeant in charge of a division, he had a car provided and Haken began travelling with him.

George Sheill came to Chatswood from Merrylands in Sydney's west and according to Haken, brought a bit of the western suburbs with him. He would go out for long lunches a couple of times a week. (Some detectives were called 'brown baggers'. The sign of a failed detective was somebody who brought their lunch to work. If you had to bring your sandwiches then you were not very successful compared to the others.) Haken had worked with Merv Beck at North Sydney. Beck wanted to know where you were all the time and kept a fairly good eye on his staff. In contrast, Sheill enjoyed a lunch and so the station became a very social place.

At these lunches detectives were treated well and would receive 'mates' rates'. There was no real purpose to the lunches other than allowing Sheill and his associates to enjoy the detective lifestyle. They would go to lunch and drink right through to five o'clock and then everyone would go to the RSL club and continue to drink. The downside for Haken, who at the time was travelling with Sheill, was that he arrived home later and later.

This lifestyle was not conducive to married life. It became such a problem that Haken had to cut a deal with Sheill. If Haken was travelling with him they were to leave at 7pm instead of 8pm. This caused friction when Sheill often reneged.

Haken and Sheill 'carried on with some dreadful things — I'm talking improper behaviour'. They often split stolen moneys and had scrum downs to thwart internal inquiries. Ironically, Sheill was later promoted to head of Internal Affairs. This suited Haken:

I had both my partners in good positions. There's George as head of Internal Affairs and my other partner Alan West in a senior position with Internal Security, and I'm out there doing [corrupt] things so I suppose I've won the daily double. It was such a waste of time. I really wish I had my life again. You want to be a part of the group, so you do what's expected of you ... but it all turns to shit really. Your marriage buggers up and everything buggers up. Big waste of time, big waste of money and big waste of your life.

Among Haken's colleagues at Chatswood was a detective nicknamed 'Kimbies', a detective who was 'prone to having a drink'. He was given the nickname Kimbies because, like the nappy, it was said that he was 'always full of piss'. True to form, Kimbies was in the Willoughby North Hotel at lunch on 27 November 1978. Kimbies was there to make sure that the pub was doing business and that there was plenty of beer when the boys came up after work, and he was doing a good job. However, across the road from the pub was the local Westpac bank. On that day, Arthur Joseph Loveday and Munci Onat were sitting in a car with shotguns waiting to rob the bank.

They wore mechanics overalls and balaclavas, and had sawn-off twelve-gauge shotguns. Loveday ran into the Bank and fired the twelve gauge into the ceiling, yelling 'Everybody down, everybody on the floor', then turned around and barked 'Where are you smart-arse tellers?' The tellers were on the floor like everybody else. At the sound of a shot, those in the pub across the road ran onto the street to see what was happening. Kimbies had retired to the toilet as he didn't want to get involved. So, although Chatswood Detectives had someone on the ground as an armed robbery was taking place, his response wasn't from the manual. Haken, recalling Kimbies reaction, laughs: 'Two guys with balaclavas and twelve-gauge shotguns ... fuck that!'

If Kimbies knew who he was dealing with, he would probably have hidden earlier. Loveday was what police would call a career criminal. Haken's view of Loveday is to the point: 'He is just a lifetime crook, a boob [jail] rat and an arsehole'. A quick review of

Loveday's history shows that Haken's analysis, while not polite, is accurate. In recent years, Loveday did time in Berrima Jail with former detective Roger Rogerson. He was a senior figure in the Bandidos motorcycle gang and has served time in prison for rape, armed robbery and kidnapping. He has escaped from jail twice. When pulled over by police on the north coast, he jumped out of the car and escaped. Says Haken, 'He basically ran a marathon and swam over a couple of rivers — unbelievable! He's just a gorilla. There is no fear in him at all. It was Onat who said that he is absolutely cold as ice. He'd go off to do a hold-up like you'd go to buy a packet of chewing gum. He'd say, "I'm just going to do a hold-up."'

The tellers at Willoughby that day had to get up on their feet when Loveday threw each of them a pillowcase and told them to fill them with money. He exited with about $25,000. When he and Onat ran back across the street, all the drinkers from the pub were standing outside. Loveday shouted to the assembled drinkers, 'No heroes!' Faced with two armed hoodlums, they complied. The bank robbers dumped the stolen getaway car at a nearby park.

Chatswood Detectives arrived and took statements. They had cars circulating in the area looking for the suspect vehicle. The place was fingerprinted but not much was found. The next morning Haken got a 'phone call from a man who ran a timber yard, and who'd heard about the robbery. He said, "Look, I don't know if it's got anything to do with anything but yesterday I saw a bloke throw something down a drain near the timber yard which is about half a mile or so away from the bank". It turned out to be a pair of numberplates that were registered to an address in Mascot.

'Ninety per cent of your work is luck and anybody who sort of kicks it the other way is having themselves on. It is a lot of hard work and foot slog, but it all goes hand and glove with a little bit of luck here and there,' says Haken.

Haken called the Armed Hold-up Squad as they had information that suggested the inquiry would go further, but Chatswood did not have any more people to investigate. Haken spoke to Roger Rogerson, 'which was sort of like talking to God in those days'. He said he would send some guys out to Mascot.

At Mascot they 'turned over' (interviewed and searched) a young suspect. He happened to be the brother of a Playboy centrefold model. At the Mascot address they found the car that had been seen when the numberplates were dumped. The Armed Hold-up Squad officers then joined the search of the house.

Haken noticed that the youth was lying on the bed and did not get up, which was unusual behaviour. As he was full of bravado and cheek, Haken began pulling him off the bed, telling him to 'get up'. At the same time, another detective turned over the mattress. There, they found a large number of one dollar and two dollar notes, evidence that he was a minor player who had been thrown the bones of a decent haul. A thorough search was then carried out.

Detectives could not get access underneath the drawers of a built-in divan and so they ripped it off its mountings. Beneath were two sawn-off shotguns, which were apparently those that had been used in the hold-up. Following the locating of the guns, the youth's sister gave up the location of the armed robbers. 'Once you've got something to charge somebody with, they're more likely to give you assistance,' says Haken.

The youth's job was to meet up with Loveday whenever they decided to do a hold-up and give them the guns and a stolen car. In addition, the youth got a set of 'cold plates', plates that would not have been reported stolen. The youth would go to a shopping centre carpark at the last minute before they were going to do a job and steal a set of plates.

This was the case with the Westpac robbery. When Haken checked the plates the next day, it appeared that they had nothing outstanding on them. In fact, they had been reported stolen but were put in a Crime Report instead of a Stolen Motor Vehicle Report. After finding the shotguns, detectives spoke with the youth's sister who was concerned about her brother. She decided she would tell police where the other people involved could be found.

Haken told the Royal Commission that Detective Sergeant George Sheill, Detective Sergeant Alan West and three others from Chatswood turned up at a unit in Lane Cove with Detective Senior Constable Ian Donald and police from the Armed Hold-up Squad, including Detective Sergeant John Bourke and Detective Sergeant Roger Rogerson.[8] This operation was to be an 'A-grade' event.[9]

Loveday and the others were on the third floor. The unit was surrounded by police. Alan West stood at the door of the unit with his shoes and socks off in the belief that the crooks would look under the door and not suspect that the police were outside. Haken then heard Detective Ron Morris call out, 'Get back inside or I'll blow your fuckin' head off!' At this Haken pulled West away from the door, believing 'we were going to be blown away'. Loveday was on the balcony and was about to dive from there to escape. When he saw the ring of heavily armed police he changed his mind and went back inside.

Loveday was found sitting on a mattress on the floor. His hair was cut extremely short and bleached blonde and so he was not easily recognisable. Burke was the detective who realised it was Loveday and was shaking with excitement. He shouted, 'Fuck, it's Loveday in there!' Haken thought, 'Finding Loveday was like finding the golden goose. He would lead to a lot of money. And we fucked up and didn't get any of it. That shows you why you don't spread your information around!' Loveday placed his hands together, waiting for handcuffs, and said, 'There are no guns here'.

In evidence eventually given before the Royal Commission, Haken stated that Chatswood detectives found $1500 in Onat's car but the remainder of the money was not found.[10] Onat was taken with the $1500 to Chatswood to be interviewed, while Loveday was taken by the Armed Hold-up Squad to be interviewed in the city. The $1500 was divided six ways in George Sheill's office, the recipients being Haken, George Sheill, Alan West and three others at Chatswood. But that left a lot of money unaccounted for.

Haken was told where a good percentage of the money went. 'I heard that some of the hold-up squad blokes got it. Loveday had been out for a while and done a lot of robberies. He was on the lam [on the run and wanted] at that stage.' Haken was told by Ian Donald that some of the Armed Hold-up guys had done a deal with Loveday not to lock up his girlfriend (for harbouring a criminal or whatever charge they wanted).

Donald had worked with Haken at Chatswood and was now with the Armed Hold-up Squad. Haken told the Royal Commission that Donald had got into trouble with others in the squad because he made a suggestion that they ought to think about dividing 'the whack up' with the blokes from Chatswood because it was their job in the first place.[11] Donald was told very smartly that if he wanted to work at Chatswood then he could go back, but he should remember he was now with the Armed Hold-up Squad.

CHAPTER 6

FROM DRUG SQUAD TO PHILLIP STREET

In 1982 the Stewart Royal Commission into Drug Trafficking had heard evidence that, over the years, detectives in the Drug Squad had recycled confiscated drugs and fixed court cases involving drug offenders. Some detectives had these offenders sell drugs on their behalf. While some of these detectives had resigned by the end of 1978, others were untouched and promoted into positions of even more responsibility. For Haken, going from Chatswood to the Drug Squad was like 'leaving Earth and going to another planet'.

The Royal Commission was to hear from Haken that corruption in this squad was systemic.[1] Once you were in the Drug Squad you were definitely 'playing A grade'. Haken's evidence was that the business of taking money from people 'you turned over' was an everyday occurrence at the Drug Squad. The only thing that varied was the amount of money involved. Haken was asked by Justice Wood why he had engaged in these corrupt practices for so long when he had also performed properly his duties at other times. He told Justice Wood that 'It didn't appear to me at the time to be grossly improper.' 'It was in line with the behaviour that had been accepted throughout the time I had been in plainclothes.'

Haken was reported as telling Justice Wood: 'If one could get a personal benefit by short circuiting an inquiry, there was nothing wrong with that. It didn't seem through the course of my service there was great difficulty in finding somebody to carry out untoward activity with.'[2]

Another newspaper at the time of the Commission reported Haken's evidence that the majority of the squad were involved in stealing money from offenders, manufacturing evidence, 'loading up' suspects and warning offenders of pending raids.[3] Offenders were aware that if they were arrested it was possible to get off a charge if they paid the right people. As Haken states, 'It was a way of getting off the charges, basically. If you are going to be locked up, what better way is there than to be fined at the scene and go on your way? You pay the fine now, and everybody's happy.'

It was good money for Haken and the other detectives who participated, but most of it was 'pissed up against the wall' in long lunches at the best places in town. 'It cost a bomb of money to live in the Drug Squad, because it was just a forever drink; they were just absolutely mad, they seemed to have a death wish of wanting to spend money and drink and … it was crazy.'

Detectives lived in their own world. Former Police Commissioner, John Avery, told the *Sydney Morning Herald* how some detectives 'would swan around the office with more style than a French madam and if they spoke to a uniformed bloke at all it would be with condescension.'[4]

It used to be said that drovers were overnight millionaires — they would be paid one day and be broke the next. That seemed to be the way of the Drug Squad; no one went home at the end of the day. 'You wouldn't last long in the squad if you weren't a part of everything that went on.' Apart from getting drunk there was the serious business of putting people in jail by whatever means available.

On one occasion, detectives from the Drug Squad had taken a quantity of heroin from a householder in a block of flats in the eastern suburbs. They wanted to plant this heroin on Henry Charles Landini. Landini was alleged by police to be a known heroin supplier who had successfully avoided being arrested by police. They decided his time had come and Haken agreed to participate in 'loading up' Landini.

Haken told the Royal Commission that it was agreed that drugs would be planted on Landini so that he would be locked up.[5] He added that Detective Senior Constable Glen Ross revealed the plan to Haken who was given the task of cutting the heroin. The reason for this was to increase the quantity of heroin that would be 'found'. It would also give the appearance of it being ready for sale. This would give the Drug Squad the option of charging Landini with supply. Haken cut the heroin with icing sugar and placed it into a number of five-gram plastic bags.

Further on, Haken added that the squad, composed of detectives Glen Ross, Steve Chidgey, Les Knox, Tony Gardener and Michael Leary, drove out to the Penrith area where Landini lived.[6] Les Knox was the president of the Leonay Golf Club and, as it was near Landini's place, they waited there, drinking until he left his home. The squad had had quite a few drinks by the time Landini left his home, but this was not going to be a difficult operation. Landini's Mercedes Benz was stopped along the freeway to Sydney and detectives placed the heroin in a pair of shoes in the boot of his car. Landini was arrested for possession of heroin and pleaded guilty in the District Court.

Another incident involved Graham 'Abo' Henry. Henry was a first-class crook. He had been in and out of jail for a long time. He had a tattoo that said, 'When I die I'm going to Heaven because I've done my time in hell — Grafton Jail.' Grafton Jail was a tough jail for prisoners who were classified 'intractables'. It was a maximum-security facility that operated until the mid 1970s. Prisoners were 'flogged' (bashed) as soon as they arrived and for most of the time they were there. They would do most of their sentence stuck in their cell. When they were allowed out for exercise, they would walk along a yellow line with their chin on their chest. If they looked up they were flogged. Grafton Jail was a violent hellhole and Abo Henry was a graduate.

Abo was targeted by the undercover section of the squad. Detective Bill Mansell was undercover and met Henry to arrange a buy. This resulted in an arranged sale of one pound of heroin for an agreed price of about $90,000. Haken thinks that it was probably Neddy Smith's 'gear' (drugs). Henry and Mansell met atop a high-rise building. Abo said to Mansell that if anything was to go wrong 'I'll be back up here and [pointing to the ground below] you'll be down there.'

The sale was to take place in Henry's car in Mount Street, North Sydney. Police were not going to take any chances with Abo. Surveillance was put in place and squads of men surrounded the streets around his vehicle. There was a parked panel van with detectives Rousos and Moss inside while Haken and Michael Stevens were parked directly behind Henry's vehicle but several cars back.

They were all in position for a quick response and arrest once the sale took place. Mansell had a hidden electronic device that he would press once the buy had taken place. This would be the code three signal that went back to the control car. The control car would then announce to other vehicles via radio that it was time to move in.

The Royal Commission heard that when the code three signal was announced, Rousos and Moss ran from the panel van towards Henry's car. Rousos fired a twelve-gauge shotgun through the driver's window.[7]

Haken recalls that Mansell was 'burnt-out nervous', and ran vomiting from Henry's car. The blast from the shotgun put paid to any suggestion of Henry trying to escape. Henry had been a boxer and his reflexes were such that he moved in time to save his life.

Detective Steve Matthews who Haken says they squad nicknamed 'the Moth' — that is, someone who always comes out at night and is attracted to the bright lights — was a part of the operation.

Haken told the Royal Commission that Matthews opened the passenger door and dropped a small silver pistol onto the floor of the car.[8] As Matthews dropped the pistol, Henry looked up and said, 'not you, anyone but not you'. A search of Henry's car revealed another handgun, an old-style dark-coloured revolver in the centre console of the car. Both guns were lodged as evidence. Henry was charged with supplying a large quantity of heroin and for possession of guns. Bail was refused and he was jailed for nearly seven years. Detective Rousos later resigned from the police service, but before he did he came into contact with Frank Avery.

Frank Avery was an old crook who was selling heroin at the Palace Hotel in South Dowling Street. He was arrested by Rousos and Ross and made a deal to get out of going to jail — he would become an informant. The information that came from Avery was good and led to the investigation of the Painters and Dockers drug supply in Melbourne. Mick 'Jukebox' Drury and Joanne Norman were New South Wales police who both worked as undercovers on a heroin supply operation which centred on a person named Williams. The information and investigation led to his arrest. Drury went on to become an anti-corruption fighter who lectured at the police academy.

Darren Goodsir identifies Rousos as the detective who Rogerson asked to see Drury about the Melbourne drug case.[9]

While there is no dispute about this aspect, there are two conflicting versions of the events. It was the Crown's case in bribery charges brought against Rogerson that Rousos made the approach on behalf of Rogerson offering money to compromise the evidence in the Melbourne trial of Williams. Rogerson vehemently denied this version of events in court and maintained that he had an informant who had come to him with information about the drug operation in Melbourne saying that something strange was taking place. The approach from Rousos was to speak to Drury so as to alert him of these concerns and to check the information from Rogerson's informant.

Sometime after the approach from Rousos, Drury was shot by an unknown assailant through the window of his house. It has been alleged that it was Christopher 'Hitman' Flannery who shot Drury, but as Flannery disappeared many years ago, supposedly buried beneath the freeway to Newcastle ('he's the speed humps near the Central Coast') or in the sandhills around Sydney, we'll never know. Luckily, Drury survived the shooting but things got messy for all those involved in the matter. Anyone involved in the passing of information from Williams to Drury about the Painters and Dockers ended up dead.

As Haken describes it, the informant Avery 'turned into an instant heroin addict' — that is, he was given a 'hot shot' (a lethal overdose of heroin, forced on the victim). Haken contends that this is a classic way of covering a murder. The two men who introduced Drury to Williams were found dead under suspicious circumstances. 'One of them was found shot dead on the highway.'

According to Haken, soon after, Williams' brother was walking down Williams' driveway when a gunman forced him to his knees and pointed a gun to his head. The brother said, 'You've got the wrong man', to which the gunman replied, 'Bad luck'. He was then shot dead.

Towards the end of his time at the Drug Squad, Haken worked with Mal Brammer. Brammer was very well thought of in police circles. Together they worked on an undercover drug supply operation involving a man named Sam Scott in the Queanbeyan area. Scott was a former safe breaker with what Haken describes as 'more form than Phar Lap' (Scott was referred to as 'the horseman' in the Winchester inquiry). As part of this investigation, undercover police officers, detectives Kippax and Mennie, attempted to buy cannabis from Scott. Haken told the Royal Commission that Mal Brammer did not trust the other drug squad officers and so did not tell all the officers (apart from Haken, Kippax and Mennie and two Queanbeyan police) of Scott's identity.[10] Haken claimed that this resulted in a lack of surveillance and crucial intelligence relating to Scott's method of operation by police.

One of the undercover officers was shot at by Vincent Kimber (one of Scott's associates), bashed around the head and dumped beside a road. Scott and Kimber disappeared immediately after the assault.

The situation was serious and so a meeting was held at a hotel in Bowral between Jim Willis, the officer in charge of the Drug Squad, Mal Brammer and Bill Cullen, the senior detective of the Southern Highlands. Haken attended the meeting but was excluded from the conversation. The next morning at Queanbeyan, Haken was told that Scott had told Cullen on the phone the location of the pistol used in the shooting. Haken and other police searched unsuccessfully for the pistol in the area described.

Later that day, Cullen and Brammer located the pistol. Haken was to tell the Royal Commission that they bragged to Haken that it was in exactly the place Scott had claimed, wrapped in a shirt, and that the detectives had obviously not looked properly.[11] Haken stated to the Royal Commission that he did not believe them, and suspected that the pistol was obtained directly from Scott. Shortly after the finding of Scott's pistol, he gave himself up to Detective Sergeant Cullen. Brammer and Haken charged Scott with attempted murder and associated matters; Brammer was recorded on the charge sheet as the informant.

Following a dinner meeting between Michael Knight (the Queanbeyan police prosecutor), Brammer and Cullen, the attempted murder charge was dropped although the charges relating to armed robbery remained. It was thought that there was insufficient evidence to proceed with the attempted murder charge.

Haken gave evidence to the Royal Commission that he was unconvinced and suspicious about the finding of Scott's pistol.[12] He spoke to Detective Max Chapman (at the time a serving detective in Queanbeyan), who told Haken that Scott had borrowed a large amount of money to have the attempted murder charge withdrawn.

Chapman and Cullen did not get on. Haken's evidence to the Royal Commission was that he and Brammer argued over the case and the charges.[13] Following the argument, Brammer and Haken's working relationship was strained. 'We were outsmarted by the crooks, and because of that, I suppose, we had more of a fallout than we had had previously.'

A short time after this incident, Haken was transferred to Phillip Street Police Station by Willis, a move that Haken described as a punishment for questioning his superiors over the Scott incident.[14] 'I was told by somebody else that it was pending, and then one day you just get hauled in and they say, 'You're going, see you, you start tomorrow.' There is no right of appeal. There's just, you're on your way.'

Going from the Drug Squad to Phillip Street was a demotion for Haken. 'It was a shit hole,' he says. Luckily for Haken, he was only there a short time. He had formed strong associations with the majority of those at the Drug Squad and as a result, he soon got a job at the Drug Task Force. This was a promotion from Phillip

Street. As he puts it, 'You're kicked in the face but then you manage to kick back.' Haken's short time at Phillip Street has remained memorable for all the wrong reasons.

Phillip Street was seen as a punishment station. 'You're doing a city beat in an office with people who didn't want to be there.' The office was the old courthouse and the meal room was a table in the alleyway that led to the toilet. When it rained, the room couldn't be used. The courthouse leaked, so the offices leaked, and when it rained police would use wastepaper buckets to catch the drips coming through the roof.

Haken tried to get people working on jobs but it was a station with notoriously low morale. 'It was a hopeless place, full of hopeless people. One bloke used to come on night work and he had a key to the Lord Nelson Hotel. He was obviously well known to them and they gave him his own key. So he'd walk out of the station at eleven o'clock soon after he started and stagger back in at seven o'clock in the morning to finish.'

According to Haken, one detective, now thankfully out of the job, used to bring his surf ski and would row up and down the lake in Centennial Park. Police wondered why he could never be found. He didn't do a lot of work but he kept fit. Another uniformed officer would come to work the late shift. He brought his fishing gear and would go and sit on the wall of the Opera House and fish. He wore a cardigan to cover his police uniform and if anybody really wanted him they knew they could find him there. These two uniformed police were both senior officers in charge of the station during various shifts.

While such matters were never really discussed at the Royal Commission (they had bigger fish to fry), they are breathtaking examples of a demoralised organisation without proper management. When the Royal Commission was looking into the behaviour of Graham 'Chook' Fowler it was well documented that if police wanted to find 'Chook' after a certain hour, they would start by looking in the Sir John Young Hotel.

There was plenty of work available if anyone wanted it. 'It's just astounding really, but nobody wanted to do anything.' Haken's enthusiasm and drive was channelled into finding work, but of course it had a silver lining. 'We kicked on and got some terrific jobs going and we made some good dollars, you know. What can I say?' The job was getting done and they lined their pockets as well.

Haken gave evidence to the Royal Commission that on one occasion a number of men were arrested in the eastern suburbs. During a search of the premises police found a large quantity of bottles of alcohol and two outboard motors, one being a black Mercury. None of the property was accounted for officially at the station and it was divided among those police involved in the matter. Haken received a dozen bottles of alcohol (tequila, scotch, brandy) as well as one of the outboard motors. Haken stated to the Royal Commission that the other motor was given to Detective Sergeant Bruce Shields.[15]

As mentioned, shortly after Haken went to Phillip Street, he was transferred to the Joint Federal and State Task Force into Drug Trafficking (JTF). Haken told the Royal Commission that it was while he was at the JTF that he sold the motor to Ray Donaldson for $100.[16] The *Telegraph*'s Ray Chesterton reported that Donaldson denied the charge to the Royal Commission but admitted that he and his son owned boats that the motor would have fitted.[17] A former friend, protected witness JTF6, told the Commission that he sold a boat to Donaldson's brother and asked that the receipt be for less than what was paid. Haken alleged to the Royal Commission that Donaldson later off-loaded the 'Shields' motor to another party. Donaldson would go on to attain the rank of Assistant Commissioner, Regional Commander North of the NSW Police Service. He would face many more questions about his time at the JTF.

CHAPTER 7

JOINT FEDERAL AND STATE TASK FORCE INTO DRUG TRAFFICKING

'If it was a perfect world, sir, the people who were guilty would plead guilty. It's not a perfect world ... it's like fronting up to somebody and saying ... Marquis of Queensbury Rules and they kick you in the balls. It's not like that out there ... it's a big game and the criminals tell lies, the police tell lies ... and if you played by the rules the whole time, you'd lose.'

JTF8, *PROTECTED WITNESS*[1]

The Commonwealth and State Joint Drugs Task Force (JTF) was set up by the federal and state governments in 1976. It included crown prosecutor Greg Smith, with Nicholas Cowdrey and Graham Blewett on the management committee. The purpose of the force was to be a completely independent and well-funded investigative body against drug crime. It was an amalgamation of federal (the Narcotics Bureau, the Commonwealth Police and ACT Police), and state (NSW) police. Something like this had not happened before; its powers were widespread, including the authority to move across borders. The Joint Drugs Task Force was a bold initiative and so being a part of this team was a position of great status; recognition that you were accomplished and on your way up.

During the Wood Royal Commission evidence of corruption within the JTF was presented by a number of JTF members. They eventually corroborated Haken's evidence and admitted their own involvement in such activities as extortion, laying false charges, receiving bribes, planting drugs on accused, the perversion of justice by perjury, the leaking of confidential information, fraud, paying money to receive confidential information, theft and receipt of stolen money.

The Royal Commission was to report that it seemed that members from each service brought prior experience of corrupt practices to the JTF. It questioned the adequacy of the supervision and organisational direction of the task force and commented that those senior officers who claimed to be not involved and unaware of the true state of affairs seemed to remain in that 'blissful state'.[2]

There were a number of protected witnesses who were given code names such as JTF6, JTF7, JTF8 and JTF16. One of these witnesses was once quoted as saying to the Royal Commission about his time at the JTF that 'we were worse than the criminals'.[3]

The effect of evidence given by Haken and many others to the Royal Commission about the JTF was devastating, although it was acknowledged that not all police at the JTF were corrupt. By way of response, legislation was rushed through Parliament enabling police identified as corrupt in the commission to be sacked immediately by The Minister of Police Paul Whelan, with no right of appeal.

When Haken joined in 1983, his duties were initially those of an intelligence officer. Inspector Paul (Pag) Lawrence was in charge. Under Lawrence was a man with an unfortunate surname, Harry

Bendt. Rod Harvey was another investigator from NSW Police; he would later become Chief Superintendent, and Commander, State Major Incidents Group. Harvey's position was declared open during the Royal Commission.[4] Other NSW police at the JTF were Terry Kilpatrick (Snoopy), Ray Southwell (Magoo), Richard Paynter (Docker), Brian Meredith (Lumpy), and later Mark Keane, Bruce Johnston, Geoff Hoggett, Mario Zanatta and Peter Scott. The Federal Police (AFP) investigators were deputy leader John Travers, followed by Rob Milner and then Phil Lawrence. The investigators included Ken Hardiman, Chris Dent, Michael Tracey (Schooner), Glen Matinca (Tinkerbell), Alan Taciak (Tash), Denis Pattle (Ace), Laurie Grey (NAS, 'nervous as shit'), John Cushion ('Two Storeys', for his height), Dave Allen (Clint), Terry McNamara, Frank Gillies, Kay Parkins (Daphne) and Vali Jadescro.

In Haken's evidence to the Royal Commission, he clearly asserted that neither the leader (NSW) or deputy leader (AFP) were aware of any corrupt activities at the JTF. Haken told the Royal Commission that his first recollection of corruption at the JTF was shortly before he joined the task force when he overheard a conversation between Ray Southwell and Richard Paynter in the main office of the JTF. He said that he had told David Kelleher (a drug dealer) that for $8000 he would make sure that Kelleher was omitted from a brief. According to his evidence, this offer was accepted by Kelleher and Southwell received the money. Haken described how he realised that the JTF was no different from the Drug Squad in regard to corrupt practices referring to an incident involving Ray Southwell's personal car.[5]

Haken also told the Royal Commission that Southwell had damaged the front suspension of his car and rather than pay to have it fixed himself, Southwell borrowed Ray Donaldson's Commodore and swapped the front ends of the cars.[6] He then took Donaldson's work car to the government garage at Woolloomooloo and left it there to be repaired. NSW taxpayers footed the bill. Protected witness JTF6 gave evidence to the Royal Commission that involved another investigator's car.

The evidence of JTF6 was made public in a newspaper report under the heading 'Officers Linked to Crime'.[7] JTF6 and Bob Lysaught had been drinking and had driven home in separate cars when JTF6 hit a parked car. JTF6 stated that Lysaught told him to drive around the corner while he called Ray Donaldson to ask what they should do. As the vehicle was badly damaged, he advised that the vehicle should be dumped in a back street in Paddington and reported as stolen to Kings Cross Police.

The Royal Commission was to hear that corruption at the JTF was more than scamming repairs for investigators vehicles. Evidence of secret witness and former AFP officer JTF7 into Operation Bing also came to light.[8] This operation resulted in the arrest of a target named Pat Curry who was later convicted after heroin was found in a hollow partition in the wall of a taxi school which he owned. After Haken and JTF7 interviewed Curry one night, the JTF received a note from his solicitor complaining that there was no furniture in the house and that everything had been taken from the house (including a refrigerator). JTF7 told the Commission, 'Just about everything that wasn't nailed down was gone.' JTF7's assertion was that 'it was common knowledge that John Cushion had taken it', and that Ray Donaldson, then a commanding officer in the JTF, had ordered the goods be put back.[9]

The JTF practised a policy of 'target policing' — that is, identifying persons of interest and targeting them. At the end of December 1983, Operation Pickup investigated the drug activities of two people, Salisbury and Powley. The operation would also involve the corrupt behaviour of police at the JTF. The JTF had Salisbury and Powley under surveillance for a number of weeks. A controlled buy of drugs was organised from Melbourne. This involved a buyer being monitored from Melbourne and carrying money that had been recorded by Victorian Police. The buyer flew to Sydney, where he was watched by Task Force surveillance as he made contact with and bought drugs from Salisbury and Powley. He flew back to Melbourne, where Victorian Police arrested him.

Haken gave evidence to the Royal Commission that Salisbury and Powley were in an undercover parking area of a block of units on Sydney's northern beaches. A garage had been rented by the pair and it was secured by an automatic door and security device. After leaving the carpark, they were followed for some distance and eventually surrounded and arrested by Task Force members. A search was made of the garage area and over two kilograms of cocaine was found as well as drug paraphernalia.[10]

According to his evidence, Haken stated that the drugs were all properly accounted for but the money was not. The drug dealer must have known what was to take place as he said to JTF10, 'Someone will get a nice new brick veneer tonight.' There was a hard-sided briefcase and a soft bag full of money. The money that was recorded by Victorian Police was set aside; the rest was taken back to the Task Force office.

As an intelligence officer, Haken had been in the office all day but was still to be a part of the split of the search money.

Haken's evidence at the Royal Commission stated that a meeting took place between Haken, Harry Bendt, Michael Tracey, Terry Kilpatrick and others. They decided to divide the money among the police who worked on the brief. Those who were present on the night would receive $13,000 each, while those who were not would receive $1000 each.[11] This split was subsequently referred to as 'the Christmas club' because of its proximity to Christmas and because 'it was a nice little present'.[12] Haken put the money for those not present in the safe in the intelligence office, and handed the split to most of those who were away on the night.

Haken told the Royal Commission that every police officer at the JTF received money except the leader, Paul Lawrence, deputy leader AFP Milner, Laurie Grey and Kay Parkin. Laurie Grey (NAS) was present during the job but went home feeling sick before the split.

The *Sydney Morning Herald* reported the evidence of JTF 10 at the Royal Commission that a senior officer, Harry Bendt, had tried to get him and two others to give him their $13,000 split for a real estate venture he had in mind. They declined as, according to JTF10, 'he would have ripped them off'.[13]

The money that had been sent from Victoria was retained and placed into evidence. However, as the money was being booked up it was discovered that some of the Victorian money was missing. Haken and Terry Kilpatrick began to feverishly call around to try to locate the missing money. Haken told the Royal Commission that Dennis Pattle said that he had received the missing money from protected witness JTF16. Haken drove to Pattle's home and picked up the money.

Haken never placed corrupt money payments in the bank but spent it instead. Haken's mother comments, 'The money that he got that he shouldn't have got he put into things like house payments and high living.' There was a lot of bad feeling from other police at the JTF as a result of the uneven split of money from the Christmas club.

At the time of their inquiries, Royal Commission investigators executed a search warrant on JTF16's house. They found PVC pipes stuffed with money buried in a garden bed. It was reported that in another part of the garden (set in concrete buried under a tree) was a Smith and Wesson .38 police issue revolver belonging to another AFP officer. They had had a dispute and so JTF16 stole the officer's gun and buried it.[14] Losing your service revolver is a serious offence. JTF16 told the Royal Commission that he accepted money while working at the Federal Bureau of Narcotics, in the AFP and during the time of the taskforce and accepted money stolen from drug raids and the sale of confiscated drugs. He told of Haken's plan to steal the floor covering from a commercial premises in their office in the Westfield towers. JTF16 said this was 'the best one he ever came up with'. Of course, the plan was hatched after a particularly long session of drinking at a hotel. Haken gave roles to his task force comrades and with what JTF16 described as 'military precision' the carpet was taken and evidently used in Haken's home. JTF16 was eventually dismissed from the AFP and served periodic detention. 'The last time I heard of him he was selling cars,' says Haken.

Haken gave evidence at the Royal Commission that protected witness JTF4 and another person were running a drug importation business with an individual from Hong Kong.[15] Operation Post was set up to target this importation but it went terribly wrong when the operation orders were stolen from a JTF car. Full operational orders contained names of all the crooks involved, all the addresses of safe houses (a house where crooks can go in an emergency to hide out, where they can store drugs, make telephone calls and be reasonably certain that the lines aren't intercepted) and telephone numbers (of main houses, safe houses, associates and dealers). Such orders represented a detailed running sheet on the whole operation.

JTF16 and his partner left their JTF car and their bags were taken. The operation orders and their guns were in their bags. They should not have had their operation orders outside the office, nor should they have left them in their vehicle. They were in serious trouble and returned ashen-faced and pleaded with other officers to help them. And so Haken and other police forced the boot with a jemmy to make the 'break-in' seem legitimate. There was a suggestion that they might have been bribed to release the orders but Haken does not believe this. However, the papers did fall into the wrong hands. A crook by the name of Leighton Dunlop contacted JTF4's partner and said to him, 'I have some papers you would be interested in'. As Haken describes it, 'Operation Post went arse up'. After that, the JTF was determined to get JTF4, his partner and the others identified in Operation Post.

According to Haken's evidence to the Royal Commission, around Christmas 1983, the JTF received information that a certain Eric John Honeysett was going to be at a Christmas party at the Erskineville Hotel; even 'Black Santa' (an Aboriginal Santa Claus) was making an appearance.[16] Honeysett was seen going into the lane at the back of the hotel. The JTF positioned people at both ends of the lane — Michael Tracey, Terry Kilpatrick and nearly everyone from the Task Force was there. Haken was in the hotel with 'Daphne' Kay Parkins. 'We wanted to get him [Honeysett] and it was on the cards that a number of them [police] had decided that he had to go and they would let rip [shoot their weapons].' However, not everything went to plan.

They tried to shoot Honeysett in the back lane and missed. Honeysett climbed a fence and up on to the roof so some police tried to shoot him on the roof and again missed. He then jumped down into a backyard with members of the JTF in pursuit. Dick Paynter cut his upper arm as he tried to get over the fence. Honeysett kicked in a door of a house and started to run through it. Inside the house were two large Greek men. It was a very hot day and they were sleeping in the hallway to try to catch a breeze. As he ran through the house, Honeysett tripped over the Greeks who then jumped on top of him. 'You fat bastards,' he cried. They were too heavy to get out from underneath and so, with the help of 'my big fat Greek captors' Honeysett was finally captured by the JTF.

Honeysett was charged with the attempted murder of Paynter. Rather than state that Paynter had cut his arm climbing over the fence, JTF police said Honeysett was armed with a knife which justified police shooting at him. Haken recalls, 'There was no knife so we had to put a knife into the scenario somewhere and so (the Fed) JTF14 took a knife and threw it back over the fence and of course when the scientific guy was photographing the scene the next day he found the knife.' In his statutory declaration to the Royal Commission, Haken told how Honeysett was taken back to the Drug Squad office at the CIB where he was kicked whilst attempting to run out of the office.

Haken's version of events was confirmed during the Royal Commission investigation of the incident. Detective Paynter, who retired medically unfit from the police service in 1986, had denied to the commission Haken's version of events. Firstly Honeysett told the commission that he 'definitely did not stab Detective Paynter'. Then, protected witness JTF14, an AFP serving detective superintendent was brought back from the United Kingdom (his posting with the Federal Police) and corroborated Haken's evidence. He testified that Paynter had not had his arm cut with a knife but had cut it on a fence.

The incident was reported as 'Federal Officer planted knife at scene of arrest,' and that the Fed JTF14 was told by Detective Dick Paynter that he was going to claim that he was stabbed by Honeysett.[17] He [Paynter] came up and spoke to me and indicated the injury to his arm and he said 'I'll add a bit extra and I will claim that I was stabbed by [Honeysett]. Paynter then gave the Fed JTF14 a knife and asked him to take it back to the scene. He had gone in a car driven by Ray Donaldson with the knife. Donaldson drove him to a lane behind the house where the Fed JTF14 threw the knife over the fence. Justice Wood asked the Fed JTF14 if Donaldson knew "full well" what the Fed JTF14 was going to do and he was told "I think that it would have been fairly obvious, the fact that I'd gone back to the house with him with — yes.' Donaldson interviewed the residents of the house and the knife was found following a search of the garden. The scientific police then came and photographed the knife as evidence of the attack on Paynter by the target Honeysett. Justice Wood asked the Fed JTF14 if his actions were 'utterly inexcusable and impermissable' to which he replied 'yes.' JTF14 said that he agreed to plant the knife out of 'misguided loyalty' to his task force colleagues.[18]

The Royal Commission heard evidence from two former AFP officers, protected witnesses JTF15 and JTF16, who said parts of their statements used to support the police case against Honeysett were false. Their evidence was reported as stating that task force police had met to devise their statements before Honeysett went to court. JTF16 said, '[Det Supt Ray] Southwell and I and other members of the task force sat down in scrum format and devised our statements.' Southwell denied to the Commission that this 'scrum down' took place.[19] Another report of the evidence of JTF10 given at the Royal Commission mentions that the doctor treating Paynter's cut disagreed that the injury was consistent with a wound from a knife. The police told her that it was a pity she couldn't say it was, as the criminal had 63 convictions for rape and assault on women. The doctor then asked 'where do I sign?'[20]

There were further reports of the evidence of JTF15, who said that she had signed a statement containing untruths concerning the alleged wounding of Paynter. Her recollection was that she did not prepare or even read the statement but signed it.[21] Meanwhile, another JTF officer, JTF12 also signed the statement containing untruths because 'it was requested of me'. Mr Southwell was reported by the *Herald* as denying any part of the statement he made had been fabricated, he told the Royal Commission, 'I still firmly believe Paynter was stabbed.' At one stage, Honeysett was facing the possibility of life imprisonment for the alleged attack until he pleaded guilty to a lesser charge.

The press had a field day with the story. Ray Chesterton wrote how the decision of former colleagues to 'assist' the Commission by refuting their earlier favourable evidence for Paynter has left him and Detective Inspector Ray Southwell as the only ones supporting the stabbing theory. He likened Paynter's stabbing in medical terms to a phantom pregnancy. Chesterton described how Southwell and Paynter were hurt by the 'whip of ridicule' from the Commission and the defection of old workmates.[22]

In evidence before the Royal Commission, Southwell also denied the allegation that the JTF fabricated admissions from Honeysett. The counsel assisting the Commission, John Agius asked Southwell, 'You were dealing with a hardened criminal and he made admissions about nearly everything you asked him about?' Southwell stated, 'He did make admissions, yes.'

Counsel assisting, John Agius, asked Paynter at the Royal Commission, 'you know you are a shot bird on this one don't you?' Justice Wood was told by Paynter that he had no idea why colleagues had refuted earlier evidence. Wood suggested to Paynter, 'Could it be that they are telling the truth and you are not?'

The Fed JTF14 lost his job with the Federal Police after giving his evidence about the planting of the knife and the subsequent scrum down and false statements. Haken is appalled at the lack of follow-up:

I don't know quite what happened, someone must have convinced him [the Fed JTF14] to say 'well this happened' and that he'd be okay to go back to England and live happily ever after. One would think that's an open-and-shut case for prosecution. You've got a Federal Police superintendent coming back from England saying, 'Yeah righto, that's what we did' and there's all these other people saying that's what happened, but no prosecutions! I believe that Paynter received a $2500 payment as a result of a criminal compensation payment for this incident. If you have a look at his history, he's claimed for injuries in motor vehicles and other things. Mate, he's the most injured man in history. He shouldn't be able to walk, he should be like Raymond Burr ripping around in a wheelchair!

The DPP hasn't prosecuted the majority of people who ought to have been prosecuted out of the Royal Commission, and people haven't asked why. The DPP should be asked to explain this.

The JTF at one stage targeted some South American drug importers. 'They were so fuckin' organised it was frightening,' says Haken. One importer–wholesaler entered Australia and went straight to the domestic terminal and flew to Melbourne. He then hired a car and drove to the south coast of New South Wales. By this stage he had picked up a kilo of cocaine from a package that he had sent in previously. He met with a known Sydney drug supplier (Neville Stevens, who was buying large quantities) who had ridden a motorbike from Sydney to purchase drugs from the South American. The JTF was there and arrested both men in the act of supplying and purchasing. The South Americans' method of concealment was fascinating. They had dinner sets packed in wooden crates and flown into Melbourne. The police knew that the drugs were in this shipment. Despite all the testing, no one was able to determine the exact whereabouts of the drugs. They eventually found them inside the pieces of wood that made up the packing cases. There was at least a kilo per case.

The importer had photos of his home in Miami. On show was a large room on the scale of the foyer of a hotel, with a number of lounge suites that looked out through two-storey high windows onto the open sea. Outside was a jetty with several speedboats tied up. These were the trappings of big-time dealing.

Haken gave evidence to the Royal Commission about another operation mounted on a cocaine importer and supplier named Gomez. Bruce Johnston was in charge of the operation and Matinca, Kilpatrick and Haken were involved, as were the majority of the Task Force members. The JTF had followed Gomez around and established where he was storing things. A search warrant was executed at a motel in the Double Bay shopping centre. Gomez was in the shopping centre with his female associate when police arrested him. They took them to the hotel room, where money and cocaine were found. Haken also found a wooden plank (part of the same method of shipment) in the motel room. The other storage points were searched, including the lockers of Oxford Street bus station and the domestic terminal at Mascot. Gomez and his female associate were taken back to the CIB to be interviewed.

Haken told the Royal Commission than an amount was taken and divided by Haken and Matinca. There was a 'whack up' of the money that was taken from Gomez (about $5000). It was shared among Haken, Matinca, Kilpatrick and Johnston.[23]

Due to legal manoeuvring Gomez was released on bail. He fled Australia on the cruiseship *Fairstar*. Incredibly, Ray Southwell had taken leave and had the plum job of security on the *Fairstar*. Haken recalls that this was a great lurk for police in the past, who would take holidays and act as 'Master of Arms' on a ship. There would generally be two detectives per cruise but sometimes four detectives on big ships.

On board, Southwell recognised Gomez and phoned from the ship to inform the JTF. The first port of call was Noumea, so the JTF arranged for the French police to meet the boat when it docked. Gomez departed the boat and they followed him to a hotel, where he was later joined by another male who had flown from France. When police entered the room, they were in the process of placing Gomez's photograph into a stolen passport that the second man had brought from France. He was subsequently arrested and extradited from Noumea.

David Kelleher became a major target of the JTF while Haken was there. He had been a known drug dealer for years, mainly dealing in heroin. Haken had spent months in a surveillance position monitoring Kelleher and his associates. During this time it became obvious that not only were the criminals involved in drug importation, but so too were some of the lawyers with whom he was involved. A prominent Sydney lawyer was regularly taped in conversations with Kelleher, advising him on methods of avoiding investigation into his heroin importation business. It was a close partnership that was obvious to police. This surveillance went on for months and following the arrest of Kelleher and his associates for large quantity importation, a decision was given that the lawyer would not be prosecuted because of professional privilege. Says Haken, 'This sort of behaviour stuck in the craw of all police who had witnessed the blatant criminal behaviour. The lawyer used his position to sidestep prosecution. It was scandalous. You talk about the brotherhood!'

On another occasion, the JTF had received information that Dennis Keane would be at his home in Sydenham with an amount of drugs. The JTF executed a search warrant and found his wife, Kim Mary Keane, and her children present but not Dennis. Police discovered a five gram bag of heroin in a brown paper bag in the rangehood of the stove. Kim Keane claimed that she did not know about the drugs and was charged with supplying heroin and goods in custody of about $9000.

Haken told the Royal Commission that he was approached by Peter George, a detective sergeant who had worked with him at the Drug Squad. George offered Haken $2000 on behalf of

Dennis Keane to not get in the way of an attempt by Kim's legal counsel to have her brother Wayne Alexander plead guilty to possession of the drugs.[24] Wayne Alexander was in jail at the time doing a sentence for armed robbery and said that he left the drugs at the house. Haken comments, 'As if any good junkie would leave five grams behind?' There were some holes in this defence as the person he claimed to have bought the drugs from had been murdered a month before he said he bought them. Nevertheless, Haken accepted the offer and his plea was accepted. Kim Keane was discharged. The charge in relation to goods in custody was also discharged. Haken says, 'I got another $500 out of that for returning the $9000 before his solicitor could get his hands on it.'

Jancine Nicholls was a high-class prostitute, a heroin user and the girlfriend of informant Leighton Dunlop. Dunlop was the receiver of the stolen operation documents taken in Operation Post. Jancine was with Dunlop all the time and was an important witness for the JTF. Haken had regular contact with them during the time of the prosecution of Operation Post. Charlie Low and Honeysett had both been arrested and were before the courts, along with other members of the same conspiracy to import heroin into Australia.

During the prosecution, one of the principal accused, Tony Cameron, was in Long Bay Jail. There was no doubt among the police involved in Operation Post that he was targeted by some of his fellow accused. They had heard that on the following Monday the prosecution would be producing a mystery witness and so among themselves they decided that one of them 'was off'. If you are suspected of giving evidence against your co-accused, it can be a death sentence.

Tony Cameron was well-connected in Kings Cross. He had been a health inspector with the city council and was a heroin importer. His mother ran a nightclub in Orwell Street in the Cross. Unfortunately for Tony, his co-accused thought that he was to be the mystery witness at Monday's hearing. He did not live to see Monday morning — he died in jail sometime on Sunday afternoon. On Monday morning, all other co-accused except for Honeysett and Low, pleaded guilty. The mystery witness, Leighton Dunlop, appeared.

It was believed that Cameron had been injected with air bubbles, which caused his death. However, Charlie Low told Haken at the time that the diagnosis 'was bullshit' and that Cameron had died of a heroin overdose. Low was correct, it was a heroin overdose. It's Haken's view that this was no accidental overdose but that Cameron had died as the result of a forcible injection (a 'hot shot'). Hours after Cameron's body was found, the co-accused would find that they had killed the wrong man.

Jancine and Leighton were both under the protection of the JTF. They had a safe house away from Sydney where Haken kept in touch with them during the conduct of Operation Post, paying their rent and making sure they kept out of trouble. Included in witness protection is the idea that you 'lay low' and stay out of sight. Unfortunately, Haken had to explain to Jancine that her habit of sunbaking topless in the backyard was not what they had in mind. The neighbours certainly noticed Jancine's presence. 'She was a great sort, spectacularly pretty and extremely well spoken.'

In 1992, while working at the Drug Unit, Haken had been contacted by uniformed police and requested to go to William Street. It was there that he again met with Jancine who had asked police to contact him. She knew that Haken was working in the Cross and was concerned that she'd seen Charlie Low in the area. Low was now out of jail.

Jancine asked Haken to help get her out of the country as quickly as possible to join an ex-boyfriend in New Zealand.

This would have only cost a relatively small amount of money. Haken said that he would do what he could but he found it very difficult.

> I chased through all the channels that were still there from the Task Force days. In the space of two days I couldn't find anybody willing to give her assistance. Everybody shunned the responsibility. 'Oh the Task Force is finished' or 'It wasn't my job' — you know, that type of thing. And 'Whoever took over from the Task Force, you'll have to see them'. 'Whoever was her case officer, you'll have to see him.'

Two days after Jancine pleaded for help from Haken, she was found dead in the Pleasure Chest (a shooting gallery–brothel) in Kings Cross. Haken recalls, 'It was another classic overdose. Nobody saw anything, nobody knew anything. She was found between the wall and the bed, and it appeared to me that there'd been some form of struggle. She'd obviously been given a hot shot.'

Jancine's death still upsets Haken because something could have and should have been done to protect her. 'Here's a classic example of how we treat witnesses once their use-by date has been reached. And don't I know that!'

Ray Donaldson, nicknamed 'Box' or 'the Smiling Assassin', was an investigator when Haken joined but would progress to become deputy leader of the JTF. When the Royal Commission was operational, Donaldson, then Assistant Commissioner of the NSW Police Service, was asked by Gary Crooke, QC, senior counsel assisting the inquiry, 'And there's never been an occasion when you've done anything that a fellow police man would take as a want of support for the Royal Commission by you by way of word or deed. Is that correct?' Donaldson answered 'correct.'

Donaldson, however, was secretly taped by the Royal Commission in a conversation with protected witness JTF6 commenting on the inquiry. The tape was played at the Royal Commission and reported in the *Daily Telegraph*: 'The whole fucking thing's frog shit, you know. This is a hundred million, this is, I reckon, it's the WOFTAM [Waste of Fucking Time and Money] commission, mate!' 'Any team of fucking galloots could have gone up the Cross, it's been going on up there for a hundred years.'[25] Donaldson admitted to Justice Wood that when he appeared before the Commission, he had closed his mind to the possibility that police in the JTF could be corrupt.[26] If the evidence of JTF8 is to be believed, then Donaldson certainly had a way with words. It was reported that Donaldson had called Haken a 'horrible lashing little c...' when he learned that Haken had not properly shared money stolen from a drug suspect. [Lashing means dudding or ripping off your friends].[27]

Donaldson's involvement in the JTF would eventually end his career in the NSW Police Service when the Wood Royal Commission turned out not to be a WOFTAM and looked in detail at the activities of the Task Force.

Journalist Kate McClymont commented, 'Lysaught and Donaldson [who] have doggedly stuck to their position that they are not and have not been corrupt, are looking decidedly more precarious with every day that passes'.[28] The NSW Police Board did not renew Donaldson's contract. 'Donaldson out of police force,' the *Daily Telegraph* reported at the time, and quoted a police board statement: 'A number of allegations have been made concerning Mr Donaldson before the Royal Commission into the police service, all of which are strongly denied by him. There has been no finding made against Mr Donaldson by the Royal Commission or elsewhere in respect to these allegations.'[29]

Another investigator from NSW Police to be snared in the web was Bob Lysaught. Lysaught was to become the Chief of Staff to

Police Commissioner Tony Lauer and the head of the Fraud Enforcement Agency. His involvement in the JTF would also end his career in the police service, thanks to the attention of the Royal Commission and the Police Board after hearing evidence presented at the Commission. Both Lysaught and Donaldson were the two most senior police officers to be called before the Royal Commission. Katherine Glasscott told how the Royal Commission heard three taped conversations between Lysaught and protected witness JTF16, which according to counsel assisting the commission John Agius, allegedly indicated that Lysaught had on at least four occasions, acted improperly or in a way that had drawn his integrity into question.[30] Both Lysaught and Donaldson denied any involvement in corrupt activities.

The Royal Commission reportedly accused Lysaught and Donaldson of being links in a chain of corruption. Counsel assisting the inquiry, John Agius, was quoted as saying to Lysaught, 'See, you know, don't you, that you are the link between the corrupt activity at the taskforce and Mr Donaldson.' Lysaught, however, denied any involvement in corrupt activity.[31]

Former detective sergeant and protected witness JTF7 had been Lysaught's former best friend and godfather of his son while they were at the taskforce together. He told the Royal Commission how Bob Lysaught masterminded a 'bribery scam' to pass $100,000 from criminals to other officers in relation to Operation Tin. John Murphy had been arrested in relation to large scale heroin trafficking which involved millions of dollars. JTF7's evidence was that heroin dealer John Murphy (via his associate Dennis Keane, a friend of Christopher Flannery) offered NSW police money to escape charges.[32] The JTF did not have a brief on Murphy but thought they could relieve him of some money anyway.

NSW Drug Squad officers Peter George and Chris Hannay relayed Keane's offer to Bob Lysaught and other senior police who instruct them to 'snip him for what we could'. $44,000 of this money was to be shared by four officers while the remaining $56,000 divided up among the remaining police. JTF7 told the commission that Lysaught and JTF7 also spoke to Dick Paynter and Brian Meredith about this arrangement. Paynter and Meredith delivered $44,000 to JTF7 one winter evening at the car park of Koala Park saying 'here is your Christmas present'. JTF7 said that he then rang Lysaught and told him that 'everything is sweet.' At the time JTF7 gave evidence to the Royal Commission the matter, Paynter had retired but Meredith was a Detective Superintendent and a Drug Enforcement Agency commander.

JTF7 told the Commission that Lysaught claimed $17,000 when the money was taken back to the JTF headquarters and that he took a further $5000 for Ray 'WOFTAM' Donaldson. JTF7 told Gary Crooke, QC, senior counsel assisting the commission that 'Mr Lysaught colluded with JTF7 and other detectives so that each other would tell the same lies when Judge Thorley and the State Crime Commission in 1990 investigated the allegation that Lysaught and Ray Donaldson had accepted the $100,000 bribe.

The Royal Commission was played tapes from inside Lysaught's office of conversations that suggested that as the Royal Commission sat, none of the officers would break ranks before Justice Wood. JTF7 alleged that Lysaught paid him $3000 after he got secret information from the National Crime Authority and that he passed JTF7 $1500 as his share of a bribe from a heroin trafficker who was also the boss of a vehicle theft racket so that charges would not be proceeded with. JTF7 also told the Commission that Lysaught had joined other police in sharing in a $10,000 bribe so that a heroin trafficker from the Central Coast would be given bail. JTF7 admitted to the Royal Commission that he and at least 17 other officers he named were corrupt during his time at the JTF.

* * *

Towards the end of Haken's time at the JTF there was an operation conducted on Brent Peters and his associates. They were well-known drug suppliers and importers. Peters had gone to Scots College (an eastern suburbs private school) and his father was a pilot for an international airline. It was not the usual background for a crook in Sydney's underworld.

Haken's view is that Peters' group was well connected with senior police. He didn't like Peters and knew him from his days at the Drug Squad. 'We turned him over [in the Drug Squad] a few times. He was always involved in heroin. He was a huge man and extremely violent. He was known to sexually assault street prostitutes with bottles. He was just a cruel filthy grub that should have been eliminated, the sort of person you don't do business with.'

Peters lived with a prostitute named Cassie Christie. He was once in partnership with Peter Forster. 'Forster was ex-military, a hard bastard, running drugs from New Guinea for other criminals and included some NSW Police.' During the course of the operation, the JTF were informed that Darlinghurst Police were going to search Peter's house. Two of the JTF (Dave Allen and Mark Keane) were invited along as observers. While searching Peters' house they located a large amount of money under the mattress of the baby's cot. This money was taken by all the police present and a deal was struck with Peters. (It was established at the Royal Commission that the money from Peters had been picked up and divided among members of the JFT.)

Haken felt that no such deal should have been made for such a high-profile target and for such a 'low-life'. He explains: 'I know it sounds hypocritical, but there were always people who you just didn't deal with and Peters was in that bracket. My gripe wasn't that I wasn't in on the whack-up of money. There were rules about that type of thing. As Harry Bendt would say, 'You're not there, you're not in it.' We just should not have done business with Peters.'

Haken told the Royal Commission that Allen worked in the same office as Haken and so Haken saw him return from the raid. Allen was holding a black-coloured clutch bag that was full of fifty dollar notes. Haken knew what had happened and asked if they had done business with Peters. Despite the bag that he had with him, Allen denied that any deal had taken place. A passionate argument about the rights and wrongs of such a deal followed, which Allen continued to deny had taken place.

Allen told Donaldson about Haken's complaint and this was passed on to Jim Willis (Superintendent of the JTF). When Peters went before the court, he did not make any complaint about money being taken by police. Willis said to Haken that this proved that there was no substance to his allegation and that he would have to be transferred to maintain harmony in the Task Force.[33]

'I was told, "You're going, see you later." So he got rid of me.'

Trevor Haken was ordered to go immediately to Central. He was then transferred to Central Detectives at Campbell and Smith Streets, Surry Hills, the location known as the 'old hat factory'.

CHAPTER 8

CENTRAL DETECTIVES I — A MONUMENT TO INCOMPETENCE

During the time that Trevor Haken was at Central Detectives there were organisational changes within the police service. Haken moved from the 'old hat factory' to the Sydney Police Centre. The Phillip Street Detectives (known as The Rocks Detectives) were amalgamated with Central Detectives, which later became known as the City of Sydney Detectives. These detectives shared a room at the Sydney Police Centre with Darlinghurst and Redfern Detectives. The whole of the City region was contained in the one room, with their cars parked in the basement downstairs. It was a move that Haken contends was not fully thought out. 'It was a monument to incompetent people's egos. It was a huge disaster that never had a chance of working.' Because of the delays that arose from being located there and trying to get anywhere else, Central Detectives were then transferred back to the old station in Central Lane, between George and Pitt streets.

The theory supported an American model of basing all police in the one centre, while having mobile patrols out and about and retaining only a few officers in the station at any one time. The idea was to have all available officers out on the road, but Haken felt that it was unworkable. The response time to any event in the city was huge. 'You can imagine going from Surry Hills in the peak hour to an armed robbery at the Rocks. You were adding twenty minutes to a half-hour to get to a job.'

As a result of the amalgamation, vehicles were removed from the detectives, an example of creative accounting that resulted in chaos. Further to that, detectives suffered from a loss of identity. Darlinghurst Detectives were no longer Darlinghurst Detectives. Any *esprit de corps* that had existed was lost. There was one meal room for all these detectives who were used to having their own facilities. The open plan style of workplace was not conducive to efficiency. There were four glass rooms for the officers in charge of the detectives, and then everybody else was in one open space. 'It was basically a place where nobody wanted to be.'

If a telephone rang a detective wouldn't know for whom the bell tolled — for Darlinghurst, the Rocks, or for Central. The jobs allocated to the detectives were still defined by boundaries, but if something came in and there was no one from that office, then someone else would take the job. For example, former Darlinghurst detectives could be called to Redfern. They would then try to piece together a case in an area they were not familiar with. They would also be working without the knowledge or assistance of local informants. They would have no in-depth knowledge of local criminal identities, whereas the local detectives would know where these people could be located at any given moment.

This system did not make sense to detectives and it seemed to be a policy driven by ideology. In Haken's assessment:

Instead of spending the money and upgrading individual police stations, they created this monster that was just out of control. It was created mainly for the specialised areas such as ballistics and scientific squads. They got parking areas and huge workspace, but for the working police it was a disaster. They then tried to send everybody back to their districts after it was found to be a failure, but in the interim, of course, they had disposed of the properties. Darlinghurst Police Station had been given to the Health Department I think, and was a drug referral centre, so all the Darlinghurst Detectives went back to Kings Cross Station, which was absolutely out of control. Later, when I went there it was one room in a basement, which used to flood when it was very wet. You had twenty-five guys working in a room that would have comfortably sat six.

When Haken left 'the concrete bunker' of Sydney Police Centre and returned to Central Police Station there were very few senior staff left. Vince Rhynn (OIC) and Des Johnson (2IC) had moved on, while some had taken permanent sick leave. In effect, Haken was one of the few senior, working detectives present at Central Police Station. The uniformed police were on the ground floor, with the detectives on the first floor. At one stage, the floors above the second floor at Central had been condemned by the Board of Fire Commissioners as being dangerous and unable to be occupied.

Central Detectives was located on the corner of Campbell and Smith streets in Surry Hills. This is where divisional detectives were based. Central Detectives was one up from Phillip Street in the pecking order of stations. Haken recalls:

I was pretty pissed off. I thought that everything had come good at the Task Force; it was a prestigious gig and then it fell apart. I went from travelling in cars to back on the train again. Central was just a joke, that was all there was to it. Of course, there was money to be made and drinks to be consumed. It was a drunk, bigger than a drink.

Detective Senior Sergeant Vince Rhynn was in charge and he, or his second in charge, would work out the roster for the day. There would be two detectives to a 'job car' (cars allocated to respond to the daily workload) and there were three cars at Central. The job cars would involve six of the staff at Central, while the rest of the staff would continue with their own outstanding work. The three job cars would run most of the day doing shoplifters ('shoppies'), or frauds, or whatever else might come in. The majority of the work normally involved shoplifters. As Haken says, 'You'd be going to Grace Bros or David Jones just booking them up. Occasionally you would get a good shoppie in, but they were few and far between. Most of the time it would be 'El Shahib' just doing the family shopping for clothes.'

There was a tradition in Sydney of professional shoplifters. The shoppies ran with the crooks from Glebe and The Rocks. It was a big operation; professional shoplifters would steal from trucks, from the wharves and from the containers. In contrast to some sixteen year old stealing a CD, they might take Hugo Boss suits — in fact they might take a rack of suits without any difficulty.

They're unbelievable, they're like spirits! If people would turn around, they would have taken shops! They are good at what they do. If there were electronic devices on goods, they would just take them off. Nothing fazes them, believe me. I had one bloke who was a middle of the road shoppie, very good at what he did, but a junkie. When I was at the Cross, we had him in custody. No one believed me when I told them what he could do, so he took two blokes I worked with down to David Jones. They said, 'You can't do what you say you are doing.' He took about half a dozen suits off a rack and walked out the door with them and nobody noticed him. It was just a matter of doing it.

This guy used to get dressed in blue denim shirts and shorts like an ordinary worker, take an antique chair and walk out. Nobody says anything, it's a matter of having the gall. He had given himself up, he was a gig of mine who would give himself up every so often, because he would say, 'I want to go to jail for a few months otherwise I'll end up killing myself'. He said, 'Look, I've done this and I've done that' — he confessed to taking thirty sewing machines and they said, 'Bullshit'. I said, 'If you think he's lying go down there and he'll do it', and of course he did. He once took every bottle of Grange hermitage out of the stand in the restaurant at the Hyde Park Grand.

The shoppies provided another opportunity for corrupt police to make some money. In certain instances, when they were arrested they would try for any concession and this would come at a price. In one case Haken arrested a shoppie named Christopher John Purcell and his girlfriend for shoplifting at Grace Bros. Purcell was a well-known shoppie who offered Haken and another officer $1000 in order not to lay charges against his girlfriend and instead charge Purcell with the items stolen. It was agreed and Purcell later paid the money to Haken and the officer over a period of time at the Royal Oak Hotel in Double Bay. Everyone walked away with a result — Grace Bros, Purcell, his girlfriend, Haken and the officer. It was much more satisfying than dealing with the courts! Anything was negotiable.

Even when a shoppie had been charged, there were things that could be done before the court passed judgment. Keith William

Bonney was a shoppie with a long history. If he was arrested and his full history was revealed to the court, then his sentence might be substantial.

Haken was first made aware of outside interest in Bonney's case when he was approached by a senior police prosecutor in September 1986. The prosecutor knew Haken and knew that he was open for business. The prosecutor explained that Bonney had been arrested in relation to the shoplifting of goods of substantial value and asked Haken to alter the criminal history record. In return for the favour, Haken would receive around $2000, which was being held by Graham 'Abo' Henry.

Haken needed to change the fact sheets: the court copy held by the prosecutors, the station copy held at the central charge room and those held by Haken himself. He would have to substitute these papers with amended documents. Haken did so and indicated on the fact sheet that Bonney had a minor record. Haken maintains that he never received the money from Abo Henry. The Independent Commission against Corruption (ICAC) later approached Bonney's lawyer and asked why he had not placed the information about Bonney's past before the court. The lawyer told ICAC that it was not his job to do so. Haken was visited by ICAC officers who searched his office looking for documentation, but nothing further came of the matter.

There were times when goods were received in lieu of cash and cops would send their shoppies out on an order basis, along the lines of, 'I need a 42 regular Hugo Boss suit, see you on Wednesday'. Haken tried to avoid this option.

I didn't receive goods in kind, I was fairly cautious about it. How dangerous is that? If it turns to shit down the track, as it often does, what do you do? All they need to say is that he's got a 42 regular Hugo Boss suit, a Sony stereo, some

Sidchrome tools, and if they find this gear you're gone.
Whereas there's no way of tracing money.

Royal Commission investigators caught a notorious light-fingered detective. So flagrant was his theft among other police that he was given the nickname 'Klepto'. A number of crooks had alleged that, when they were arrested, some of the property they had stolen was taken and kept by this detective. The crooks were not in a position to be believed and so Klepto got away with a lot of stolen goods.

The justification for such theft was that these were stolen goods that were most probably covered by insurance and it was only taking from thieves. When Royal Commission investigators executed a search warrant on this detective's suburban house they discovered a large number of curious trophies that he had accumulated over the years. Behind a large blue and white pleasure boat in the driveway was the double door garage. There wasn't a lot of room for a car or anything else in the garage. It was full of junk, but this guy couldn't help himself. It wasn't so much Aladdin's cave as Aladdin's junkyard. Apart from possessing enough watches in his bedside table to last a month of changes, there were confiscated martial arts weapons including num-chuckers, swords, knives and what seemed to be enough rifles and ammunition to cull the entire kangaroo population of Australia; there were also a lot of tools, including a set of Sidchrome tools.

Investigators were looking for a number of specific items following complaints from crooks and one of these items was indeed a set of Sidchrome tools. According to this detective, his wife had purchased the tools at the markets, and she supported his claim. The tools the investigators were looking for had been engraved with the initials of the original owner. The detective had scratched over the engraving but an X-ray revealed the original engravings. In the end, Klepto left the police service and was charged.

A detective on the make would have to be reasonably careful in all areas. The view of police was that it was easy street for the shoppies because most times they got off the charge, and all a court fine meant was another ten minutes' work to make up for the lost income. Most of the professional shoppies would steal to order. The saying was that there were more suits sold in a certain Redfern pub than there were in Grace Bros. People would go into this pub, or any other haunt, and say, 'I saw a grey pinstripe size 36 suit in the men's department at David Jones, can you get it for me?' And the shoppie would answer, 'I'll see you tomorrow at four o'clock'. The next day at four o'clock there would be the suit, and instead of being $450, you'd get it for $150.

Haken knew a shoppie by the name of Winter, whom he describes as 'an old-style crook'. Winter complained to Haken that he'd been arrested by a constable and some others from the South Region Anti-theft Squad. Haken recalls, 'The Anti-theft Squad were all young uniformed police put into plainclothes without any supervision.' Winter had no real problem about being arrested, that went with the territory. His complaint was that during the hearing of his case, the constable in the witness box was wearing one of Winter's stolen leather coats.

One time, Central got a phone call from John Pardoe Menswear in Castlereagh Street. At this time it was said to be the kind of place that you'd have to throw a handful of fifties onto the floor to even gain entry. (Or, according to Haken, it was like gaining entry into the office of some well-known Sydney criminal lawyers!) John Pardoe was one of two stores who handled Zegna clothing, the other was David Jones, in the days when when they were an exclusive line. To put the value in context, in 2002 a US edition of

Vanity Fair magazine advertised Ermenegildo Zegna couture cotton cashmere suits at $US2850.

A man had walked into Pardoe's with two Zegna sports jackets and said, 'I'd like these altered'. Not a problem, but Pardoe couldn't believe his eyes because the labels had been taken out of the jackets. This when everybody knew that if you bought a Zegna sports jacket, you would not only want the labels to show, you would also want a large 'Z' on the sleeve to show that you were wearing a Zegna. The guy gave a story that he'd bought these two coats overseas and wanted them altered, again an unusual thing, because coats were always fitted when purchased.

What is not commonly known is that sewn inside the lining of every Zegna garment is a number. Pardoe looked at the numbers and contacted Zegna who told him that the coats were on consignment to Australia. As these coats had not come to Pardoe it was safe to assume that they were stock from David Jones.

Haken was called and went down to Pardoe and then on to David Jones. David Jones confirmed that they had received a consignment but told Haken that the jackets were still in stock. Haken asked David Jones to check the twelve garments that they had received. They said that they were in bond (locked inside a wire cage), and there was no problem as they couldn't be touched there. Despite the security they checked, and there were only ten jackets. They then checked the numbers and confirmed the two missing coats were at Pardoe's. Clearly, the crooks had access to any part of David Jones, including high-security areas. This was later substantiated when it was shown that the shoppies had keys to storerooms.

The man who had brought the coats to Pardoe's was a travel agent. Haken pointed out that he had a bit of a problem with the coats as they hadn't come from overseas, but were, in fact, from David Jones. The travel agent said that he bought all his clothes from the same Redfern pub, and it seemed like a pretty good deal as he got them for about a quarter of the retail price! Haken arrested him.

The accused was brought before the court with a magistrate presiding. A barrister represented the travel agent who pleaded 'not guilty' to the charge of receiving stolen goods, because it seemed they were looking for a lesser charge. The case was thrown out of court, and nobody could understand it. At the first hint of the case being thrown out, the barrister was on his feet saying, 'If you throw it out, we won't be asking for costs'. He clearly hoped this would be an incentive to dismiss.

According to Haken, the magistrate's basis for throwing the case out was that it couldn't be assumed that the travel agent would have known that the garments were stolen, even though police could prove that they were stolen, because the magistrate knew many people who bought their clothes from hotels. Haken cited this case as an example of the stupidity of the law and as a justification for their actions in dealing with shoppies. Given the same circumstances, if the travel agent had said, 'Listen, take the sports coats or take this money and we'll call it quits', it is clear which way Haken would have gone. 'The bloke just kicked his heels and said "See you later" and there was nothing we could do.' This was not an isolated case, according to Haken. The police had a system that seemed to work a lot better. Haken explains, 'Why bother letting the court make a mockery of justice; why don't we do it? At least we'll make sure they get fined.'

CHAPTER 9

CENTRAL DETECTIVES II — A CUP OF TEA IN CHINATOWN

To be a part of any game you need to be accepted by the other players. Those introducing you have vouched for you and so from that moment you are in on the game.

Haken told the Royal Commission that when he first went to Central he was introduced to Frank Hing by Peter Tippett, who was a detective sergeant attached to Central Detectives, and Graham 'Chook' Fowler, who was in charge of detectives at The Rocks. Haken stated that he believed Hing was looking for police to protect his influence. The Commission heard that Hing had been introduced to Haken as a businessman who had interests in restaurants, gambling, prostitution and massage parlours.[1]

At the time of Haken's introduction there had been the makings of a Chinese gang war on the streets of Sydney's Chinatown. This has continued into recent years with stand-offs between police and suspects in siege situations, drive-by shootings, escalating gang violence and the increased use and possession of hand guns by gang members. Haken cites these as examples of what happens when things are out of control. 'When the cops have their fingers on the button, those sorts of things don't happen. We dealt with things before they got out of control.'

Haken's evidence to the Royal Commission was that, at that time, Frank Hing was one of the movers and shakers in the Chinese community. He acted as a go-between for the Chinese community and other groups. Haken recalls him as being a 'smart-arse Chinese' who could speak English fairly well and knew a lot of cops. There is an adage that 'it never hurts to know a copper'. Haken agrees and elaborates: 'This is something that should be put in flashing lights above the bloody MLC Tower, and it was to *everybody's* advantage. It stopped all the rot at ground level. If anything was going to go wrong, you'd know about it before it happened.'

If one could find an advantage in associating with a community, as a policeman, then that was all to the common good. 'If you could make a quid out of it as well, then that was even better!' And there was plenty on offer.

Every time Haken saw Hing there was money being thrown around. Haken gave evidence to the Royal Commission that he and Hing would meet over food and drinks at Chinese restaurants, normally in the company of other police such as Graham Fraser, the active officer in charge of detectives at Central or Peter Tippett.[2] Hing would pick up the tab for all the police as well as giving them money under napkins. He would often walk a police officer through a gambling club, which Haken believed was meant to improve his standing amongst the Asian community and further to provide protection for various establishments that Hing purported to represent[3]. It appeared that everyone was happy with this arrangement. Haken estimates that he would have received several thousand dollars over a few months. He spent most of the money on socialising, in particular, drinking.

In Haken's assessment, gambling and drugs go hand in glove. Gambling, he says, is part of Chinese culture: 'If you say Chinese, you say gambling'. Haken's experiences in Chinatown have left him embittered. His view is that the Chinese have always been involved in the heroin trade, but that it was predominantly sold outside their community. 'I never saw a Chinese junkie and if you look around for a legitimate Chinese businessman ... you keep looking.'

Jensen Liu was a businessman with a lot of varied interests. Haken met Liu when he first went to Central in 1986. Haken's evidence to the Royal Commission was that Liu ran the Shanghai Village in Dixon Street and a video reproduction and rental premises specialising in dubbing Asian 'soap operas'.[4] Haken met Liu when he was asked to organise off-duty detectives as security for Asian concerts that were being promoted by Liu. Haken stated to the Commission that he was employed on three to four occasions and was paid on an hourly rate. He was aware that some of those involved in promoting the concerts were connected to the 14K Triad[5].

Haken also assisted Liu with the investigation of Asian video-pirating operations. Haken stated that there were no official arms of inquiry available to Liu at the time for copyright infringements. Bob McDougall, a retired ex-licensing sergeant from Central Police, acted as an investigator for Liu's video business to try and prosecute the backyard pirate copiers for copyright infringement. Even Liu's legitimate competitors would pirate his material and put it in their own shops contrary to copyright laws. Haken describes the operation:

There would be Chinese men in home units in Epping with ten video recorders set up and dubbing each day's 'Days of Our Chinese Lives', or whatever they called their soapies.

You might not think it's a big earner but when it's seven days a week tax free, it soon adds up. This practice of Chinese pirating was huge, it stretched from Cabramatta to Sutherland to Hornsby and I've no doubt well beyond. They have no regard for Australian law.

Haken told the Commission that he and McDougall were paid about $300 on a per job basis.[6] Haken also executed search warrants and split the fee with other police who assisted. They did around ten jobs for Liu.

Haken's evidence was that through Frank Hing, he met John Chai, also known as 'Sambo'. Chai ran a gambling club in Dixon Street underneath the Maysun restaurant. Haken stated that he originally thought the gambling club was owned by Hing, but later learnt that the club belonged to Chai and that he had been paying money to Hing on the understanding that Hing was paying money to police.[7] Chai was not happy with this arrangement and approached Haken about it.

Haken told the Commission that he believed Chai also paid some members of the Gaming Squad, as he never expressed any concern about the squad interfering with his business. Haken was told that he was to come and have a 'cup of tea' with him. Haken explains that 'the tea was all green crinkly stuff [money], and he was the start of a cup of tea in Chinatown.'

Haken received about $100 a week for a couple of months, which he shared with Fraser. In his time before the Royal Commission, Justice Wood sentenced Chai for what was then the largest importation of heroin ever intercepted, at around 69 kilos. While Haken was getting his 'cup of tea', Chai swore to him that he was not involved in heroin importation. After his arrest, Haken saw him and asked, 'What's the go with you, you told me you're not into the "white gear" and you're in it up to your neck?'

Chai told Haken that he wasn't involved, but that he had just financed someone else's business. Haken said, 'Hang on, that's heroin importation', to which Chai replied, 'It doesn't matter what it is, we don't ask about other people's business'. Haken saw this as the philosophy the Chinese businessmen lived under, and that it was useless to fight. It was easier to go with the flow and take whatever advantage it offered to both the force and him. 'It's very easy to close your eyes to what happens, if you write it off as "that's business"'.

Haken was sought out because he was a detective who was seen to be active, to be 'sniffing around on the ground'. Those involved in illegal activity in Chinatown would not want their business to come undone, and so would approach detectives such as Trevor Haken. Haken still sees himself as having been a hard-working detective. 'They never sought out those who sat on their arse doing nothing.' At the Royal Commission Justice Wood made reference to working on 'the sunny side of the street'. Haken sees it differently, and points out that a policeman can be both hard-working *and* taking advantage of what's offered to him [corruptly]. He could still effect arrests while playing the game. Of course, there were those who crossed farther into that territory and actively sought out opportunities, and sometimes created them. Opportunities abounded in Chinatown and the temptations proved too great for many.

Let's face it; none of us are Alice in Wonderland. It becomes very tempting to want to be thought well of by all the crooks. They ring you up and say, 'Listen, we've got a problem', you go and see them and you become a person who becomes perhaps ... even well thought of by yourself. And that's a funny thing in a job where everybody thinks you're an arsehole.

The amount of money in the 'cup of tea' varied from $150 to $500. Every time a policeman would see one of the 'businessmen' in Chinatown, he would be invited in for a cuppa. There were no specific favours asked in return for the 'cuppa', but they knew that if you were open to the cuppa then, when they did require a favour, you would help them out. 'They knew you were open for business,' Haken says. These contacts were also useful if you wanted to know what was going on. Haken saw the Chinese as a community that by and large looked after itself, and would only call upon the police if things got out of hand.

Haken gave evidence that it was during the late 1980s that Hing had created a protection racket and had sought to utilise his association with police to his own advantage. He formed an association with Lenny McPherson and George Freeman ('the bloke who bundied off with an asthma attack'). They decided that they would have a very lucrative association in Chinatown. This was to be a standover tactic offering a security service to Chinese merchants. This 'service' had only been going a week when a Chinese merchant approached Haken. In what seems to be a contradiction, Haken is at pains to point out that he had associations with many good Chinese people as well as the undesirable element but then adds, 'My view of the Chinese society is that there is no other element other than the criminal element; they're all into everything. There is no use saying anything nice about it, the long and the short of it is if they can make a buck out of it, they'll be in everything. Their view on business is to take "the wide eyes" down for as much as you can while you can.' He adds, 'You talk about racist comments — they make them all the time, they hate us with a passion.'

Lawrence Tsang ran a Japanese barbecue restaurant in Little Hay Street called the Sinju Taipan. According to evidence given before the Royal Commission, Tsang called Haken and told him about a standover threat to him.[8] The approach was made under the guise of Hing being a part of a security company, whereas both Tsang and Haken saw the approach as extortion. The fact that Lenny McPherson and George Freeman sat together in the restaurant as Hing made his approach made it pretty obvious what was going on. Tsang told Hing that he didn't want to be a part of it, nor could he afford to be a part of it. The amount demanded was about $150 a week from the merchant, although this varied from place to place.

Haken told the Royal Commission that he and others spoke to Tsang and obtained what information they could about the scam, and then spoke to others to corroborate this story.[9] Haken then went and 'buckled' [forcefully confronted] Frank Hing about this scam and simply told him to shut it down. Hing was interviewed, with his solicitor Ray De Rubeis present, on 12 January 1988. Hing made no admissions but was told to 'close it down and tell the other blokes to piss off, otherwise there's going to be trouble'. Of course if Hing had not paid Haken in the past then he would have been pursued and probably charged. Haken admitted to the Royal Commission that the investigation was compromised by his association with Hing. Hing's 'cup of tea' had paid off.

This encounter occurred late in the week, and the following Sunday there were revelations in a Sunday newspaper by Peter Ho (husband of Helen Sham Ho, the Independent politician). Ho claimed to have evidence of a standover scam in Chinatown, and would reveal details in the newspaper. According to Haken, by this stage it had been exposed, closed and finished by those who really looked after Chinatown. Nonetheless, an inquiry was established by then superintendent Tony Lauer and both Fraser and Haken were summoned to Lauer's office where they were informed that they were to take no active part in the inquiry.

Although the solution was seemingly simplistic, Haken views this as a result of their arrangement. The system in Chinatown was

'Play the game, do what you will, tell us what's going on, but if you overstep the mark you'll be told to shut it down. And if you don't shut it down, you'll go in.' This was a system used by many within the police service. It was the system that begat the 'Green Light', the method that Neddy Smith was to use in his association with the disgraced former detective, Roger Rogerson. Haken concedes that New South Wales was operating under the Green Light system, but it is his view that it had a very capable and active Red Light as well. If something got out of control, if someone crossed the line, then they could be shut down. Most worked within this system. Of course, there are examples of those who did not want to be controlled, and they sometimes met with disaster.

From the police point of view, people didn't really want to know what went on behind closed doors as long as it didn't end up on the streets or in the newspapers. And so it appeared to be a game — a game that had rules as well as winners and losers. There were obvious advantages for those detectives 'out there and sniffing around'. Detectives were able to wine and dine in Chinatown at no expense while pocketing some extra cash and seemingly keeping the peace.

While businessmen in the 1980s turned the long lunch into an art form, some detectives in Chinatown didn't do too badly either. One particular dinner was held at a restaurant where there was a lobster tank in the front window. There was also a pond inside the restaurant, which held more lobsters. After a few hours of eating and drinking, the lobster in the pond came to Trevor's attention. In fact, he felt drawn towards the water. 'It seemed like a good idea at the time — some people have to go to the tropics to go swimming with lobsters, I didn't have to go that far, did I?' And so Trevor took a jump into the pond. 'The owner was pretty pissed about it, but what could they do? Yes, lobster hunting at its best.' These were also the days when Trevor's alcohol intake was considerable, even for a policeman. 'I used to enjoy life pretty well, and you could in Chinatown, because no one would tell you no.'

The detectives were treated with respect although they knew that behind their backs a different view might be expressed. They were aware that order was kept by Chinatown's own code of behaviour. Police acknowledged among themselves that this form of community policing (albeit perverted) was more effective than anything they were able to achieve. They compared Chinatown's sense of order and 'justice' to the judicial system, which they viewed as a constant failure. To everyone involved, this parallel system of justice appeared to work.

There were a number of Chinese brothels in the Haymarket and in Kings Cross. Haken and other detectives would be taken around to the brothels that were in the southern end of the city and the Haymarket. If you went down George Street and took a right turn into Goulburn Street, entered the first doorway on the left and climbed a flight of steps, you would be in one of the brothels Haken visited. There it was, in the heart of the CBD. There was another in Cunningham Lane, just off Pitt Street. They were everywhere.

To gain entry to these brothels, the door at street level had a buzzer. It was one way in and one way out. Once inside, you would climb a narrow flight of stairs to the top where there would be a locked door. The operators would have to let you in at this point and you would be in a room with a number of chairs around the wall. On each chair would be a woman for your choice and another woman would be sitting at a table acting as a receptionist. There were a number of small rooms that led from this area. In most of these brothels there were no bar facilities for patrons, and so as Haken describes it, 'It was a simple matter of "wham, bam, thank you ma'am".'

The detectives, however, would sit drinking with the operators even though the majority could not speak English.

I had a fairly good relationship with everybody that I ever did business with. I never ever stood on anybody; it is not in my nature. And why bother, you didn't have to! I could have made a million bucks if I'd stood over people, but I didn't, I didn't have to. It was one rung further up the ladder that you didn't really go. I mean, that's the same as going out and doing armed hold-ups. It happened — there were guys that did it, and they've never ever been brought to task. There were lines of cut-off, lines of demarcation, if you like, that said, 'You go this far, but you don't go that far, and you certainly don't go into the high jump.'

Security in Chinatown being another area where the locals looked after themselves, there were always people inside the brothels and clubs to respond if there was trouble. Suffice to say that the police were never called to deal with a problem patron, but they often saw the results. Haken was called out early one morning to a savage assault that happened at a restaurant in Liverpool Street. Some fairly well-to-do young men had been drinking at the Oaks Hotel at Neutral Bay and had then moved on to Chinatown for dinner. The youths were drunk and their behaviour quite obnoxious so were asked to leave. They did not want to leave or to pay and so were ushered out of the place. When they reached the street they were met by men with baseball bats who beat them senseless. Problem solved. As Haken puts it, 'Twelve baseball players, all batters, no ball and all hitting home runs'.

The beaten youths were taken to North Shore Hospital but did not want to take the matter any further. One of the youths pleaded, 'For Christ's sake leave us out of this, next time they'll kill us'. That is how security worked in Chinatown. Someone makes a phone call and says they have a problem and 'the boys' come and fix the problem. Haken says 'they're just cruel, cruel people; they will beat the shit out of you with baseball bats until you are a broken mess on the ground'. This was not an uncommon event. For those in the know, security in Chinatown was only a phone call away.

Haken told the Royal Commission that while he was at Central, Vince Rhynn was in charge and his second in charge was Des Johnson. As well as Sergeant Peter Tippet, there was Peter Yeo who was attached to The Rocks. Peter Regan and Alan Clark were in the same office.

Work was not a high priority for a number of police at Central. One of the officers in charge would give the synopsis of the morning, which was about going through the daily crime of the previous day, keeping in touch with the hierarchy of the CIB upstairs and allocating the jobs that required following up. This done, the officer would then have a cup of coffee until the time the pubs opened, and would spend the rest of the day drinking. The location would be anywhere that served a drink before lunchtime and then, from lunchtime onwards, the Irish Bar at the Hilton. He would come back to work at five o'clock inebriated, collect a police car and drive home.

This was the situation when Haken arrived from what he describes as the enthusiastic, efficient but corrupt Joint Task Force. 'Going from the Joint Task Force to Central was like dying and going to hell.'

Central was a station totally lacking in enthusiasm. The young constables who were there loathed the sergeants with a passion, and that is why Haken says it was like a breath of fresh air for them when Haken was attached to Central. At least he got out and did things. If any jobs came in that required attention, Haken would go with the constables and he got results. It is still Haken's view that he got good results because of intelligence he gathered from such figures as Frank Hing. Haken maintains that a police officer can work both the sunny and dark sides of the street, asserting that an officer can be making legitimate arrests and 'cleaning up' inquiries while taking bribes from criminals. Haken insists that this improper association provided information that was invaluable. It represented a modus operandi that Haken maintained for the rest of his career.

The regulations for dealing with informants were viewed by Haken and most other police as a joke. It is today a matter of known fact that the NSW police service leaked like a sieve. If a criminal was registered as an informant, it was only a matter of time before it was public knowledge within the criminal community. For many, this was a death warrant. As a result, the type of informant who would come forward under this system was one of little intelligence value, of low ranking within the criminal society and therefore out of touch with what was going on.

Haken's view is that police without associations with criminals were not effective. 'It would be of no advantage to a crook to associate with so and so — what's he going to do, go up and find him in the Irish Bar in the Hilton pissed every day?' Ironically, there were some criminals who did not like heavy drinkers. 'Louis Bayeh [Bill's brother] despised police who drank; he used to see them all the time. He thought they were a waste of time. A lot of the crooks in Sydney, particularly the Chinese, used to give police a drink as soon as they walked into their premises. Their view was, if you could get someone on side with five to ten dollars' worth of beer, how easy is that?'

One of the many disturbing lessons of the Royal Commission into the NSW Police Service was how easily and cheaply police were bought. An occasional liquid lunch, some 'small change' from a drug dealer and a few gifts of jewellery in Sydney's western suburbs bought a licence to deal. This was the way that most police were bought, and it was the way that Trevor Haken became enmeshed in this lifestyle. 'I was the master at it, for years. You'd walk into a place and they'd say, 'have a drink, or have a meal' and you'd think well, this is terrific. What does it result in? An early divorce, that's all.'

Haken saw many detectives deteriorate quickly because all this was so readily available, and they were swallowed up by the lifestyle. Of course, the crooks used this to their advantage. Haken would speak to Bill Bayeh more than Louis Bayeh. Bill would tell him what Louis really thought about those he was dealing with and it was something that Haken eventually realised. 'Once you're not drinking yourself, you can see exactly how these people are playing you, but it's very hard to see it at the time.' From the first day that Haken was in plainclothes, the message was loud and clear: 'Never trust someone who doesn't drink, and now let's go have a drink'. It has been a revelation to Haken to look back and see how easy it was to fall into the lifestyle and how easy it was for them to be manipulated and to lose sight of who was really winning. Haken says, 'The Chinese were masters at it. Very few of them drank much, and when they did they would drink something more up-market than beer or champagne. It would be Hennessy XO, and I have no doubt they were celebrating the last fifty kilo importation or something.' Anything was available to the detectives if they wanted it, yet more often than not they could be bought off with a few beers and a $500 dinner while the dealer was making $50,000 a week.

At around three o'clock one Friday afternoon in early 1989 while Haken was still at Central Detectives, two uniformed police officers were called to a bank in George Street where a fraud was taking place. The offender, who was trying to use bogus credit cards, 'threw an almighty tantrum' when confronted, and sprayed the two police officers with mace. At the same time, a number of media people attending a conference above the bank they were standing outside having a smoke. Some had their cameras with them, and so this whole altercation in the bank was captured on film.

Meanwhile, two females waited across the road in a Mercedes sports car with the engine running. The women saw a highway patrol officer arrive on his motorcycle and they took off at high speed. The officer drew his pistol and fired shots at the tyres of the vehicle. The Mercedes hit other cars in its escape and was chased into East Sydney, where it made a bad turn and ended up mounting the front of another car.

Haken was the officer in charge on the scene and had to make sense of the chaos. There were people screaming, cars damaged and a general sense of the unreal. He felt poorly about the fact that the highway patrolman had discharged his weapon in such a public place and wondered whether it would be possible to keep him out of trouble in the report. A press photographer had captured most of the event, including a photograph of the officer aiming his gun at the tyres of the Mercedes.

A female police officer who was to search the two females in the Mercedes Benz soon discovered that they had a surprise of their own. In a very Sydney scenario, one female was the offender's girlfriend while the other was in fact a transvestite named Chris Foster. The officer came over to Haken and declared, 'You know that girl, she's not a girl!' Haken says, 'You would have thought it was a woman except for the five o'clock shadow.' The officer certainly got more than she bargained for in that search.

Haken recalls that Detective Graham Fraser had a passionate dislike of men who were homosexual and became involved in an argument down at the Taxi Club in Darlinghurst. 'He was goaded by some poofter and didn't take too well to it, so he gave him a flogging.' As a result of this incident, Fraser and another officer, Strizick, were dismissed from the police force. According to Haken, Strizick took the fall for another officer who was already in trouble with Internal Affairs. Due to the police code of sticking together, Strizick protected the other officer, not thinking that he would be punished severely.

The Old Windsor Tavern was right in the heart of the city. It was the kind of pub where you could get a good inexpensive meal and drink. If you were a detective, it could be a very cheap meal indeed. Most detectives were able to eat and drink without dipping into their pockets and so it was very popular with detectives from Central and even Kings Cross. 'There were more coppers there than anyone else,' says Haken.

John Morgan managed the tavern and was a good mate of Haken's. One of the owners of the pub was actually a civilian working at police headquarters. Morgan was from an Irish background and, according to Haken, resembled an overgrown leprechaun. On Saint Patrick's Day, much of the police hierarchy would start the day at the tavern and some would not leave. 'They'd all go down and be singing songs. You'd swear it was the reincarnation of the CIB.'

John Morgan liked a bet and having a TAB inside the pub provided him with the temptation to bet more than he could afford. Morgan called Haken and told him that he was in deep trouble, he had gambled the weekend takings of the hotel on the hotel TAB and had lost it all.

According to Haken's evidence to the Royal Commission, he agreed to help Morgan by fabricating a report of a hold-up at the tavern.[10] He decided to use his mate Graham Fraser to help him create a robbery scene. In his report made through City of Sydney Detectives, Haken stated that Morgan was in his office at the hotel doing the banking for the weekend when a person entered, held him up, then locked him in his room, where he was later found by a delivery person. Fraser was the one who had gone into the hotel and locked Morgan in the office.

Fraser and Haken received a small amount of money from Morgan for their efforts (less than a thousand dollars) as there wasn't much money after the betting loss. They had helped out a mate and he was grateful. When Morgan died a few years later, his son Sean called Haken to say that his father had asked him to call Haken to say goodbye. Haken carried his funeral notice with him for many years and gave it to legal counsel at the Royal Commission when telling his story.

While at Central Haken's dissatisfaction continued to grow. And he and his fellow staff were not content with the changes Avery made to policing. Avery dissolved the Pillage Squad (which was alleged to be the most corrupt squad in the CIB), 21 Division, then the CIB.

Haken was short-staffed in the detectives' office. At best there were two detectives at his disposal. There was one other detective sergeant attached who was on permanent sick report and therefore of no use. Another officer had come from the Child Mistreatment Unit and 'was burnt out and did not want to be there'. With the exception of those, Haken had all 'A Listers' who were uniformed people in plainclothes. Further to that, the staff consisted of 70 per cent to 80 per cent probationary constables in the uniformed area. This was the unit looking after the Central Business District and was, in Haken's view, 'totally useless'.

The Avery machine just kept on refusing to address the problems. There were shortages of police in the city, and you couldn't operate on that level. We had a reduction in cars. We were virtually catching buses to go and do jobs. It got to the farcical stage where if you arrested somebody you had to either walk them back or catch a bus or ring a uniform truck and wait. It was an absolute nightmare. Every time the issue was raised through official channels, they just kept saying, 'Do your best, just hang in there mate, it'll get better.' I was still enjoying the social life, but we were all working our arse off and getting nowhere. The hierarchy were lying their head off saying, everything is all right, we've got tonnes of people — and really it was beyond a joke. It was at the stage where people were ringing up for you to go and do a job, and you'd say, 'I'm terribly sorry, we don't have anybody here to send down. If you really want to follow it up, come up and see us.'

Haken decided to do something about it. He approached Candace Sutton at the *Daily Telegraph*. Graham Fraser had told Haken that Sutton was someone who would 'have a go' in the press, and not give anybody up. Haken met with Sutton and told her what life was like as a detective working in intolerable conditions. She appeared enthusiastic about running the story, but it would be necessary for her to validate what Haken was saying. Some documentary evidence was necessary before the story could be printed. To that end, Haken had to meet with John Hartigan, the then editor of the *Daily Telegraph*, and Candace Sutton in a restaurant in a side street near the Strawberry Hills Hotel.

Haken brought with him reports from Detective Senior Sergeant Alan Ross and Detective Sergeant Brian Murchie who had filed complaints about understaffing at Central. These reports were submitted to their district superintendent, but Haken feels they would have been ignored, filed and forgotten. In the complaints, Ross stated: 'Having regard to all the circumstances it can be readily seen that the workload has greatly increased on the existing staff. One can only guess at the outcome of this continuing increased workload'. Murchie stated: 'I can foresee some difficulties arising in satisfactorily concluding some investigations unless the present staff level is lifted with the addition of experienced investigative personnel.' In addition to the complaints, Haken handed the journalists a copy of the rosters which showed the lack of numbers.

The *Telegraph* could see there was substance to Haken's claims and decided that this could be a big story. Hartigan said to Haken, 'The people of New South Wales will thank you for this.' The *Telegraph* then sent their own reporters out and found 'the lone ranger', a solitary probationary constable who was the only station police officer on duty one night. The *Telegraph* found that in the whole of the Central Business District there were only two probationary constables on the truck (paddy wagon), two on the beat, and one in the station (from Chinatown to Bridge Street). It seemed that Probationary Constable Bruce Whitehead — an officer with barely six months' experience — was the thin blue line!

Haken had provided the *Daily Telegraph* with a good story and it was run on the front page on Monday 20 June 1988:

WAR ON CRIME A FIASCO: POLICE
by Candace Sutton

Sydney police claim new policies are making a mockery of the force — to the extent that on one occasion they had to take an arrested suspect to the police station by bus. On one day last week only one plainclothes and one uniformed police car were operating in the central city from Haymarket to the stock exchange — a staff smaller than that in many country towns.

Compared to a decade ago when 34 detectives operated in five police cars from Hay to Hunter streets in the city, now only 10 detectives have virtually only one car to deal with an increasing number of assaults and robberies.

The unnamed source said, 'Criminals in Sydney are drinking in pubs all over Sydney and laughing at their good fortune.' The source accused the police force hierarchy of 'trying to cut police expenses back to the stage where there are no police on the street'.

NSW Police Association president Tony Day backed the sources and statistics. Police are working on the street with insufficient resources to keep people safe.

The *Telegraph* continued with a daily reporting of the situation. The editor had built up a head of steam and asserted, 'We need investigating police to get the crooks into court. We then need sentences which show the city's scum just what society thinks of them.' More headlines followed: 'Detective Shortage a Fiasco', 'Thinnest Blue Line in Need of Thickening', 'Lone Ranger has the Beat to Himself'.

Over the week the newspaper continued to give examples of robberies with people commenting that there was no police presence in the city. By midweek, the commissioner declared the *Daily Telegraph* 'offside'. On Wednesday the *Daily Telegraph* responded with an editorial:

Sh-h-h-h-h

Police Commissioner John Avery has adopted a policy of silence towards accusations that his force is unable adequately to patrol the streets of Central at night. Mr Avery yesterday accused this newspaper of distorting facts ... and then retreated into his bunker.

Do something.

By Thursday 23 June, NSW Police Minister Ted Pickering admitted to the *Telegraph* that the state's detective force was undermanned. Haken had created a furore and was about to pay the price. It was apparent that Haken was the one who had blown the whistle on conditions at Central Police Station.

A detective sergeant (first class) named R.N. Murray was sent back to Central to address the problems that were highlighted in the press. Haken told the Royal Commission that he believed the reasons Murray was sent back to Central (he had been promoted away previously) and for his 'almost immediate attack' on Haken was the publicity given to staff shortages and the correct belief that Haken was responsible for the publicity.[11]

There were a tirade of bogus allegations made against me trying to get me in trouble, over bullshit. To give you an example, they conducted a departmental inquiry and suggested it was my fault that we were occupying inadequate premises within the police station. It made no sense. But what they said was that seeing as I was the senior detective at the police station, that I should have made some attempts to obtain better premises for the detectives. We'd been put there by the hierarchy, that's how farcical it was.

Departmental charges were brought against Haken by Murray with the concurrence of Divisional Inspector Norm Graham, and it was recommended that Haken be transferred to uniform duties under strict supervision. There would be a departmental inquiry.

While Haken awaited the result of the departmental inquiry, another controversy flared. With great fanfare, Police Minister Pickering declared Hyde Park a safety zone. The night after it was declared a safety zone, Sergeant Trevor Hile from the Police Centre was walking across the park on his way to work when he was set upon by three youths who bashed his head with a full wine bottle. These three attackers had appeared before the Children's Court in Victoria for similar crimes and were ordered to leave the state.

The attack on Hile was savage. Haken recalls, 'It [his head] looked like a watermelon, you couldn't see his eyes. They expected him to die.' The youths intended to rob Hile and when they started to beat him his cardigan came off to reveal his police insignia. Seeing the police insignia fuelled their violence. One said, 'He's a cop! Let's give it to him.' Hile was so badly injured that he never returned to work.

Haken was in charge of the inquiry with another detective who had also been sent to Central. Haken had a rough description and so they went through all the lodging houses and wound the heat up. 'We said, "either someone turns them up or we'll keep turning you guys over." That's the way it always worked: if you put enough heat on the crooks they'll eventually turn them over, and that's what happened.'

They eventually found the three youths had been staying down behind the old CIB in a refuge place. There was huge media coverage of the assault, and so they had departed very quickly. Police got the names of the youths who had stayed at the refuge and 'chased them backwards' to learn that they had originally come from South Australia. They had addresses in South Australia for two of the suspects who had since returned to Adelaide.

South Australian Police arrested two of them under warrants from New South Wales. The third was arrested and flown back from Lismore. Haken and Detective Senior Constable Paul McKay, who worked in the office at Central, went to Christie's Beach Children's Court in South Australia and extradited them to New South Wales, where they pleaded guilty to all the matters.

Whatever few wins such as this he might have achieved, however, Central had become a hell for Haken. When Murray was at the station, Haken would go out to do a job and stay out so that he wouldn't have to be with him. 'When I arrived back he was still there', says Haken. Haken had had a drink with the Chinese while doing his job but did not consider himself pissed. 'Murray said, "You've been drinking, I can smell alcohol on you. I'll see you on Monday morning". Because of what was going on I anticipated what would happen, so I went to the senior station sergeant in charge of the police station at the time and got him to make a notation in his notebook as to my sobriety. So when charges were brought later, as they were, I was able to have a factual defence.' Haken adds, 'You weren't battling the crooks, you were battling the people you were meant to be working with.'

Haken faced a departmental inquiry to look into Murray's recommendations and the reasons behind them. This was handled by Detective Inspector Barry Kennedy and the Department finding was that there was no basis for the complaints or recommendations for punishment. Then Haken was taken before District Superintendent Ken Chapman who insisted that Haken apply for a transfer to Kings Cross. This whole process took from June 1988 (the time of the *Telegraph* articles) until May 1989 (when Haken was eventually transferred to the Cross). Haken found this time stressful. 'Every time I walked into the office I was hauled over the coals for something. Chapman said, "You can go up to Darlinghurst, where there's a problem." Remember when John Hartigan said that the people of New South Wales will thank [me] for this? ... All that happened was that I nearly got sacked.'

CHAPTER 10

KINGS CROSS DETECTIVES OFFICE

'I'd died and gone to heaven.'

TREVOR HAKEN

In May 1989, Trevor Haken was transferred to Kings Cross. While he had not been happy with his transfers up to this point, there was still some allure about working at the Cross. Essentially, it was a sideways transfer for an officer of his status.

In the early days of Haken's career, Kings Cross was a place where everyone wanted to work. The Golden Mile, as Darlinghurst Road was known, offered many illicit opportunities to those looking for them. The growth of the drug trade had hardened Kings Cross over the years, and those involved in drugs and prostitution were younger and younger. Children who ran away from home were drawn to the apparent free lifestyle of the Cross. It was a place that never shut down and where everyone had a scam.

If Haken thought Chinatown was trouble, he wasn't quite prepared for life at the Cross. It had grown as one of the drug centres of Sydney where users and dealers fed off each other. The degree and extent of crime was higher than at nearly any other police posting. Consequently, there were seemingly endless opportunities for police with an open hand and a strong liver. Former Detective Stephen Pentland gave evidence to the Royal Commission how he would go for drinks at 7.30am, thirty minutes after starting work (Pentland would eventually be pensioned from the force as a result of pancreatis caused by stress-related alcoholism). Detective Neville Scullion told the Royal Commission that when he first went to Kings Cross an older policeman told him, 'There's only two things that will keep you here — getting a quid or getting a drink. This is the arse of the world.'

At the time of his transfer to the Cross, Haken's mate from Chatswood, Alan West, was in charge of Internal Security (a branch of Internal Affairs). Internal Affairs would investigate complaints made against police. Internal Security was a proactive unit which would investigate without a complaint being lodged. Corruption at Kings Cross was rife according to Haken and one had to be excessive to come to the attention of Internal Affairs.

Haken gave evidence to the Royal Commission that the Internal Security Unit mounted Operation Collector to investigate Geoff Thompson.[1] Haken states that he had received complaints from junkies and dealers alike that Thompson had stood over them and stolen their money, including that he had stood over a prostitute by the name of Karen Ress while she was held in the police lockup. Ress was known under many names, 'Sharon', 'the Princess of Death' (a name given to her by Haken and others because her boyfriends, mainly drug dealers, didn't seem to live long), or 'Poison Ivy' because of her habit of drugging clients with rohypnol and then robbing them. She was one of the first in the Cross to use this drug for this purpose.[2]

Detective Inspector Peter Thomas (South Region) was responsible for investigating Thompson. While no charges were preferred against Thompson, he was transferred to prison van security uniform duties. He later resigned.[3]

While investigating Thompson, Internal Security spoke to an informant named McNamara. He didn't have much on Thompson but told an amazing story about Detective Sergeant Larry Churchill. Churchill was warned by fellow detective Kim Thompson that he was being investigated with his famous expression, 'There's a whale in the bay'. This conversation was recorded and played to the court at Churchill's hearing. Thompson was departmentally charged for this offence.

Churchill was a loud and pretentious character. He was a detective sergeant who drove a late model BMW. He felt 'bulletproof' and was indiscreet. In a restaurant he would pull out large wads of money to pay for the bill. There were other times when, presented with a bill, Churchill would turn it over and write, 'Thanks very much, Larry!'

'Churchill had a lot of allies because he was pulling huge amounts of money and sharing it around, so everyone was happy with him,' says Haken. As if in some cartoon scene, he once held Phil Giovanni upside down to get the money 'owed' to him. On Royal Commission tapes recorded by Haken, Giovanni described Churchill as a cross between Billy the Kid and Doc Holiday. Churchill's problem was not so much that he was corrupt but that he was rubbing it in everyone's face. He looked for more and more ways to make money.

Churchill's whole corrupt operation was revealed to Internal Security and nearly everyone at the Cross was implicated. He was eventually sent to jail for his involvement in a $4 million amphetamine distribution network. He was released from jail after serving four years of a twelve year sentence. Both Kim Thompson and Graham 'Chook' Fowler beat their charges but were temporarily moved from the Cross. Despite the Internal Affairs charges, they were later returned to the Cross. Thompson was returned when he overturned Jim Bignell at appeal for the position of detective sergeant at Kings Cross.

After the Churchill affair there were many changes at the Cross. The entire station was under a cloud at the time and Haken was a replacement for officers who had been stood aside. 'There were a few people there that had stayed after the purge; they didn't actually do a clean sweep of the place. They took the majority, and they certainly took everybody that they thought they could prove had been involved in things.' Morale was decidedly low at the Cross.

The senior detective at Kings Cross was Carl Spain. He was in charge of the undercover police when Haken was at the Drug Squad. Spain was involved in the Blackburn Inquiry and left the service with a medical discharge.[4] Haken was the second senior officer behind Spain. John Swan, Jim Bignell and Neville Scullion were also working there and were the only ones remaining of those detectives who had been based at Kings Cross prior to the Churchill matter.

In evidence tabled at the Royal Commission Haken gave many instances of detectives receiving bribes in Kings Cross, including Detective Sergeants John Swan and Neville Scullion.[5] Swan and Scullion introduced Haken to the 'laugh' or the 'joke' because of his status as sergeant and because it had been established that he would accept protection payments. Haken named Graham Fowler, Kim Thompson and Peter Scott in his Statutory Declaration. Haken also told the Royal Commission that it was 'Chook' Fowler who had implemented the rule that only sergeants could receive payments. On 5 June 1995, the Royal Commission played twenty minutes of footage of 'Chook' Fowler accepting bribe money. Fowler maintained his innocence and suggested that the Royal Commission may have used an actor who clearly looked and sounded exactly like Fowler in the footage played in the hearing room.

Not all detectives adopted Fowler's approach, although at first these allegations were strenuously denied. Haken provided both audio and video evidence to support his assertions and this was played to the Royal Commission hearing room. Given the weight of evidence against them, many detectives 'rolled' and admitted their participation in 'the joke'.

As more detectives 'rolled' the Sydney press started to count the score. The *Sydney Morning Herald* reported that Detective Sergeants Kim Thompson, Neville Scullion and John Swan had admitted they had accepted regular bribes at Kings Cross. Duncan Demol also admitted receiving bribes while Steve Pentland admitted stealing and receiving bribes while at Kings Cross. There would be more allegations from Haken for the press to report.[6]

According to Haken, it took him about five minutes to see how things worked at Kings Cross. As soon as he arrived, he was tutored by some of the sergeants. They said, 'Look, there's a joke on here and there's a good dollar every week and we'll take you around to meet them all.'

Haken was indeed taken around to meet those people who were a part of the 'joke'. Everywhere they walked there was a 'drink', and everywhere they went there was money exchanged. He was introduced as 'the new bloke that is here for a while'; those he met welcomed him and wished him well and gave him something 'for his troubles'. It wasn't hard to handle such introductions as there were no overt requirements for the benefits he received; 'I'd died and gone to heaven', he says.

Haken reported that he was subsequently introduced to the people who were paying money to police for protection, these included Steve Stavrou (Skinny Steve), Steve Armatis (Fat Steve) and Frank Amanti (Ashtray), Steve 'Spiro' Hardas, Con Kostas (real name Kontorinakis) of Playbirds and John Ross of Kardomah.[7] Although Hardas initially denied Haken's allegations, footage of Steve Hardas paying bribes to Trevor Haken was played at the Commission. The effect of this footage was devastating, Hardas rolled and admitted that he had previously lied to the Commission and confirmed that he had paid police protection money in the ten years he had been in the Cross, including Detectives Scullion, Swan, Thompson, Graham 'Chook' Fowler and sergeants Meizer and Kelso. Haken told the Commission that Kostas met with police from other squads including the Consorting squad, the Armed Holdup Squad and the Vice Squad.[8]

In evidence given by protected witness KX11 (a confessed cocaine dealer) at the Commission, Hardas was said to be the go-between for bribes from drug dealers to police. Hardas bribe money was paid to protect interests in clubs such as Madame Butterfly, Pink Pussycat, Pink Panther, The Barrell Strip Club, Illusions, Action Cinema (Oxford Street) Taboo Night Club and Lasers Amusement Parlour. Haken's 'Crim-Cam' tape of Hardas was one of eighty video and audio tapes recorded with Haken's undercover assistance and which helped corroborate his evidence.[9] After Hardas' evidence was given, an officer who was named over fifty times in evidence, tried to commit suicide by taking sleeping tablets. He was taken to hospital and survived.

'Skinny Steve' was also caught on tape putting $2000 into the console box of Haken's vehicle. Evidence played to the Royal Commission, stated that Fatty and his partner Skinny Steve had paid over $200,000 a year in bribes. Skinny Steve had told the Commission that he had paid bribes because the police were corrupt and would close his business or load him up if he didn't. The Royal Commission played footage in the hearing room, as the *Herald* said, 'to show that he had been lying and that he had actively tried to recruit police'.

Counsel assisting the Commission, John Agius, asked Stavrou if any of the evidence he had previously given to the Royal Commission was false. Stavrou replied 'no'. Agius asked, 'It was all true?' Stavrou replied, 'Sort of, I told mostly the truth. Agius asked, 'You didn't tell any lies? Stavrou replied, 'No, I don't think so.' Agius asked, 'Were those answers true?' Stavrou replied, 'No'. 'They were false?' Agius asked. 'Yeah' replied Stavrou. The Royal Commission said that although Fatty and Skinny paid several hundred thousand dollars a year in bribes, their tax returns showed that their business made only $35,000 a year.[10]

Most of the time at the Cross, the 'requirement' for receiving bribes was simply to turn a blind eye to the activities of those who paid him. Sometimes there was more than that required. 'We'd love to see you come to the club and have a drink, but please don't come when the clients are there.' This system had developed long before Haken got to the Cross — it was the way things were. Haken recalls, 'The Cross was a twenty-four-hour drink. It was one of the most difficult areas to work for someone who wanted to keep on the straight and narrow, if there is such a thing. All the devil's temptations were there — the only thing not there was racehorses … [he then adds with a laugh] and they were at the TAB.'

Haken recalls one time when fellow Kings Cross detective Kim Thompson took a number of friends with him after the football to the Bourbon and Beefsteak Bar. While they were standing around drinking, the manager, Mike Connors, had the front table in the window set up with a big silver bucket filled with bottles of Crown lager. Connors said to Thompson, 'Your table is ready.' Thompson replied, 'I feel very humble.' Haken comments, 'It doesn't strike you until later that while it was a nice thing to do, we were so easily bought. We would spend thousands of dollars in there anyway.'

Evidence later given by Detective Senior Constable Duncan Demol at the Commission corroborated the picture Haken had painted about working in the area. Demol had said that at one stage he was partnered with Haken because, 'I was sizable and he was an alcoholic'.

Demol was attached to the Drug Enforcement Agency (DEA) Support Unit when he gave evidence. He said he had worked with

Sergeant Haken from 1989 to 1993 at Kings Cross and had at first considered him honest and hardworking. Demol was aged in his early twenties when he was sent to the Cross and, like Trevor Haken, he too might have thought that he had died and gone to heaven or hell, depending on his predilection.

Demol's original approach to the Royal Commission was one of denial; he would state that he thought Detectives Haken and Fowler were not corrupt. But as before, Haken's damning video and audio evidence would turn the tide. Demol was asked by the commission if he had ever discussed a NSW Crime Commission affidavit with Haken. After initially denying the allegation, Demol and the hearing room were show a video tape of this conversation on the large Sony monitors, with subtitles lest there be any confusion. Demol was played more tapes of some of his meetings with Haken and asked to 'consider his position'. Demol rolled.

Demol described to the Royal Commission his first days on the job as a detective at Darlinghurst. His partner, Constable Stephen Worsley, took him to the Barrel Brothel. In a back room, the two drank beer while naked female prostitutes sat on their laps. Like some football team captain saying 'welcome to the big league', Worsley turned to Demol and said, 'Get used to it, this is the way it is here!'

It wasn't long before other misbehaviour was also evident. Demol told the Royal Commission that in his first week, Demol and Worsley were pursuing a stolen car when Worsley asked Demol to drive into the vehicle. He did so and later signed an affidavit by Constable Worsley saying the car had hit them. It didn't matter, they had stopped the car, and the problem was resolved.

Demol confirmed that police would often charge people with the trifecta — offensive language, resisting arrest and assaulting police — irrespective of what took place. He also confirmed Haken's evidence that Demol and Haken searched a house in

Menai and found nearly $5000 of alleged drug selling profits in a wardrobe. The money was taken, and Demol was given $1500 of this by Haken.

In his evidence to the Commission, Demol said drinking on duty was rampant and that detectives would regularly collect free beer from local clubs. Officers considered it a mark of pride to drink through night shifts. Demol said police would collect free beer from local clubs and that the order was, 'You're not a cop until you've worked pissed'. At the time Demol gave his evidence, the public gallery sniggered. Justice Wood pointed out the sadness of this situation, where young officers were so quickly corrupted. Justice Wood was reported as saying, 'The situation is, once compromised, they are hooked and can do nothing about it in the future. Far from being an occasion for humour, it is an occasion for extreme sorrow.'[11]

Haken gave evidence about a series of incidents within weeks of his arriving at the Cross. During one, he was called out in the early hours of the morning to Sweethearts Cafe, a drug distribution point.[12] There was a breakfast client lying in the toilets of Sweethearts, as Haken recalls, 'stone-motherless' dead. The proprietor of Sweethearts was an Asian woman by the name of Regina Ashley-Riddle. She was known to all as 'the Princess'. It struck Haken as being odd that the Princess continued counting money in the cafe whilst there was a dead man in the toilet.[13]

The victim, Ali Ghazzawie, had been bashed and shot in the head. The 'uniforms' (uniformed police) had secured the scene and both ballistics and scientific police were on the scene. The other man involved in the incident was Benny Puta. He had been shot in the thigh and had been taken to St Vincent's Hospital under guard.

Puta was a notorious drug seller and it was clear that he had 'dispatched the deceased'. According to Haken, Puta was part of an Albanian drug connection. When Haken arrived in the Cross, the

Romanians were in charge of drug distribution and to an extent continued to do so until they moved out of active drug selling when the Lebanese took over. They still maintained a foothold in dealing as the middlemen between the Lebanese and the Chinese.

Haken said that he had never met Puta but he was aware of his size and reputation. When asked to describe Puta, Haken replied, 'What's Mount Everest look like? A big Slavic-looking man, over six feet — big head, shoulders and arms.' Both Haken and Detective John Swan went to St Vincent's to see Puta. He was lying on a small metal hospital bed with policemen on either side. The first problem they faced was getting handcuffs around Puta's enormous wrists. Haken and Swan gave up on this idea and Puta, who was quite amenable, didn't present a problem during the interview that then took place.

Puta's story was that Ali Ghazzawie had approached him at Sweethearts about the sale of some gold. At one point Puta had gone to the toilet and because the men's toilet at Sweethearts was so small he had gone to the ladies. Puta stated that he was washing his hands and that Ghazzawie, as in a script from a B grade movie, had said something like, 'This one's for Johnny,' while levelling a hand gun at Puta. To this day no one is quite sure who 'Johnny' was meant to be. Puta wasn't telling; he had been a suspect in a number of murders and 'Johnny' may well have been one of the victims.

Haken says, 'You have to understand that these people have no respect for life or laws — survival is the only thing that matters.' Puta turned around to Ghazzawie, grabbed him and pushed the gun down, and as a consequence was shot in the leg by Ghazzawie. Haken recalls, 'Puta was a mountain of a man and Ghazzawie was quite small. Puta said, very matter of factly, in a voice resembling that of Arnold Schwarzenegger, "I pick up a brick off the floor and I hit him two times ... two times very hard".' The post-mortem examination showed that Puta certainly had hit him very hard, as he had caved in Ghazzawie's skull.

Puta stated that after he had hit Ghazzawie with the brick, 'I pick up the gun and I shoot him two times', and he made the sound of two gunshots. When Detective Swan was typing the record of interview he chuckled as he asked how he should type the sound that Puta made when describing the gunshots.

Haken was the officer in charge of the investigation and charged Puta with murder. It seemed to be a fairly straightforward case and the matter was handled by the book up to this point. Swan and Haken took statements from everyone at Sweethearts and they were in accord with what Puta had said. Puta stated that Ghazzawie's initial approach was to sell him some gold rings. The question raised at the murder trial was that if this was the case, what had happened to the gold rings? Of course, this was Kings Cross, and there is ample evidence that if anyone stumbled, fell or died, they were robbed within thirty seconds.

Puta was what Haken describes as a 'hard head', someone who had done time in prison and had good connections. As Haken describes it shortly after the initial record of interview, Swan and Haken were approached by 'the Princess'.[14] As well as running Sweethearts at the Cross, she also ran a gambling club in Bondi and gambling clubs in Cabramatta. The Princess asked Swan and Haken to do what they could for Puta in the upcoming trial. As it turned out, this wasn't necessary as Puta was acquitted. Puta's defence was that his life was clearly in danger and he had defended himself. Puta stated at the trial, 'Ladies and gentlemen, I was frightened for my life.' His barrister expanded on this succinct statement and it appeared that once someone pulls a gun on you, all bets are off.

Prior to the trial, Puta, the Princess and their friends were frightened that Puta was going to 'be given a hand [by police] to go down'. They wanted to ensure that no further incriminating evidence would be placed before the court. Puta and his associates knew that police could fabricate or plant evidence, and it is Haken's interpretation that he and Swan were paid to ensure this did not take place. Haken and Swan were 'playing this one straight up and down', and received $5000 each for their trouble.

According to Haken, the Princess then offered Swan and Haken $500 a week to protect Sweethearts, which was also a cocaine distribution point. Swan and Haken agreed to the proposal and thereafter picked up the money from either Puta or the Princess at the gambling club the Princess ran in Bondi Road. Haken's evidence to the Royal Commission about this arrangement was corroborated when John Swan finally rolled in July 1995 and admitted that this took place.[15]

Some time after Puta's acquittal, Haken picked up the clothing of Ghazzawie and took it to the Sydney Police Centre exhibit section, where it was booked up for disposal purposes. Sergeant Bob Brown contacted him to say that he had found some items from the Ghazzawie killing and asked if Haken would come round and pick them up. According to Haken, it seemed 'like a pain in the arse at the time' as the matter had long been dealt with. The items could not be disposed of until they had been properly released. Haken decided to get someone to pick up the items and 'book them up' with the original exhibit at the Sydney Police Centre. Then he would seek a direction and have them disposed of.

There was a furnace at St Vincent's where items such as these could be burned. Haken received a phone call from the exhibits officer at the Sydney Police Centre. He said that he had a problem; he had searched the clothes and found gold rings in the pocket. The scientific people at the crime scene had missed the rings in the search. The defence barrister would have dearly loved this evidence at the trial. The discovery of the rings certainly gives credence to Puta's version of events.

Years later Haken would tell Puta, 'Mate there are to be no more murders in the Cross'. Puta laughed and replied, 'I do somewhere else'.

With a few exceptions, like the late Reverend Ted Noff's establishment, most places in the Cross had a scam of some description. There were the landlords who charged exorbitant rents for premises being used for drug distribution. For instance, there was a doss house above a restaurant in the Cross, part of a whole complex of rooms that should have been condemned in the 1950s.

One of the owners would collect his own rents and the rent from the restaurant as well. At that stage in the 1980s, the restaurant, which wasn't a big place, was paying $5300 rent a week, an amount that certainly could not be made via restaurant takings. This restaurant was very nice in comparison to most in Kings Cross; it was run by someone who lived in an expensive mansion in an exclusive Sydney suburb; this individual was successful because he, like everybody else in Kings Cross, seized every opportunity that came his way.

The owner was known within police circles as a receiver of stolen goods. A typical incident involving him would go as follows: a friend of his might want to dispose of a quantity of precious metal; the 'owner' would arrange to meet him; then, at that meeting, it would just so happen that shortly after they sat down, the police would walk in and ask this person to show them what was in the bag. The owner would then strike a bargain with the police to get the bloke out of trouble. Of course this was all a set-up between the owner and the police. Everything was an opportunity to make money, and the owner was into anything and everything.

Haken was aware that the restaurant was being used by the Romanians to sell drugs. The owner received a percentage of the sale of drugs within his restaurant. He provided, for a fee, a safe haven for junkies. Haken likened it to Aladdin's cave, where 'you could have searched forever and not found anything'. There was a trapdoor in the ceiling that led to a storage room. The owner had storage areas at the back and many other areas where things could be hidden. The point was that nobody was really looking anyway. 'The owner' has never been convicted of a crime.

Danny Riciutti however, was a multiple convicted felon who worked for a number of people including the owner. Danny was an accomplished thief and forger. He was employed as a kitchen hand but he would boost the owner's business by moving a lot of stolen goods through him. The goods ranged from gold and diamonds to alcohol brought in by airline attendants. Haken stopped a steward from Singapore Airlines early one morning carrying a bag with the airline stickers still attached. The steward explained they were poorly paid and this was a way of surviving. Haken could understand this reasoning and let him go. The owner's was one of the only restaurants that could process a couple of hundred American Express vouchers without any meals being served!

Similarly, there was a notorious Private Hotel which had around a dozen rooms. According to credit card records, they had let out one hundred rooms. The 'owner' was onto the same scam. The junkies would bring in a hot credit card and they'd run off about six or eight meals on it and get anywhere between thirty to fifty cents in the dollar per transaction. A lot of premises used this scam. A clothing shop nearby sold more clothes than it could possibly fit onto hangers.

The report of the Royal Commission into the NSW Police Service stated that before the Lebanese network of drug distribution and sales, there had not been an organisation involved in the distribution of heroin and/or cocaine at the time that Haken arrived at Kings Cross. It was suggested that it had been an ad hoc affair prior to the Lebanese moving in, but Haken disagrees with this view. He states that the Romanians were well and truly ensconced. Unlike the 'businessmen' of Chinatown, the Romanians would not toe the line. 'They were totally out of control. You couldn't tell them what to do or what not to do; they did as they pleased.'

The Romanians' operation appeared to be based at the TAB in Rushcutters Bay. The kingpin in the group went by the name of Mischa, who was connected to a former Kings Cross detective and was therefore left alone. It was an unstated rule that you 'left other cops' people alone'. None of Mischa's workers was a user. Their lifestyle was simply getting together, drinking coffee, drinking alcohol and selling heroin in large amounts. As they were having trouble handling the Romanians, police looked for those with whom an arrangement could be made. They started to make arrests among the Romanians, hoping to squeeze them out of the Cross. The squeeze resulted in this group becoming more involved in the wholesaling rather than the retailing of the drug.

The Kings Cross Drug Unit was started in 1991 and made a concerted push against most dealers. 'It didn't take much shaking to move people on; you only had to turn them over four or five times and they'd get the idea they weren't welcome there.' In Haken's view, it was inevitable that some dealers would remain. The idea was that those remaining would be cooperative with police.

It was very difficult; you were trying to police a place that traded twenty-four hours a day when you only worked eight hours. You were working five days a week and they were working seven days a week. It became very obvious at one stage that when we went home, they came out, like moths to the light. We started doing tricky things with the Drug Unit; we started working back-to-back shifts. You'd work eight hours, then work another eight hours, which was, strictly speaking, against the union, but the boss at the time didn't have any objection to it. In the second eight hours you'd do a lot more than you ever dreamt of doing, because it was expected that you wouldn't be there.

At the Cross, you'd have three deaths per shift. Not necessarily ODs, but three deceased. We were so understaffed and the workload was terrifying. It used to rattle me a little bit when I was at the Cross, when one day people I knew were walking around and the next day they'd be ass-over-head dead. You would take that on the chin and say, 'well that's the way it is'.

In his declaration to the Royal Commission, Haken stated that the Hampton Court Hotel was selling wholesale marijuana among other things.[16] Around the corner from the Hampton Court in Kellett Street was 'Fat George's' brothel. A little farther along there was another brothel, which purported to be a dancing club. The manager of this room was there from the time Haken was in 21 Division in 1974 until he left the Cross nearly twenty years later.

Today, when asked to describe the room, Haken says, 'You couldn't describe it; it was a figment of the imagination of Lucifer when he was let rampantly loose in hell'. It was dark and sleazy. There was a birdcage made of rubber bars in which a woman would dance. You would go down some stairs and there would be a bar area with a chair where the manager would sit like a feudal lord. He kept a sawn-off shotgun or a pistol within hand's reach.

The manager would have a few runners working for him. At night, the room would fill with men who would drink and buy and sell anything they wanted while girls danced lewdly around them. 'They were pretty ordinary shows, I can tell you.' Women also worked the rooms upstairs and would come downstairs and take clients from the main floor area. It was basically a low-class brothel.

The manager drove a big Mercedes, had a huge house in the western suburbs and surrounded himself with Rottweilers. He wore large quantities of gold jewellery and claimed to be a karate expert. He was well known to police as he made alcohol freely available to them. When Haken went 'on the town' with 21 Division, the first place they visited was the manager's. 'You would go in and there'd be cans of beer handed to the boys, and he'd say, "Hello boys, come on in, have a good time" and all that sort of bullshit, typical of the Cross. You could buy anybody for a couple of cans of beer.'

Haken says of the room, 'It's one of those places that should have been condemned about a million years ago'. Haken was not sure if it ever had a licence but it had traded for as long as anyone could remember. 'I always thought Licensing should be a job for clerks, not cops.' During all the years that Haken was at Kings Cross, this place was raided only a couple of times.

Ironically, and in a pathetic show of police bureaucracy, a cafe nearby came under scrutiny. According to Haken, they served good food at cheap prices and at times they would take dinners up to old people who could not get to the cafe if they were not feeling well: 'The kind of thing you'd read about in *Good Hearted Magazine!*'

Mike Kelso, licensing sergeant at Kings Cross busted the cafe for keeping two dozen cans of beer in the fridge which would be sold to people to have with their lunch. They would charge a dollar a can, so they probably made a few cents on each can. They'd buy the cans at the local pub. 'Meantime, there's Sodom and Gomorrah going on next door, and the cafe owner ends up being prosecuted and brought before the court. In all the time I went in there, he never offered me a can of beer.'

The Cross was a place of great hypocrisy. With all the illicit activity that went on in some clubs, others were charged for not displaying the licensing sign above their doorway. Haken reported that Kelso charged John Morgan for not displaying the name of the licensee on the door of the premises in Oxford Street.

It was important to be tough in the Cross. Those with bravado seemed to get away with a lot, but it was a dangerous game. Danny Karam was a typical creature of the Cross. His first convictions were in 1985 and included heroin use, theft and possessing an unlicensed pistol. While in jail, he built up a strong physique through weight training and developed the jailhouse attitude that he used to his advantage when he returned to the streets. His record reflects this lifestyle with convictions for serious assault, robbery and the possession of drugs.

Karam gave evidence at the Royal Commission that he worked for Bill Bayeh and Sam Ibrahim protecting their interests and ensuring that all street dealers were on side. He claims to have made up to $10,000 a week in 1995. He was a heroin user and eventually went it alone, having fallen out with the Bayehs and Ibrahims. He was part of a violent criminal group that was wanted for at least four murders and sixteen shootings in Sydney. There are many stories about his strongarm tactics on the street, though some, Haken suggests, could have been his own publicity. There is no doubt that he must have offended someone. In 1993 a gunman, in search of Karam, got the wrong address and shot dead Karam's neighbour, Leslie Betcher. Karam was one of many players in the Cross; he lived large for a while but was eventually a victim of the brutality he himself visited on others. In 1999, after he had given evidence against Bill Bayeh, he paid the ultimate price when he drove to a meeting and while waiting in his car was shot dead.

Danny Karam had a huge number of people who did not like him and when his neighbour was mistakenly murdered instead of him, Neville Scullion, who lived nearby, put forward the theory that the hit was meant for Karam. This proved to be correct but was knocked at the time as being only a wild assertion. Scullion also put forward the theory that a certain Baartman was the likely shooter and detectives went looking for him around the Cross where he was a regular. Baartman was also a standover man and a career criminal. He was freelancing and had made a big mistake.

Looking for a gun, Haken says, 'We turned over a number of people and in fact found a .32 calibre automatic pistol in a room at the Majestic Private Hotel occupied by a crook from Melbourne'. This gives an idea of the capacity that police had to find something if there was a concerted effort. "Listen, business is going to stop unless you help us", I said. We want the prick with the gun and the gun itself. This attitude produced significant results and that's how we found it.' Haken found a gun but it was the wrong gun.

Sometime after that, an ambulance attended an overdose in a Potts Point flat. Baartman was there with a girl and while treating the patient the ambulance officer found a .32 automatic underneath his unconscious body. They called the uniformed police who took Baartman and the pistol back to the station, where Haken interviewed him.

The girl in the flat with Baartman when he overdosed was the former de-facto of known criminal Terry Ball (who is alleged to have once tried to kill Neddy Smith before they sorted out their differences). Haken asked Baartman, 'Whose gun is this, mate? It's either yours or the girl's.' Baartman replied, 'I'll do the white knight thing, mate, it's mine.'

Haken was contacted by Homicide Squad members handling the murder who wanted to see him urgently. They confirmed that the gun was the murder weapon in the Betcher murder. They wanted to be reassured that Haken hadn't planted the weapon on Baartman or substituted it for the weapon that had been located. 'That's a fuckin' bad reputation, isn't it, when it gets to that stage? Come on boys, this is murder, not drugs!'

In related events, the girl's flat had a listening device placed in it by the Homicide Squad who were trying to see who was associated with the murder. Shortly after, they were contacted by those listening and were told that police or men purporting to be police were in the flat carrying out what appeared to be a robbery.

Haken went to the flat with Swan and others. They came across a man whom Haken knew as a drug addict named Watson, who had just left the flat. He said he had just been robbed of a large amount of money by two people who claimed to be police. Haken found out that two people who had left the units had gone into a local club in Challis Avenue called Benny's, which at that stage of the day was locked and in darkness. Detectives gained access to the club through the owner John Ross, who also owned the Kardomah Club. Ross was told to open the club and then police surrounded it. Inside the club they found two well-known crims, Bert Kidd and Gary Page, both of whom had multiple convictions. A search of the club revealed the gun that Watson said was used in the robbery in a garbage tin, underneath the black plastic liner. Watson had left money with the female member of the flat and she had arranged for a bogus robbery so that they could split the money and blame the robbery on the police. 'They didn't have fake ID or anything, but had suits and a gun,' says Haken. As Haken told the Royal Commission, Ross had paid the police to keep them out of his club and to leave his customers alone.[17]

This was the world Trevor Haken was inhabiting on a daily basis. Haken still feels that to have any sense of order on the streets, you needed to be able to stand up to this type of people and take them on. Many of the problems of the Cross have moved to the south west of Sydney. 'That's why you need the old-style police force that existed, and officers with a bit of ticker that would walk up and close places down and close people down. Say, "Righto, you've been out of order, you're out."'

He goes further:

> In all probability we should have done more about the Vietnamese in the early days, but I was at the Cross and we didn't have a problem with them. Any time they came our way we either had them arrested or chucked out of town. It was quite easy to do because there weren't many of them there. They were running their own race out there at Cabramatta and obviously it has developed into a disaster.

Haken continues to argue that drastic times call for drastic measures and that the old way of taking these gangs head on (as in 21 Division days) should be readopted. 'At least we had some measure of order. You do whatever you have to do but get rid of them, and that's what people want.'

CHAPTER 11

KINGS CROSS BADLANDS — BILL BAYEH IN THE CROSS

*'There was no sort of situation
where he thought enough is enough.
Like all people in that sort of industry
they can see the stars, and want everything.'*

TREVOR HAKEN

The Lebanese moved in to the Cross to fill a void left by the Romanians. As Haken puts it, 'One mob moves out and another moves in within minutes, like blowflies to a dead carcass.' When the Lebanese moved in and became the main criminal force in the Cross, the Romanians stayed involved in a different capacity.

They were still running gear [drugs] between the Chinese and the street sellers, and in all probability they were supplying a lot to the Lebanese. To try to catch up with who was supplying who, was impossible. There were too many players in the field, and if you tried to chase through the Romanians it was a closed wall. They were unbelievable.

You can't terrorise people or even question people who have got nothing to lose. Their street presence disappeared.

Sam (also known as Hassam, Sam Sard and Jim Azar) Ibrahim had convictions that included offensive behaviour, assault occasioning actual bodily harm, found in a gaming house, hinder police, assault, possession of a prohibited drug.[1] Ibrahim admitted to the Royal Commission that he protected street drug dealers ('I'm a good fighter') in return for free caps of cocaine. With his brother John, he opened a club called The Tunnel in Earl Place. John Ibrahim managed to buy a twenty per cent stake in The Tunnel at the age of 19. He admitted to the Commission that he was a friend of Bill Bayeh for over 12 years but they had fallen out over his brother's Sam's cocaine habit.

In a covertly recorded tape by Trevor Haken, Bill Bayeh referred to Sam Ibrahim as a large scale dealer. Bayeh estimated that the Ibrahims were making ($100,000 a week).[2] When the tape was played to Ibrahim at the Royal Commission he recognised Bayeh's voice but denied Bayeh's assertion. When asked what he did for a living, Sam simply replied 'the best I can'.

Individuals known to the police fronted a lot of the businesses in the Cross. Prior to the Royal Commission the ownership of these clubs and businesses was generally unknown. When the Commission revealed details, the owners were seen to be living in Sydney's most exclusive suburbs, such as Point Piper, Elizabeth Bay, Vaucluse, Rose Bay, Bellevue Hill, and included one-time members of the *Business Review Weekly* rich list.

Most business in the Cross was done with a nod and a handshake. And you wouldn't back down on it, because you'd be terribly, terribly dead. You really didn't know where

McPherson, Bayeh, Domican, or Freeman stood in any area. You knew that Domican was paid to stay out of the Cross.[3] I had no idea why bloody McPherson was there or what his holdings were, so you really just didn't have a chance. The only way to keep your head above water as far as knowing what was going on was to talk to a lot of people.

Bill Bayeh was running what Haken calls a 'back door' situation. Bayeh had another brother, Fred, who lived in a house behind the station in Victoria Street, and he did business out of there. 'It's not like one Woolworths store trading, it's like a lot of corner shops that don't even have corners.' Haken suggests that in Victoria Street alone there may have been up to fifty dealers. Haken joked, 'What Bayeh did down the track was to try to do what Woolworths did — that is, put other people out of business. Not by cutting the prices or anything, just cutting their legs off.'

Haken had an excellent group of informants at the Cross and could find out within hours of someone new turning up, and what was happening. At one time, he heard that there was a new heroin dealer in the Cross called Ted Barker. Barker was sitting in the front window of McDonald's when Haken turned him over, that is, interrogated him. Haken immediately recognised Barker as unique, even by his weapon of choice. It was the first occasion in years Haken had found someone in possession of a cutthroat razor.

Barker told Haken that he had met him years ago with Les Knox, an associate from the Drug Squad. Haken and Barker spoke and Haken recalled that he had had dealings with Barker and Knox. He had found him to be 'a trustworthy kind of fellow' in relation to those dealings, in that, he could be trusted to keep his end of a deal. Barker told Haken that he wanted to develop a kind of franchise of dealing in the Cross and that he was to be in partnership with Bill Bayeh. Haken recollects, 'That's how I met

Bill, and things went from there to the way they existed down the track.' Barker told Haken that there was 'a giant dollar to be made' and asked him, 'Why don't you let somebody work here that you can trust, rather than all these bloody monkeys running around the traps? This way, nobody's going to get hurt and there'll be good quality gear going on the street instead of rubbish. There'd be no battery acid and that type of thing.' Haken adds:

> I know it sounds terrible now, but when you're living in that sort of environment, you think to yourself, hang on, this'll overcome a lot of the problems that we've got. You have to remember that there were people running around carrying caps up their arse, using internal carrying — it was just a matter of course. You know they were whipping caps out of the inside of themselves and putting them into their mouth and passing them out to other people who are breaking them open and injecting the substance. The thing was horrifying when you think about it.

Haken and Barker spoke about his suggestion and Haken thought it had merit. Barker suggested paying Haken $500 a week 'just to kick' (to start with). Both would benefit financially and it seemed that a sense of order could be restored. Haken would be dealing with people who he felt would toe the line. It seemed a win–win situation.

Barker and Bayeh hired a small gaming room to run 'a clean operation'. By a 'clean operation' he meant that they would only be dealing to adult junkies. It was supposedly a primary consideration 'to keep the kids out of it'. Of course, Haken admits that the overriding consideration of everyone concerned was to make money. It didn't stay clean for very long.

Everybody up there was scheming or scamming to make a buck. You know, they'd talk about the old days when the Yanks were in town, and how everybody really made a dollar then. They wanted to try and get that level of money going again but the scene had deteriorated mainly into drug dealing. Although everybody complained about it, everybody was trying to get a portion of the drug dollar. So whatever was going on, no one was saying 'we've got to stop this'. Bayeh was to run the 'okey doke' [cocaine] while Barker was to have 'the hammer' [heroin].

This arrangement did not last long. In 1992, Ted Barker died of a heart attack while being arrested at North Sydney. Bayeh then took over the running of the whole operation. Haken says of Bayeh, 'There was no sort of situation where he thought enough is enough. Like all people in that sort of industry, they can see the stars and want everything.'

But as one door of opportunity closed, another one would always seem to open. There were countless opportunities in the Cross.

In his evidence to the Commission Haken stated that Angelo Ivanoff had run a drug selling operation from the Mansions Hotel.[4] Haken reported to the Commission that Fowler suggested Haken have a drink with Ivanoff. When they got together, it was arranged that Haken would share money (amounts up to $500 a time) with detectives Fowler, Scullion, Thompson and Scott for turning a blind eye to Ivanoff's dealing. This arrangement came to an end when Bill Bayeh moved into the Cross.

As Haken further reported to the Commission, Bayeh took over a small place that was being run by Phil Giovanni.[5] Giovanni had run a snooker room at the Cross above Porky's, which was a drug outlet. This room was basically a retail outlet for cocaine.

177

Haken believed that room was protected by Fowler who told Haken to leave it alone. Thompson and Haken met with Giovanni and $500 per fortnight was suggested as payment for leaving the premises alone. Giovanni ran it as a simple set-up and did it very well.

Of course, having the police leave you alone in Kings Cross might not be enough to keep in business. Giovanni complained to the Royal Commission that he was driven out of The Penthouse Snooker Room. Giovanni was reported to have said that street dealers had broken his machines and that the landlord had increased his rent. He told the *Daily Telegraph* that he had heard that Bayeh had wanted him out.[6] The *Sydney Morning Herald* meanwhile reported Giovanni's complaint that he found his rent was increased by the lessor Dimitri Karageorge and that Dimitri had been offered a 'substantial offer' of what Giovanni believed to be about $3000 a week.[7] Haken kept in contact with Giovanni and would meet regularly and pass on information.

Bayeh was accepted quickly into the Cross by detectives as the new player. Former detective Stephen Pentland first met Bill Bayeh when Pentland was visiting his former partner Larry Churchill in Long Bay Jail. Bill Bayeh and John Ibrahim would later chip in to help pay the bill for Pentland's 30th birthday party. Pentland would tell the Royal Commission that the CIB cricket team had received funding from brothel owner Fat George and nightclub manager Skinny Steve to help it get to Perth.

Bayeh muscled in on every premise available to spread his network, using Danny Karam to get rid of opposition dealers on the streets.

If what used to happen regularly at the Cross happened in a normal suburb, it would be a major crime. Someone would get carved up something dreadful, we'd go to the hospital and ask if they wanted to make a complaint and they'd say no, so you'd just throw it away. There was a saying at the time that if people really knew what happened on the streets of Kings Cross, they'd surround the place with barbed wire and flatten it with a nuclear device.

Working at the Cross as a cop, you not only formed a different view of life, you also developed a different view of the way crime was dealt with. Haken likened taking the train from Town Hall to Kings Cross to catching a rocket ship to Mars. At Central and Town Hall there were normal people, but at the Cross it was just insanity. 'You got off and it was wall-to-wall junkies and crooks from all over the place. If someone got out of jail anywhere, you knew they'd end up here.' If the rest of the city stopped at five o'clock, the Cross was just starting to hum. As soon as you got there, the work was rolling and there was no such thing as down time.

For Haken, it seemed that the police being promoted weren't the right type to get the job done. The primary consideration of the hierarchy was to keep within budget. This made them look good in district meetings, but it took no consideration of the working unit at all. The unit's arrest rate in the Cross was good despite the difficulties they faced.

When the Drug Unit was formed at the Cross, they were not even given a vehicle. Haken took matters into his own hands and bought a second-hand Datsun 180B from a friend for $200, using the unit's petty cash. The driver's seat was broken and there were two milk crates behind it to keep it stable. It was therefore impossible to put anybody behind the driver's seat and so it was effectively a three-person car. People who were arrested were taken to the station in the Datsun. The car seemed to fit in with the surrounding madness.

Haken saw the arrangement with Bill Bayeh not so much that police were protecting Bayeh's people but that they weren't 'being worked on'. 'If you grabbed someone inadvertently, then bad luck. But you knew which places to work on and which places to stay away from.' There was no shortage of people for Haken's detectives to work on. 'Our arrest rate was at a higher rate and a higher quality than the south region, which has never been argued by the hierarchy. The majority of the people that we arrested pleaded guilty. They were caught and caught fair. The only thing was that we were selective in who we were targeting.'

Among the dealers that Haken reported as paying into the 'laugh' was Mia Thorne. She was a large scale dealer of heroin in Kings Cross, who used to sell heroin out of the Tudor Private Hotel in Darlinghurst Road.[8] The hotel had a security system built in so that when junkies would come to the ground floor door, they would be 'buzzed in' by the doorman. Thorne would negotiate the sale inside the premises. For this service, the hotel charged five dollars per person for every junkie admitted.

Haken turned over Thorne. He put it to her that 'we can go a number of ways here. You're going to jail forever or you can steer us onto your main man.' No one wants to go to jail and when faced with such choices, most dealers 'turn up' the next level of supply.

Ilya Kraizelbird was a dental prosthetist who was also a supplier of heroin in Bondi — a member of what Haken calls the Russian mafia. It appeared to be common knowledge that Kraizelbird supplied and yet no one had touched him. The Kings Cross Drug Unit later 'did a job' on Kraizelbird where he was supplying Thorne with ounces of heroin. However, the drugs went missing during the sale (Thorne took them) and they had to be withdrawn from her and placed on Kraizelbird by the squad to effect a successful prosecution. That is, Kraizelbird was loaded up for the drugs by Haken and his partner at the time, Peter Scott.[9] The sentence he received for his was light and non-custodial but Kraizelbird was subsequently arrested by the DEA for a one-kilo heroin supply transaction. Haken recalls,

> He was obviously guilty. It was house cleaning. He had off-loaded the drugs to our informant and so we simply returned them, as good housekeepers do.

Kraizelbird pleaded guilty. This approach was used again with the person who took over from Kraizelbird in supplying Mia Thorne with heroin (another Russian dealer). He was arrested while supplying Thorne with an ounce of heroin. Once again, Thorne decamped with the drugs from the sale and the squad had to load another dealer. Thorne had paid the dealer thousands of dollars in a paper bag for the heroin. When the arrest was made, he dropped the bag and denied any knowledge of it. Similarly, the bag had to be 'put back' into his possession to enable a successful prosecution.

There is no such thing as a free interchange of information in the police force. If you had a good job, you wouldn't give it to anybody. Haken had a falling out with his second in charge, later known at the Commission as KX6, when he realised that KX6 was giving information away about good jobs to his mentor, Bob Lysaught. Haken alleged that he leaked information about a number of their operations.[10] 'He was desperate to get to Lysaught's task force [one of the DEA task forces] or to the South Region Drug Unit. So he would give this information away to ingratiate himself with the South Region and to give Lysaught the ammunition to get him into the unit.'

Lysaught originally took KX6 from country New South Wales to the Joint Task Force. JTF members were asking, 'Who is this guy and why he is coming from the bush to the JTF? It was simply because he was Lysaught's mate.' KX6 then resigned from the JTF and went and operated a business for a while. Under a scheme introduced to entice people to rejoin the force, KX6 came straight to Kings Cross. Thereafter, he worked with Lysaught at the Fraud Enforcement Agency (FEA), 'where he never would have been accepted as a recent rejoinee if he hadn't had an association with Lysaught'. What frequently went on in the police was that mates looked after each other. KX6 admitted his involvement in corruption at Kings Cross and the JTF.

The Royal Commission heard that Steve Hardas leased nearly all his business premises, such as the Pink Panther, the Pink Pussycat, Nugatty, the Butterfly (later called Playbirds). Teamed up with Robert Daher, he also ran some smaller low-class strip clubs and brothels. These coexisted with Bill Bayeh's places since they didn't step on each other's toes. Haken points the finger at some of the faceless owners of these premises who were charging exorbitant and 'who must have been aware of the only type of activity in their premises that could generate that amount of money was drug dealing.

Meeting those who were a part of 'the joke' was something that needed care. With a phone call or a word to one of their men, Haken could track down those he wanted, to meet and receive the money. These people were in the Cross all the time and if they weren't then they were contactable on a mobile phone. If someone was stalling, Haken would call some of his contacts to shake them up. The Cross wasn't a big place — Haken would eventually find who he was looking for.

As a rule, the payments Haken received and then distributed to other detectives were purely for leaving the dealers who were 'on side' alone. Haken provided information about police, such as staff movements, investigations and police gossip. The crooks provided information to Haken regarding other dealers and what was happening on the street.

In evidence to the Royal Commission Haken described the early dealings with Bill Bayeh where the payment of $500 was divided evenly between Detectives Kim Thompson, Neville Scullion, John Swan, Peter Scott and Haken.[11] Haken would get four envelopes and put $100 inside each and mark them for the relevant detective. A skull symbol for Scullion, a swan or a bird for Swan, 'Katies' for Thompson and the initial S on the left corner and the initial T on the right corner of the envelope for KX6. When Bayeh pushed out Giovanni from the Pool Room and took over the third floor above Porky's the payments increased to $1000 per week, which Haken personally received from Bayeh.

Steve Hardas, Fat George and Bayeh all had their own camps and ran their own shows. This was common knowledge but there was never any documentation or paperwork to confirm such relationships. In this business there were no receipts issued. For this reason, if someone had asked Haken how much he had made over the years, he would have found it hard to determine.

Meetings took place in cafes, in cars and in clubs. Money might be handed over underneath a napkin, or placed in an envelope or passed during a handshake. It was all cash, which Haken, as bagman, immediately divided among those in 'the joke'. It was very rare that anyone else other than Bayeh himself or other principal dealers would hand over a large payment to Haken. To trust someone else to do this was too dangerous. The exchanges took place very quickly, as video evidence played to the Royal Commission would later show.

When Haken first met Robert Daher, he was one of the doormen at the Love Machine in the Cross. He was short, stocky and clean-cut and struck Haken as being more intelligent than most doormen. It surprised Haken to hear that Daher was suddenly running the Pink Panther with a number of other Kings Cross identities. Daher used the Pink Panther as a front for cocaine distribution. Haken eventually gave evidence to the Royal Commission that it was at this time that Malcolm Bigg (a detective at the Drug Squad working with Haken) approached Haken on behalf of Daher and offered $300 a week between the two of them to 'turn a blind eye' to Daher's operation.[12]

The Commission was told that Bigg had told Haken that Daher's group would do whatever they were told to do and that there would be no problems. Haken accepted the proposal and Bigg would be the one collecting the money on their behalf. Haken's evidence stated that Bigg and his cousin, former Detective Sergeant Geoff Thompson, had a very close association with Joe Bayeh (cousins of Louie and Bill Bayeh) because of Joe's brothel in Parramatta, the suburb where Bigg and Thompson had previously been stationed. Haken stated that Joe Bayeh had wanted to move in on Daher's drug operation, but that nothing further transpired.[13]

Daher and his associates took over the private hotel known as the Budget Inn above the Pink Panther and focused the cocaine operation out of there. Haken gave evidence that despite the arrangement with Kings Cross detectives, Daher's operations were raided by a Drug Unit from another region who Haken said had a close relationship with Bill Bayeh.[14]

Daher's operation at the Budget Inn went on for some time until Bill Bayeh's operation across the road was 'damaged' by one of Daher's men.

Daher used a man by the name of Tony Achmar, who was also known as 'the Inspector'. The Royal Commission heard that the Inspector was a go-between for the police and the crooks.[15] He hoped to develop a similar role as Frank Hakim had in Haken's days at 21 Division. The Inspector would purport to do a deal with police on behalf of a crook. Haken stated that he would often only pass on a percentage of the money received or he would receive money from other crooks while not actually doing anything that he promised.

In evidence, Haken told how the Inspector planted a stash of drugs, on Daher's behalf, in Bill Bayeh's club Lasers.[16] He then reported the whereabouts of the drugs to Kings Cross detectives while Haken and Bigg were off duty. The junior police on duty rushed to Bayeh's club and found the stash where they had been told (in the column of a white plastic pedestal table). This caused a problem in Bayeh's camp. It was not long after that Bayeh heard who was responsible for the set-up. Louis Bayeh provided protection for his brother's premises, and this behaviour by a competitor was a serious and untenable situation.

The Royal Commission heard that Louis Bayeh then bashed Daher outside the Majestic Coffee Lounge. This bashing was seen as a great insult to Daher. Later the same day, Louis Bayeh's home in Ermington in western Sydney was shot at. Bullets smashed through the windows and doors of the house. Bayeh's wife and children were inside at the time and were fortunate not to be hit.

It was then that this tangle of corruption became even messier. In evidence to the Commission, Haken stated that Daher's men (Norman Korbage and Assif Dib) were responsible for the shooting.[17] Louis Bayeh went to the press and claimed that the police had shot his house. The Royal Commission was told that Louis Bayeh approached a detective in Sydney's west to arrange a meeting between Daher, himself, Dibb and Korbage at Bayeh's house. Dibb and Korbage pulled out of the meeting as they were aware that Bayeh's house was under surveillance.

The Royal Commission was told that Dibb and Korbage feared that they were being set up to be shot dead.[18] At the same time, Haken and Bigg were approached by Daher to 'safely arrest' Korbage (now deceased) and Assif Dib. The two police were offered $5000 to make this happen and to accept Korbage and

Dib's version of events and not investigate the matter fully.[19] In short, Haken and Bigg were paid for not loading [fabricating evidence to ensure conviction] Korbage and Dib and keeping them alive.

Although Haken had a strong association with Bill Bayeh, he disliked Louis Bayeh intensely. Louis Bayeh and his associates would eat at Pinocchio's (a restaurant known for its good food), next to Porky's strip club. Bayeh would have his driver park his Mercedes with its blacked-out windows right in front of the restaurant in the no standing zone. In comment, Haken says,

> [Louis Bayeh] acted was like some Mafioso boss wanting everyone to see him, so I'd wait until his food was served and then tell him to piss off out of there. He didn't like it. It was like a contest of importance. He was showing everybody how important he was, so I'd show him that he wasn't. I couldn't do business with him. He was so heavily involved with others that I thought he was dangerous, and that proved to be the case.

Daher's concern was that if his men gave themselves up to anyone else there was the likelihood that they would be shot by police when they were located. And so an arrangement was made that Daher's men would give themselves up at the Bankstown Police Station in the early hours of the morning. Bankstown was selected because the station was not involved in the dispute and no one there would have been looking for either person.[20]

Haken and Bigg were heavily criticised for this action as the inquiry was considered to be in the control of detectives in the western suburbs. It was suggested that the interviews were conducted in an improper manner, giving Dib and Korbage the opportunity to beat the charge of shooting at Bayeh's house. As

Haken later admitted to the Royal Commission, this was the case, although it was denied by Haken at the time.

The Royal Commission heard that during the preparation of the brief for court, Korbage called Bayeh and begged forgiveness.[21] Bigg had told Haken that Bayeh had offered Daher not to give evidence if, in exchange, Daher paid $50,000 to save face. Bill Bayeh confirmed this with Haken.[22]

The story that Korbage and Dib put forward was that there was a third party involved and although they were present at the time they could not identify the shooter. As pathetic as this story sounds, it was accepted by the Department of Public Prosecutions as reason enough not to proceed to trial. Of course, the matter was not helped by the fact that on the day of the committal of Dib and Korbage, the majority of witnesses, including Louis Bayeh, his wife, some police and some ballistics and scientific officers failed to attend. Ray De Rubeis represented Dib and Korbage at the committal.

The fallout from the Bayeh shooting was that Bayeh, through his connections with the police, organised for a special investigation to be mounted against Robert Daher with a view to eliminating him as their main competition on the street. This investigation would involve Haken and was one of the many reasons that brought the Royal Commission to speak to Haken. Ironically, the Bayehs' decision to bring on this investigation would ultimately lead to an investigation of their own organisation by the Commission and eventually lead to the jailing of Bill Bayeh.

In the event, Haken told Bigg to tell Daher to stay out of the Cross.[23] He had contravened the rules and was banished. The Bayehs stayed in the Cross. Haken reported to the Royal Commission, that Daher installed another man, Antoine Chapelle, as the manager of the drug-selling operation in the Budget Private Hotel.[24]

This seemed to calm things down. Haken told how he knew Chapelle from when he was running the brothel, Nevada. Chapelle had a close association with Chook Fowler and detectives Scullion and Thompson. Haken began receiving payments from Chapelle of around $500 per week.[25]

At this time, the Crime Commission began an operation looking into Daher's activities. This was another good reason for Haken to keep Daher away. This begs the question of what would have been done if Daher came back? 'We'd load him up and bust him so many times that he would never get out.'

At the end of 1993, Haken was ordered by South Region Inspector Bob Waites to transfer immediately to A-district headquarters in the Sydney Police Centre. There was no stated reason for the transfer. Haken thought that he was transferred because of the trouble in the Cross. Bayeh was still pushing for Haken to get into trouble for what he saw as Haken's 'desertion' to Daher's camp.

Things do not go well if you are a police officer with a summons standing over you. 'South Region probably found out that the toe-cutters [either Internal Security, the Crime Commission or the NCA] were doing a job on me and they wanted me moved.' Waites told Haken that two men had visited Alf Peate (Superintendent in charge of South Region) and immediately after they left the office, he directed Waites to transfer Haken to A–district headquarters. 'Which is basically, "Here's a desk, sit at it for eight hours and don't do anything". This normally results in people going on sick leave and not coming back. It's a clear indication that something's going on and they either want to protect you or protect the integrity of the department. They obviously didn't want to fuckin' protect you, so draw your own conclusion.'

Haken was only at A-district for a short time when he spoke to Chook Fowler and arranged to go down to City of Sydney as a non-operational unit, which means that he was restricted to office work. He still maintained contact with Daher and Bayeh, and was able to supply information to them on what was going on. Haken continued to receive 'the joke', and pick it up and split it. This continued with Skinny (Steve Stavrou) and his partners for some time.

In evidence to the Commission, Haken revealed he met with Ray De Rubeis at his office with Daher and Korbage and was told that Dib had gone missing.[26] He was played a video tape of Dib expressing concern for his safety just days beforehand. This video tape was eventually handed to the Royal Commission. Haken believed that Dib showed up and was later arrested for bail infringements in Kings Cross.[27]

A detective from South Region Drug Squad spoke to Haken and told him that Daher was subject to 'a huge police investigation' and that Haken 'was off' (the target of an investigation) because he had been taped speaking to Daher on a phone tap. Haken would normally have ignored this except that he had called from a phone in the picture theatre complex in George Street. This confirmed that he was 'off'. The detective had a good leak in the organisation. Knowing that, Haken stopped seeing Daher but maintained contact with his solicitor Ray De Rubeis.

The Royal Commission heard that Haken would go and see De Rubeis in his offices in the Hong Kong Bank building in George Street.[28] De Rubeis was quite nervous about receiving him. He would usher him inside and turn the radio up loud as they whispered to each other.[29] Haken would confirm that Daher 'was off' and that the investigation was going on. It was Haken's understanding that Daher was going to leave the country. De Rubeis would never pass Daher's money to Haken inside the office in case there was a camera and so would often go out to the fire stairs. Haken received a number of $500 payments from Daher.

Haken told the Royal Commission that he would pass on information to Daher through De Rubeis.[30]

Haken did not speak to Daher again. On the day that Haken had arranged to meet Steve Hardas at the Pink Pussycat, he noticed that he was being tagged by a surveillance car. Haken tried to 'dry clean' the tag and went to places where he would not normally go and the vehicle stayed behind him.

Haken didn't keep the appointment but he did drive through the lane at the back of the Budget Inn where he had arranged to meet Hardas. There he saw a number of obvious police vehicles that Haken did not know (similar to Task Force vehicles on operation), so Haken continued on. Haken went back to City of Sydney and told Fowler that he was off and wondered if he'd heard anything. Later that day, Haken learnt that Daher had been pinched and was in custody somewhere. 'There's no two ways about it, Bayeh was behind all of this.'

This caused great worry to anyone who had contact with Daher, including De Rubeis. Not that long after the arrest, Haken was contacted by Guy Pianta from Internal Security and summoned to appear before the Crime Commission.

CHAPTER 12

THE GAME AND HOW IT CHANGED

'The crooks lied and cheated to stay out of jail and the cops lied and cheated to try and get the crooks into jail.'

TREVOR HAKEN

For those police involved in corrupt behaviour there were rules of a kind. While they did not see themselves as crooks, they would do what was necessary to maintain some order in an environment that seemed uncontrollable. Largely left unmanaged, corrupt detectives were free to develop a code of behaviour that was passed on to those who followed.

> As far as the cops being crooks, the money we got was just the spoils of war. If it was a case of just doing business, the crooks were paying for concessions while the cops were sticking their neck out to give them a free passage. It was necessary that somebody paid something. You're not going to stick your neck out for nothing. The stupidity of it was that most stuck their neck out for next to nothing.

There were cops who were crooks. They were those who would blatantly rob junkies of their last fifty dollars. There were cops who dealt drugs, and that was taboo. There was acceptable and unacceptable involvement in criminal behaviour. Assisting in the violent crimes [armed hold-ups] was out of order. Anything that was a 'victimless crime' was seen as okay. At least with controlled crime you had your finger on the pulse.

There were unwritten rules that crooks who 'were given the advantage of a blind eye being turned to their operation' were expected to keep. The first rule up there was not to sell drugs to kids.

Virginia Perger was a dealer who was based in Woolloomooloo and was involved in the notorious 'love boat' scandal that supposedly involved NSW politicians. She sold heroin for well-established Romanian dealers and was a major drug supplier in the Cross. With her background, it came as no surprise that Perger sold drugs to people of any age. 'If you ever picked up kids [under sixteen], they would have got their gear from either Perger or her runner, Ray Oxby.' Oxby had a double lining in his underpants, like a swimming costume, where he would store the caps of drugs. If Oxby was searched by police he would soil his underpants to deter all but the most determined of searchers.

When Haken was recruited by Jim McCloskey, the officer in charge of Kings Cross, to form and operate the Drug Unit, Perger and Oxby were targeted and arrested. 'It was the first time that she'd been touched in years.' Every time Perger came into the Cross, the police would turn her over, and so eventually she moved her operation out to the inner south of Sydney.

Another rule was that dealers were not to carry guns and not to murder anyone in the Cross. After Benny Puta's 'breakfast at

Sweethearts', Haken did not want any unnecessary attention brought to the Cross.

Haken states that these rules related to controlled crime as opposed to uncontrolled crime in the Cross. There were always murders in the Cross, but they were not committed by those who were in on the 'joke' or 'laugh'. 'If they wanted to do something it would be away from the Cross — that's where you'd find bodies in blankets out in the bush.' Haken says that this system worked very well until the 'Daher camp' shot up Louis Bayeh's house.

Dealers would be expected to toe the line. 'They would do what they were told. If dealers were becoming too prominent [the operation too big and noticeable] they were told to pull their heads in [scale down the operation]. The most important rule was that dealers in on the laugh were never to hurt police. One group of dealers who operated out of the newsagency and its surrounds in Darlinghurst Road chose to ignore this rule and showed little respect for police. The group leader would 'stand police up' — that is, he would refuse to be searched and scream obscenities at police. 'Once they become aware of their rights according to lawyers, some had a view that they were above the law and the handling of law by police.' When approached, he became too physical and the uniformed officers would walk away rather than persist in trying to search him. 'He tested the waters and when he got away with that sort of behaviour, it got worse.'

Haken was involved in an incident where an off-duty police officer from outside the Cross was bashed so severely that the officer required a metal plate be put into his skull. He explains that, 'Off-duty police from outside the Cross had a terribly bad habit of coming to the Cross and wanting to be police.' In many instances they would be beaten up by criminals in the street. 'It wasn't a place to fuck around, it was coming from Z grade to A grade. For instance, if a constable from Pymble, where the most serious thing he sees is a housebreaking report, comes to the Cross, he is like a lamb to the slaughter.'

Police from stations outside the Cross would often go there for a night out. They would get very drunk and try to get into strip clubs for free, get drinks for free, get prostitutes for free, and of course this caused friction. 'We would get calls from strip club operators saying, "Look, we've got five drunken coppers here, can you come and get rid of them".'

The crooks, dealers, doormen, thugs and regulars of the Cross would know who the local police were and would not touch them. However, police outsiders coming to the Cross who tried to exercise some authority (while drunk) 'were really asking for trouble'.

After having bashed the off-duty police officer, the gang leader was targeted. He was 'loaded up' by Haken and other police from the Detectives office with a pistol to increase the seriousness of the offence and to minimise the risk of bail being granted. This action was meant as a clear sign to him and other street dealers what would happen if they stepped over the line.

It was one of the basic rules of the game in both the criminal and police fraternity that you did not touch the families or homes of players. 'This has since broken down. Bayeh threatened to hurt anyone who endangered his set-up, even if they were family. Asian gangs don't have any qualms about targeting families of rival gangs or anybody. It was a clear line in the sand. That is why the Drury shooting was considered totally out of order.'[1]

There was no such thing as breach of contract in the Cross. You either stuck by your word and kept in line, or you were severely dealt with. A dealer who was seen to be 'out of control' or a danger to either the police or his criminal associates could easily end up dead.

There has been much written about the death of Warren Lanfranchi. Lanfranchi was a heroin dealer who, while on the way to an armed robbery, had pulled a gun on highway patrol officer Gerry Ambrose and tried to shoot him but the gun misfired. Although he was working for Neddy Smith, who had a green light, he wasn't working for him when he was doing armed hold-ups. Lanfranchi was seen to be out of control and ended up dead.

Haken adds calmly, 'He was one of those people that needed to go — he was a violent, uncontrollable criminal. Neddy Smith couldn't control him, the cops couldn't control him, no one could. That was the thing with Roger [Rogerson], he always led from the front. There would have been no drama at all if he had let someone else shoot Lanfranchi.'

The other method of disposing of criminals came at the hands of police but by using deception on the part of their criminal associates. Haken describes Emile Massart as violent, ruthless, merciless and uncontrollable. Massart was closely associated with Frank Salvietti, the stepson of Connie Salvietti (nee Perger).[2] Frank was a housebreaker without parallel in the early 1970s. He specialised in working the upper north shore and graduated from that into high quantity, middle level heroin trafficking (he wasn't an importer, but was a dealer moving a substantial amount of heroin).

Massart worked for Salvietti. He had killed some of Salvietti's team. This was done with Salvietti's knowledge, but Salvietti thought that his lieutenant had him next in his sights. Salvietti arranged for the word to go to Massart that there would be bogus police trying to break into his place on a particular day. He arranged with his corrupt police associates for police to stake out the house on the same day with the knowledge that the offender would be returning to the house armed and probably in possession of explosives. Massart had used explosives and was alleged to have the house booby-trapped, which was later found to be the case. Massart returned to the house and when called on by police, he fired at those he thought were bogus police. Massart was shot dead.

In an ironic twist, it was the lieutenant who replaced Massart who shot Salvietti dead. 'One thing I can tell you is that when Salvietti died, a lot of police breathed a sigh of relief. He was doing business with so many police. Everybody's so temporary in that game.'

The game had run, according to the rules, for a long time. But like all good things, it had to eventually come to an end. By 1994 Haken's world was collapsing on a number of fronts. His marriage to Jane, which had been under stress for some time from alcohol, absence and the destructive culture of policing, was in a state of collapse. By June 1994, Haken became aware that he was under surveillance. 'I felt that someone had been in my house. Something had happened to the barrels on the locks of the doors, they were a bit loose. But then again, I was under a huge amount of pressure with what was happening with Jane, and I couldn't find any listening devices.'

It seems that Haken's suspicions were confirmed when he received a phone call from Guy Pianta, the head of Internal Security. He asked Haken, 'You're not at work?' Haken replied, 'No, I've gone home with a blinding headache'. Haken was told to stay at home as there would be two investigators arriving to speak to him within five minutes.

In fact, it took over two hours for the investigators to get there. Haken believes that they may have been waiting to see if he contacted anyone in the interim. The investigators simply told Haken that he was to appear at the Crime Commission the following morning, a Saturday. Haken contacted his lawyer, Eric Kelly, and he accompanied Haken to the Crime Commission.

The Crime Commission is an autonomous body set up by the state government to investigate drug and organised crime. It is located in the old National Crime Authority building. There are hearing rooms there, and a commissioner sits on the bench while a matter is heard. The Crime Commission can recommend a matter be referred to the Director of Public Prosecutions (DPP). The commission has wide-ranging powers and can take action against people for refusing to answer questions or for perjury. Haken comments, 'All the cops called it the "star chamber" while Chook Fowler called it "the Spanish Inquisition".'

Haken was questioned at the Crime Commission about his association with Robert Daher. A tape was played to Haken of him talking to Daher over the phone and he was asked to confirm that it was his voice on the tape. Haken denied that it was his voice. He did what his fraternity did: denied everything and held the line.

Lawyers can ask the same question in many different ways and so the questioning continued for a number of hours. 'What do you know about Robert Daher?' 'What association do you have with Robert Daher?' 'Have you ever met with Robert Daher?' 'Have you ever taken money from Robert Daher?' 'What did you know about Daher's operation in the Cross?' Haken was asked whether he had an association with a renowned crooked solicitor. Haken recalls, 'It was a typical Internal Affairs inquiry except it was in a courtroom. It was an attempt to get me to deny things they knew as fact.'

It appeared to Haken that the commissioner, Phil Bradley, was not happy with the hearing, as 'he left the bench in a bit of a huff'. Perhaps the Crime Commission had hoped that Haken would say, 'You're too good for me, copper! You got me, guv!'

Unknown to Haken, there were men from the Royal Commission into the New South Wales Police Service in a room above the hearing room watching proceedings on a monitor. They saw an opportunity in Haken and would attempt to make contact with him. Nigel Hadgkiss (Australian Federal Police) and John Agius (legal counsel and former prosecutor) contacted Eric Kelly (ex-CIB) and asked if they could meet with him.

On 2 September 1994, Haken, Hadgkiss, Agius and Eric Kelly met in Kelly's offices in Macquarie Street. Agius handed Haken a document which set out in a very explicit way their belief that Haken was in a position to assist the Royal Commission with its inquiries. Agius was recorded reading the statement aloud. There was not, at that stage, any threat or suggestion that unless Haken assisted them, he would be prosecuted and imprisoned. It was a request for assistance based on the belief that Haken had working knowledge of what was an active cell of corruption within the police force.

To suggest that I was offered the choice of either being prosecuted or assisting the commission is totally wrong. I had known both Agius and Hadgkiss since the JTF [Joint Task Force]. Agius was a junior prosecutor appearing for the JTF and was known to most members both professionally and socially. I knew Hadgkiss when he was conducting an allied inquiry with the JTF. I had worked with Eric Kelly when he was a detective at Chatswood Police Station.

The approach the Royal Commission adopted was very different. New South Wales police inquiries had been heavy-handed and indiscreet, whereas this was pitched to Haken in a different manner. The Royal Commission came at him from the perspective of a chance for Haken to show his integrity. 'It's a funny thing, I knew what they were talking about and it did appeal to me but integrity is like virginity, once it's gone you can't get it back. No matter how hard you try and how much you regret it.'

Friday, 2 September was a very important day for the Royal Commission. They might only get one chance to 'turn' Haken or anyone else from the Cross. The Commission team had drafted a document that would hold out to Haken a chance to join their team and perhaps salvage his integrity. They picked the one detective who was involved enough to expose the full picture at Kings Cross, who was energetic enough to work undercover for over eight months, who had a record for sticking his neck out — both properly and improperly — and whose life personally and now professionally, was in a state of turmoil. As well as this, Haken's previous association with Agius and his knowledge of Wood's integrity meant that if he was ever going 'turn' now would be the time.

The document they prepared was a good sales pitch. It revealed nothing the Royal Commission had on Haken but it was clear that the offer would not be open for an indefinite period. Both Agius and Hadgkiss were charming and persuasive. Their approach was cool and professional. Haken later confessed that he felt that he was a part of the inner team at the Commission. He worked closely with a team of young and enthusiastic investigators.

This Royal Commission was what the JTF should have been, but with greater resources, close management, advanced use of technology and no corruption. If only this type of body had been around when Haken was rising through the ranks. Ironically, the Commission was the chance for Haken to finally show what a great cop he could be. He would be taking risks, collecting evidence, helping to catch crooks and exposing the truth. The timing was perfect, and Agius and Hadgkiss were about to enlist the best witness ever to present before a commission of inquiry. The following paragraphs are from the transcript of a conversation between them.

Persons present:

JA: John Agius

NG: Nigel Hadgkiss

TH: Trevor Haken

EK: Eric Kelly

JA: Well this is Friday 2 September at 2.45pm. This is an interview between myself John Agius, counsel assisting the Royal Commission into the NSW Police Service, and Commander Nigel Hadgkiss, Director of Operations, and Trevor Haken, NSW police officer in the presence of his counsel...

JA: Trevor, do you consent to this being tape recorded?

TH: Yes.

JA: We've come here today to present you with this statement of our position and our intention for your consideration. As you probably know the Royal Commission has been established to inquire into and report upon police corruption and to that end I can provide you with a copy of the letters patent which established the Royal Commission and set out the terms of reference of the Royal Commission. The commission has gathered a large amount of evidence itself. It has a large amount of evidence from other agencies about police corruption in New South Wales and in the Kings Cross area in particular.

There is a large body of that material which indicates that you have participated in corrupt activity as a police officer and we do not at this stage propose to detail that evidence nor do we propose to interview you today about these matters. However, we believe that you're in a position to make a full and frank disclosure of all that you've done and all that you know of corrupt activity by police to nominate other police, both junior and senior to yourself, who have also engaged in corrupt activity.

We are prepared to interview you on the basis that anything that you say during the course of the interview or any document or thing that you produce will not be used in evidence against you in criminal proceedings, other than proceedings which may be brought against you in the event that any material you provide in the course of the interview is false to your knowledge.

We do not propose to commence an interview at the moment. However, you should be under no misunderstanding, you are in a very serious situation. You need to make a decision as to whether or not you will cooperate with the Royal Commission. Whether you cooperate or not, the Royal Commission will not delay its investigation or be put off its business. If you agree, and you may wish to take some time to think about this and to consult with your counsel and with your family, we propose to interview you on the basis that anything you say will not be used against you in criminal proceedings, other than proceedings which may be brought against you in the event that material you provide in the course of the interview is false to your knowledge.

Should you not be willing to be interviewed on this basis, you should know that you will not thereby avoid being examined in a public hearing before the Royal Commission, in which case the privilege against self-incrimination and any other privilege will not be available to you.

Depending on a number of considerations, including but not limited to the degree of your cooperation, the truth and frankness of anything that you say and the nature of the matters disclosed to you, I may be prepared to recommend to Senior Counsel Assisting the Royal Commission that the Royal Commission support an application for indemnity from prosecution by you in respect of some of the matters disclosed by you during the course of any interview. Any such indemnity should be conditional upon your full and frank disclosure, your giving evidence as or when required, and your continuing cooperation.

I cannot offer you such indemnity at this time and you should understand that I'm not undertaking that any indemnity will necessarily be forthcoming. You shouldn't expect that my preparedness to interview you in the way described or to recommend support for an application for indemnity will continue indefinitely. As the commission goes about its work circumstances change. For example, other people will come forward. Accordingly, you should make your decision with this in mind. Now do you understand what I've just read to you?

TH: Yes I do.

Agius then asks Haken to confirm that there had been no other conversations before or after this one concerning the Commission's plan to interview him. He cautions Haken not to discuss this matter with anyone but his legal representative or his immediate family. Haken was then told that he should think about the offer they were making and that he had seven days to decide whether he would assist the Royal Commission.

There had been a lot of talk about the Royal Commission: 'Everyone knew it was there. There was talk about who had been seconded to it but nobody really knew anything about it. It was like a secret society.' Once he had been spoken to by Agius and Hadgkiss, it was obvious to Haken that things were going to be difficult if he decided to hold the line.

Haken knew that this inquiry was very different from anything previously undertaken. There was extreme secrecy in everything they did. The people who approached Haken impressed him as being extremely thorough in their investigative procedures. They had the ability to use all forms of investigative tools by calling on the authority of the Commission. As he was told privately later by a Commission investigator, 'Mate, even if we hadn't got you over Daher, we would have killed you with the tax'.

Whatever the origins of the approach, whether he was seen to be weak, or whether it was because he was considered to have some moral fibre, Haken had a conversation with Kelly. Was he a person who was capable of regaining some form of respect if he was to assist the Commission? 'I was under no misapprehension at that stage that the Commission would be requiring more than just verbal evidence to assist with their inquiries. There was no way guys like Hadgkiss would be interested in just what you've heard about corruption.'

Haken made his mind up pretty quickly. 'You didn't have to be a genius to see that things were going to be nasty, when you put it in the context of what had been taking place over the last couple of months added to the [marriage] problems I had at home.' That same afternoon, Haken told Kelly that he would assist the commission and instructed Kelly to arrange a meeting with Hadgkiss and Agius the next day.

Haken told his wife what had taken place and that they would need to go for a meeting to have his situation explained. It was rare for detectives to discuss matters relating to receiving corrupt money. Haken's wife spent large amounts of money and so although he didn't specify the source of the money, it was obvious that it was more than he was earning as a police officer.

At the meeting, it was explained to Jane that Haken had decided to assist the Royal Commission with their inquiries into police corruption.

Jane was pretty cool with whatever happened. I don't think she considered the long-term ramifications. Actually, she may have already thought about it because very shortly after that, in fact the next week, she started moving items out of our house. As the Commission was going on, items from my house were taken away. I was told a relative of Jane said to her, 'The gravy train's over, it's time to get off.'

Once Haken had agreed to assist the Royal Commission, the Commission did not waste any time. Haken and his lawyer met with Nigel Hadgkiss, John Agius and Bruce Onley the next day.

Haken wanted it recorded on tape that he was giving voluntary assistance without wanting to know the full extent of any material or holdings the Royal Commission had against him. He declared that he would assist the Royal Commission in a proactive role and would be putting himself at risk to advance the investigations of the Royal Commission.

Haken outlined the normal week ahead of him. He would make a call in coded form and arrange a meeting at a place of his designation in Kings Cross with Steve Stavrou to collect around $2000 as part of 'the joke'. Haken told the commission that these meetings took place once a month. He explained that he would contact either Detective Kim Thompson or Detective Neville Scullion and then meet with them individually and split the money. Haken was the bagman, he would control the pick up of the 'joke' and its allocation and distribution.

Just as detectives avoided speaking on the phone about any specific topic beyond a greeting, they would also avoid meeting in the same place all the time. The calls were quick and so were the meetings. The Commission needed to know the small details of this pick-up. They were hoping to be ready for Monday and needed to know all the details.

Haken explained that $2000 was too much cash to fit inside his hand and so the money was often passed over in an envelope, a bag, a newspaper, but no set form. Haken would either meet in a restaurant or his vehicle, and so the method of payment depended on where he was meeting. One had to be more discreet in a restaurant. He explained that if you listened to the conversation in isolation you would not normally know that money had been given to him.

Haken had thus taken the first steps in revealing the sordid world in which he worked. The revelations about how many police operated in New South Wales would finally be caught on tape and become irrefutable evidence. For Haken, there was no turning back.

CHAPTER 13

THE RECKONING

'As policemen you see people in a completely different light. When you worked at the Cross, you didn't see any nice young men.'

TREVOR HAKEN

Once at the Commission, Haken would have a lot of stories to tell. To take one: On 22 July 1990, detectives from Kings Cross and their partners went to the Gazebo Hotel for a dinner function, when, after the function, the group decided to walk along Darlinghurst Road to show their partners the Kings Cross area. If they ever wanted to show their wives and girlfriends life at the Cross, then tonight was the night.

The group had walked to an area near Stripperama and the Love Machine when they came across a group of eight to twelve men from the western suburbs out celebrating, Haken's evidence was that it was a bucks' night. The group was looking for a big night and had been drinking.

Haken told the Royal Commission that the group were unruly and barged into some of the detectives and their wives.[1] One of the men in the group was reported as saying that he accidentally brushed shoulders with one of the policemen.

Haken was across the road outside Porky's speaking to Steve

Stavrou while his wife was speaking to John Swan's wife. David Langton and Swan were admonishing some of the bucks group when they were attacked by other members of the group. It was reported that after the clash of shoulders, one of the group was thrown against the side of a tow truck, and this is where the fight escalated.[2] Haken recalls:

> We were set upon by a group of thugs who were later referred to in court as 'a group of young men'. But thugs always are 'a group of young men' in the eyes of Mum and Dad. They come along to court polished up in their suits and short hair, but on the night they had blood in their eyes and were out of control. They were intent on belting the living daylights out of anyone who got in their way.

On that night, one of the group kicked Duncan Demol in the face. Demol immediately collapsed to the ground and another young officer, Paul Watson ('Turtle'), was also set upon and kicked and punched. It was then on for young and old. The fight escalated to include police, bouncers and the bucks night group. Police cars and vans were soon at the scene and the bucks group were arrested. Eight men were placed in the one police wagon. An ambulance attended to Duncan Demol who was taken to hospital, where he received stitches to his head.

The detectives and uniformed police followed the arrested men to Kings Cross Station.[3] Haken comments today that during the trip the prisoners were 'yelling abuse and banging the sides of the van'. As they drove into the underground carpark of the police station one of them looked out through the back door of the van and realised that the people they had been fighting were police and they were now waiting for them. One youth turned to the rest of the group and said, 'Fuck, we're dead!'

One of those arrested that night later gave evidence that he saw a police officer with an armful of batons handing them out to each police officer. Haken told the Royal Commission that both uniform and detectives were issued with the batons.[4] They started to bash the side of the wagon with the batons and rock it from side to side telling the young men that 'they were dead'. The men were told to come out of the van one at a time. There were two lines of police, most armed with batons, including Haken, who then flogged the prisoners as they walked into the holding cell.[5]

Haken recalls, 'It was full-on anger, so there was plenty of "Get the fuck in there", "We'll teach you to fuckin' belt us" and that sort of thing.' The beating was seen as retaliation for the groups' action on the streets. 'This type of behaviour happened all the time in the Cross. People would come on bucks' nights, flog someone and get back on their bus and disappear, leaving the damage behind for us to clean up. But this was where we worked, this was home for us, and they picked us. They expected to get away with it, but they didn't this time.'

Police were all aware that the 'Lamb method' of using a baton requires batons to be used on arms, or backs of legs and never on the back, shoulders or the neck. Batons were only to be used as self-defence and not as punishment.

Other reports at the time indicated that the last prisoner out of the van could hear the screams and thumps of those who had gone before him. He was taken out of the van and pushed to the floor. A police officer was just about to kick him when another officer said, 'Hang on, that's enough'. As the officer turned, the prisoner was kicked in the chest. He was then dragged to his feet and struck with batons as he was taken to the interview room.

Haken recollects that after the flogging, those identified as the ring leaders of the melee were taken to separate rooms and questioned. While Haken, Swan and Paul Watson were preparing the charge sheets and other paperwork, David Langton and his wife Christine (also a police officer) were 'handing out punishment'. Both of the ring leaders were 'flogged unmercifully'.

Haken says, 'Langton was really handy with his fists and was a good bloke to have on your side in the Cross, but when he got upset he was out of control'. Langton was later dismissed from the police force following a similar incident where he was convicted of assault occasioning actual bodily harm (he cracked the cheekbone of an arrested man by punching him). The assault had taken place when a prisoner had objected to being searched and so Langton punched the prisoner and then 'backhanded' him. Langton later testified to the Royal Commission that he was disillusioned with the police force and the legal system. It seemed that the court and jail system were like a revolving door. When Langton joined the force fifteen years prior to this incident, his only ambition was 'to lock up crooks'.

In relation to the incident at the Cross, one of the men arrested gave evidence that David Langton came into the room in which he was being held, shouted 'You little fuck', then punched the prisoner in the face so that he was pushed back in his chair. Langton then hit him on the forehead and nose. Langton shouted to the prisoner to stop crying and was about to hit him again when he was stopped by Haken. The prisoner later confirmed that this was the case. Langton was shown photographs of Detective Demol who was injured. He showed these to the prisoner and told him that this would happen to him if he did not sign the statement being typed.

Christine Langton followed her husband's lead and bashed the prisoners' heads into the walls and desks. The prisoners did not fight back. Christine Langton testified that she assaulted the men because she was upset that two of her friends had been assaulted and that 'a perfectly lovely night had been upset'. The *Telegraph* reported her evidence to the Royal Commission saying how she jabbed her fingernail into the throat of one of the arrested men and told him 'you didn't know who you were messing with.'[6]

One prisoner recalled being thrown up against the back wall of the office while different people took turns hitting him in the face, grabbing him and throwing him against the wall. At one stage he pretended to be unconscious in the hope that the beating would stop. Instead, he was told to 'get up or get more'. The prisoner was bleeding from his injuries and was told by David Langton to stop bleeding on the floor.

All the prisoners were then taken out through another cordon of police armed with batons for a 'Kings Cross farewell'. They were again flogged with batons, placed in the trucks and taken to Sydney Police Centre (SPC).

There was then a problem at the SPC because of the injuries that the two principals had sustained. One police officer was heard to say over the phone that 'someone had better get their arse down here real quick to explain the prisoner's injuries'. Kings Cross Police were asked how these prisoners had been so badly injured. They told police at the SPC that the injuries were sustained in the fight in the street and so the charges proceeded. 'In those days there were no problems that couldn't be overcome somehow,' says Haken.

The wives had been left behind and so the detectives returned to pick them up and then went to the Bourbon and Beefsteak, which was then a 'safe haven'. As a place frequented by police there was rarely any trouble there. 'The whole thing had slowed the night down a bit, to say the least.'

Those arrested later went to court and pleaded guilty. The man who had kicked Duncan Demol in the head was a licensed security officer who stood to lose his licence if convicted and so he fought the charge in the District Court. Haken was called to give evidence as he had interviewed most of those charged, including the appellant. Haken and some of the other detectives had 'a scrum down' before they appeared in court and agreed that they would deny the baton beating.

The evidence Haken gave to a certain point in this matter was factual, but the bashing was omitted from his evidence. Other police gave evidence and denied that the baton beating and bashing had taken place.

After evidence about this matter at the Royal Commission, charges were laid against police involved and Haken was called to give evidence. 'There were a lot of matters exposed at the Commission to show what went on in the Cross, but they prosecuted the cops for that bashing. You think, how the fuck did I get into this?'

Christine and David Langton were sentenced at trial following the Royal Commission. It seemed that at the Royal Commission the only policeman who other police could remember taking part in the baton bashing was Trevor Haken. Their memories soon returned. Haken was called to testify at the Langton trials over what really took place and although he knew what they did was wrong, still defended the actions for the most part.

Bloody lawyers sit up there passing judgment on us. How many used to approach you on the quiet and say, 'You can get twenty per cent for any briefs you send my way'. It was a common practice to steer offenders toward particular lawyers to receive a kickback, and it was common practice for some lawyers to pick up work that way.

Then there's a lawyer who was in the Fraud Squad. It's all right to criticise today, but what did you do yesterday? I mean, the Fraud Squad, what did some of them do — they ran a share portfolio for themselves, that's what they bloody did. Imagine the inside information they were getting. 'Fraud Squad Friday' was an expression used by all police to say,

Haken felt that the cross-examination he underwent at the District Court trial was trying to take the jury away from matters of fact. 'All they did was try to tear me apart in front of the jury by saying "well you're an expert witness who knows when to take your glasses off and when to put them on". And so I said that I put the glasses on to read a piece of paper and I take them off when I speak to you. I can't see you if I have them on. That's the sort of shit they go on with.'

Again, Haken is frustrated that of so many matters of corruption and misconduct raised at the Royal Commission, so few were pursued by the Director of Public Prosecutions. Matters that Haken believes involved far greater degrees of criminality were left untouched. In his case, Haken knows that what they did was illegal but he still believes that it was an appropriate response at the time and would be an entirely appropriate response in handling the current situation with gangs in Sydney.

You can't treat hoodlums like Sunday school children. You can't just hope these type of people will go away, you've got to deal with them. At the trial of the police who were charged with the assault of the group, Swan, David Langton, Watson, Christine Fish [previously Langton] came before a judge who went out of his way to say that the bucks party were innocent young men, but they were exactly as I described ... thugs. As policemen you see people in a completely different light to that which everyone else sees them. When you worked at the Cross you didn't see any nice young men.

By September 1994, when Trevor Haken had begun assisting the Royal Commission and had given up the grog, there were rumours among those in the 'joke' that someone had 'rolled'. So, although business went on, people were getting nervous. Haken and Skinny Steve had recently done business beyond the 'laugh'. One of Skinny's men, Korean John (Jun Kyu Bum), a martial arts expert, had been arrested by police at Ryde Police Station and was charged for assaulting another Asian male. 'You couldn't beat up Korean John, he was massive. He used to punch holes in windscreens of cars when he got cranky,' says Haken. Skinny Steve offered Haken $5000 to approach Sergeant Dave Greer to have the matter withdrawn. Greer told Haken that the victim just wanted to be left alone. Haken pocketed $1000 and gave $4000 to Greer, who organised the withdrawal of the complaint.

However, Haken didn't always get results. Haken told the Commission that on one occasion when Haken saw Skinny Steve, he had complained about Detective Ted Shepherd and some members of the Armed Hold-up Squad, CIB.[7] They had come to his house early one morning and spoken to him in his bedroom. They wanted to be in on the 'laugh' as well. Skinny Steve wanted Haken to speak to Shepherd and find out what was going on. Haken spoke to Sergeant Bill Mulheron, who was in charge of the squad. Mulheron denied the approach and Haken heard nothing about it again from either Skinny Steve or the squad.

By this stage, two weeks after coming on side, Royal Commission investigators had 'wired' both Haken and his car so that his meetings and involvement in the 'laugh' would be recorded in audio and video. The Commission did not know how long

Haken would continue to actively work for them because they didn't know how long his cover would remain, and so the pressure was on to deliver results quickly.

Bruce Onley was a straight talker, an 'old school' cop from the days when the police were 'the Queen's men on the Queen's business'. Commission agents stated that when you first met Onley he could appear quite stern and intimidating, but he did enjoy a joke. Most of all, he loved being a policeman. Accordingly, he chased corrupt police with a religious fervour. And so, while he recognised the incredible importance of Haken to the success of the Royal Commission, he never seemed to take a liking to him. Although neither had much choice, there was not a lot of affection or trust between Haken and Onley. Onley worked directly under 'spymaster' Nigel Hadgkiss. With the help of a few other agents, he worked and controlled Haken's operations.

Onley's office was decorated in standard police style coupled with his own unique touches. The large maps of Sydney that hung on his walls were dotted with different-coloured pins in locations throughout the suburbs. Although the pins had little meaning to anyone else, he would cover the maps when they were not in use. There was no such thing as being too careful. Onley's walls were covered with souvenirs from previous campaigns and associations, including Hong Kong and the Department of Justice in the United States. He was a serious man who had some serious background experience. He was the perfect person to be working at the Royal Commission.

In his position, Onley couldn't afford to trust many people. He would speak and work around work mates as if there was a leak. When he gave directions to sensitive operational locations, he would often point to a location on a map rather than say it aloud. Other agents joked that if he had to go to the toilet then he even pissed into a shredder.

Haken was told to line up his meetings with crooks and corrupt police on the telephone to enable the conversations to be recorded. He and his vehicle would be fitted with listening devices and hidden video cameras. Haken wasn't told where all these devices were located. The stakes were too high to have blind faith in anyone. The Commission kept tabs on everyone, including those who worked within its walls or on its behalf. The Director of Operations oversaw all teams, however, the Commission isolated each team so that other teams would not know the specifics of what was going on in another team. Evidently, the surveillance team never came into the office; they lived on the road. Interaction was kept to a bare minimum at all levels. Sometimes seals were placed on office doors overnight, offices were regularly swept for listening devices. Investigators kept diaries that would be regularly inspected by the Director of Operations. There was a person who was seconded from Washington from the military to be in charge of internal security, and he kept an eye on everyone at the Commission. Phone records were kept of all investigators. Everything done financially, administratively and of course operationally was overseen by someone else. The tapes were all kept at the Commission and transcribed there. They were later transferred to mini disk and were used as backup for the court cases.

Haken would drive this 'mobile recording studio' to the pick-up location. Onley and another agent would brief Haken before each meeting about which route he would take. Haken always suspected that the Commission was testing him. He was under strict orders not to deviate from given instructions and to return straight after the meeting to the 'RV' (rendezvous point). All Haken's meetings were short and to the point. As instructed, he would describe his journey to the tape machine as he drove, adding the time and repeating who he was about to meet. On the tapes, Haken sounded tense, but his speech was as precise as if he were talking to a jury. He was the perfect informant.

On 6 September 1994, Haken drove to meet Skinny Steve. He had done this many times before, but circumstances had changed. By this stage, Haken was one of many to receive notice to appear before the Royal Commission and had taken sick leave. To outside observers he was suddenly a person of interest to the Commission and so was seen as being 'hot'. Skinny Steve didn't want any unnecessary attention drawn to his business. Haken's influence in Kings Cross had diminished. Skinny Steve planned to tell Haken that he was too difficult to deal with and that he would look to pass on 'the laugh' through others.

Haken drove his car to a predetermined meeting place but he was unable to park because a woman was waiting to park. He continued to drive around and then signalled to Skinny Steve who was waiting on the footpath. As the Royal Commission would hear on the tapes played back, Haken's voice changed and he no longer sounded nervous. He was back to being the one in on 'the laugh', with the language and tone to match.

Trevor Haken (TH): 'Hop in mate.'

Skinny Steve (SS): 'Hello.'

TH: 'The bitch just told me to piss off.'

Skinny Steve was distracted. While waiting for Haken he had noticed someone who seemed to be observing him. It had made him nervous. As Haken drove, Skinny continued to look at his supposed observer.

SS: 'This fuckin' cunt over there has been standing there for ages.'

Haken seemed to share the concern and decided to drive away from the usual pick-up place.

TH: 'Fuck off out of here then!'

And so Haken drove away to an alternate location. Skinny Steve and Haken were both aware that things were tense around the Cross. No one was sure who had been busted and who was talking to the Commission. What was certain was that things were changing and people were getting very nervous. Haken wanted to appear normal and so chatted about the holiday Skinny Steve recently had in Cyprus. Haken then raised the fact that the Kings Cross identity Steve Hardas had been charged with approaching detectives at Parramatta Police Station to turn a blind eye to a drug-selling operation.

SS: 'Yeah, I've been told to keep away from him. I just say g'day, hello, whatever. Not that I done any business with him but things are very bad everywhere.'

TH: 'Yeah, I understand.'

Skinny sounded sheepish, he had something to broach with Haken.

SS: 'Trevor, something I want to discuss with you too is ... [he paused and then continued] we must arrange differently.

TH: 'Yeah.'

SS: 'This pick-up ... because you're a bit hot.'

Haken tried to jump in to explain that everyone was under the eye.

TH: 'Fuckin' of course, everybody is ...'

But Skinny talked over him.

SS: '... And I don't want to [he chuckles] and I'm not so hot because I just got back from holidays. [He then emphasises] ... We must arrange things differently!'

TH: 'Yeah, but what do you want me to do?'

SS: 'I don't know. Umm ... Umm ... you know, that people that you been looking after ... all right, let's face it, they're not around anymore, right? You my ... my only friend. I mean personal friend. Right? So I want to look after you, okay? Now the people are not around they can't do nothing for me. I have to get other people that are here to look after me, alright?'

TH: 'Yeah but the main man over here ...'

SS: 'Mm, he's going within the next month. If Scully's gone, I got nobody. I got to find other people in it. So tell me if you agree with that, right?'

TH: 'Well, Kim, you know ...'

SS: 'I was thinking of sending it to Kim [Thompson] for you, you know. It's very safe that way. Think about it and let me know.'

TH: 'Yeah all right.'

SS: 'It doesn't matter what happens, even if shot in the moon, it doesn't make any difference.'

TH: 'Yeah.'

SS: 'All right, I will send it to you in the moon. All right? No that, that's how I feel about it, all right? You will always be 100 per cent to me, you know what I mean? I've got to find a couple of boys over here.'

TH: 'Oh righto. Where do you want me to drop you, mate?'

SS: 'Just drop me.'

TH: 'Just fuckin' anywhere? Look, I'll go round the block.'

SS: 'Fuckin' yeah ... well next month if Scully's still here I'll throw it to Scully. How's that?'

TH: 'Mate, whatever you like.'

SS: 'This is very dangerous.'

TH: 'Fuckin' dangerous.'

SS: 'Yes it's very dangerous for both of us this way.'

TH: 'I know.'

SS: 'You know because there's no need for us to be watched driving in the car, you know what I mean.'

TH: 'That's why I fuckin' wanted to park it but that bitch told me to piss off.'

SS: 'But Scully, anyway, Scully's a local detective and a normal person.'

TH: 'Yeah.'

SS: 'Not a problem isn't it ... to have a cup of coffee with me?'

TH: 'Sure.'

SS: 'So long as Scully's here, that's what we do.'

TH: 'Yeah.'

SS: 'I'll let you know what's gonna happen for Kim.'

TH: 'Through Kim? Yeah, all right.'

SS: 'Yes, it's much safer like that, isn't it? Save a lot of fuckin' headaches.'

TH: 'Yep.'

SS: 'Eh? And ah … sure does me eh … [laughing]. A lot of headaches. You can drop me anywhere around here.'

TH: 'Right, I'll drop you at the end here. It's a bit safer. I'll see you soon.'

SS: 'We'll have a drink. Okay?'

TH: 'See you.'

SS: 'Bye.'

Haken drove away from his meeting with Skinny Steve and it was then that he noticed the sweat under his arms and on his forehead. He was still being recorded and continued to describe the route his vehicle took. He coughed and described where he was.

TH: 'Victoria Street. [then with a whisper] I wonder if this is the best place to have a heart attack?'

The receipt and division of moneys were an everyday practice for detectives. Following his meeting with Skinny Steve, Haken was to meet with Kim Thompson, give him his share of the money and let him know what was going on. In this excerpt from a listening device recording tabled at the Royal Commission, an investigator first prepares Haken for the meeting with Thompson.

TH: Trevor Haken

RCI: Royal Commission Investigator

RCI: 'With me in the vehicle is Trevor Haken. The vehicle will proceed from this location to Kings Cross for the purpose of making a telephone call and then return to this location. I'm now about to hand you a quantity of money and ask you to count it. There's $2000 there, you say that you would pay $1600.'

TH: 'Yes.'

RCI: 'Okay, it's the same configuration as the money that we acquired previously. How would you best pay that? Now give me that. That's $400 you've given me. Now please count the money there on your knee just like I'm doing here.'

TH: 'I'd put that in four envelopes — my usual practice is to put it into four groups.'

RCI: 'Put it in there. Check that when I put the wire on you.'

Haken then called Kim Thompson and went to pick him up. He described his approach. 'I'm going to go right and then I'll go right along and turn left. I'll be coming out that lane to that direction.' As soon as he saw Thompson, his language changed instantly.[8]

TH: 'Jesus. Get in there, you prick. I had to go around the block about fuckin' ...'

KT: 'Oh fuck they're low.'

TH: 'It's fuckin' beautiful.'

KT: 'Whose car is this?'

TH: It's mine, fuckin' whose car is this? Listen.'

KT: 'Why didn't you use it when you went to the Cross yesterday?'

TH: 'Didn't fuckin' go to the Cross yesterday, I went the fuckin' day before. Why?'

KT: 'Told ya to fuckin' come and see me. I'll go and do it [pick up the money from Stavrou because Haken was being watched]. If I fuckin' find out that you're up there, who's fuckin' looking at ya.'

TH: 'Well that's what I fuckin' didn't want to happen. That's why I fuckin' ... that's why I want to talk to you today. Listen, the little bloke said he's going to fuckin' see fuckin' Scully from now on all right, and then he's going to fuckin' see you through somebody else, I don't know who else. Okay?'

KT: 'Yeah I know.'

TH: 'Well fuckin' that's a matter for you it's nothing to do with me, I don't give a fuck.'

KT: 'Yeah, I want to know who he is.'

TH: 'No he just fuckin' wanted to set, set the record straight fuckin' just so.'

KT: 'Mate, don't go up here.'

TH: 'Fuck where do I go, quick tell me, hey?'

KT: 'Do a U-ey there, there, Mark Light's [another policeman] up there.'

TH: 'Yeah I know, I just fucked off out of the lane because I saw him.'

KT: 'Did he see you?'

TH: 'No.'

KT: 'He's a bit of a rumour monger.'

TH: 'Oh fuckin' rumour monger, I don't know about that, I just want to get out of here mate, fuck this. Well as long as you know what's going on, right?'

KT: 'Well I didn't until you told me.'

TH: 'Well no he just told me. He said fuckin', he's, he's just got back from holiday and he said something I'll go and see, he said I'll see Scully next fuckin' week, I'll see Thommo from thereafter through somebody I don't know.'

KT: 'I know.'

TH: 'He said fuckin' he wants to fuckin' see somebody else up there he didn't say who fuckin'.'

KT: 'I know who it is.'

TH: 'Fuckin' who mate, it's your fuckin' business, not mine.'

KT: 'That's right.'

TH: 'I'll just go round the fuckin' block, fuckin' drop you.'

KT: 'Don't go near the fuckin' Cross, mate ...'

The money was handed across to Thompson during this conversation. Haken later met with Neville Scullion. He arranged to drive by and pick him up in East Sydney. Haken would then pass on Scullion's share of the 'laugh'.

TH: Trevor Haken

NS: Neville Scullion

TH: 'Hello misery guts.'

NS: 'What are you doing?'

TH: 'Fuckin' what am I doing, I'm fuckin' shitting myself. What do you think I'm doing? Just park it and come for a fuckin' spin with me, will you?'

NS: [getting in the car] 'It's a lovely little car.'

TH: 'This is one I've always had ever since I crashed the other one.'

NS: 'Ooh.'

TH: 'Fuck. Listen, what do you fuckin' hear?'

NS: 'Lots of rumours.'

TH: 'Oh fuck, is that all?'

NS: 'That's all.'

TH: 'The way you were talking to me on the phone, I thought fuckin' what have I done.'

NS: 'Mm.'

TH: 'Jesus mate. No other fuckin' dramas?'

NS: 'Mate, there's everyone jumping around like fuckin' cats on a hot tin roof.'

TH: 'Fuckin' why wouldn't they.'

NS: 'Well ...'

TH: 'You know what happened to me.'

NS: 'Yeah.'

TH: 'I fuckin ...'

NS: 'Yes, I know what happened to you. And I tell you who's fuckin' stirring the shit, that fuckin' Louis Bayeh.'

Haken had been to the Crime Commission after complaints had apparently been made. It was rumoured that Louis Bayeh was the informant.

TH: 'Yeah well, I fuckin' know Bayeh.'

NS: 'He's fuckin', he's run to fuckin' John Hatton, fuckin' going blah, blah, blah, blah, blah, blah for what, his own fuckin' benefit, that's all it is. And he's stirring up fuckin' everyone, putting fuckin', planting seeds all over fuckin' town, trying to get all the cops fuckin' fighting among each other.'

TH: 'Well he's fuckin' doin' that pretty well.'

NS: 'That's fuckin' right. Exactly right, Trevor.'

TH: 'Well I just don't know what's going to become of it anyway. Listen but what I mainly wanted to say to you is this, fuckin' I saw Skinny just got back, right? He said he fuckin' reckoned I was fuckin' hot as fuckin' toast. I don't know whether he fuckin' told you or not. He said he doesn't want to see me anymore, so he's goin', he's gonna ... you can transfer, can't you?'

NS: 'Oh well fuckin' I told them I want to get transferred. I'm fuckin', I've had a gutful, they're just, they're just fucked, they don't know what they're doing. I'm the only cunt up there, Trevor. There's supposed to be five fuckin' blokes, I'm the only bloke there.'

TH: 'Mmm.'

NS: 'I'm fuckin' just inundated with fuckin' work and I've had a gutful of it.'

TH: 'No, I know what you're talking about. No, it's just fucked, I know that.'

NS: 'Oh it's fucked, mate. I'm not preaching to the converted, I know.'

TH: 'No, well it's just the whole thing is fuckin' out of control.'

These tapes in particular reinforced to the Commission that what Haken was telling them was true. There is no surprise expressed by the detectives when they were being handed envelopes full of money, there is no pause in the conversation. This was an ordinary moment in the life of a Kings Cross detective.

The Royal Commission was told of 'Fat George's' brothel the Pink Flamingo as well as the Battlers Inn, and that both of these places were used as fronts for drug selling. In 1992–94, 'Fat George' (aka George Page, aka Pandelis Karipis, aka George Karipis) ran a 'shooting gallery' at 48A Darlinghurst Road in Kings Cross. Video footage of one of the rooms at this shooting gallery was shown to the Royal Commission. It showed blood spurts up the walls, curtains and ceiling, and filthy mattresses piled on top of each other. Fat George ran two shooting galleries, which were said to be used as brothels as well. He rented rooms for twenty dollars so that addicts could shoot up.

According to a former barrister who worked briefly for Fat George, drug sales were big. On New Year's Eve 1993, there were approximately 150 capsules of heroin sold at $80 each and 300 of cocaine at $100 each. When he eventually gave evidence to the commission, Fat George said he was unaware of drug dealing at his premises. Haken told the Royal Commission that 'Chook' Fowler had said that there was money for protecting Fat George's operations.[9] Fowler always passed on this money himself. Haken let Fowler know of any police activities into Fat George.

Brian Ladewig had meanwhile been supplying information to Detective Chris Keene about a robbery of a Prouds store. Fat George was involved in the Prouds robbery and had a stolen painting in his possession. This information was also available to Graham 'Chook' Fowler, who at the time was the officer in charge of City of Sydney Detectives.

Ladewig was staying at a block of flats in Earl Place, Kings

Cross when two men burst through the door of his flat wearing balaclavas. They grabbed him, forcibly dragged him from his flat and threw him from the roof of the three-storey building into Earl Place below. Amazingly, Ladewig survived the fall but both his ankles were broken. Despite wearing balaclavas, he recognised one of the assailants men as one of Fat George's men. Ladewig was now slow on his feet, but not slow in taking a hint. He didn't officially report the matter to police and hobbled around on crutches for quite a while. Ladewig had earned a new nickname, 'Stickman'. He was lucky to be alive. His experience was a clear example of how informants were dealt with in Kings Cross.

Since the Royal Commission into the NSW Police Service had begun there was a strong rumour that someone among the Kings Cross police fraternity had 'rolled'. No one was above suspicion and the stakes were high. After rolling to the Royal Commission, Haken had over thirty meetings — from September 1994 until March 1995 — with police and criminal associates. During this time, he collected more than $26,000 in bribes, which he presented to the Royal Commission as evidence.

Haken understood the danger of the double life he was leading. The pressure had been building for Haken and it made him very nervous. Haken was, as usual, meeting the crooks he did business with and the cops that were a part of this business. At all of these meetings he was wired with a state-of-the-art listening device and covertly recorded every word that was spoken. Total meetings between September and March, including phone calls, added up to eighty. This was the number of meetings that were recorded and used in the hearings — there were many more over that same period. There were meetings where the recordings didn't work, or meetings that didn't serve any prupose for the court. Haken would travel a lot, drive to the central coast for a meeting, say, and then back to the city.

Being one of Haken's regulars, Bill Bayeh was also said to be the largest supplier of heroin and cocaine in Kings Cross. One of his lieutenants, protected witness KX14, claimed to have helped 'cut and cap' heroin and cocaine worth over $2.5 million over a six-month period. All this while Bayeh said that he simply ran a cafe and some gaming machines. He would tell the Royal Commission that his declared income was $35,000. The Royal Commission, however, recorded spending of over $400,000, which they estimated was still only a portion of his real income.

Bill Bayeh was a striking looking man with a very distinctive and easily recognised high-pitched voice. He wore expensive clothes and had expensive tastes. In 1993 he purchased a home in Gladesville for more than half a million dollars. He operated his drug business out of the Cosmopolitan Cafe in the Cross. Runners would go back into the cafe every fifteen minutes, pick up more drugs and then head out into the streets to sell. As a power broker in the Kings Cross drug trade, he walked the walk and talked the talk of a major criminal. His every move was shadowed by his minders, Nelson and Samson. Martial arts champion Nelisoni 'Nelson' Taione and Samson Hikuleo Fangaloka were two of the biggest bodyguards to walk the planet.

Bill Bayeh's bookmaker, Jeffrey Joseph Pendlebury, was introduced to Bayeh by former policeman turned private investigator Charlie Staunton. Staunton was a figure of interest to the Commission. The Royal Commission heard that Haken would ring Staunton if he could not get a hold of Bayeh and he would make arrangements for meetings. Staunton was present at many of the meetings with Bayeh and Haken that were covertly recorded by the Commission, such as at the Marble Bar in the Hilton Hotel.[10] The Royal Commission has many tapes of conversations between Haken and Staunton organising meetings with Bayeh.

On one occasion, Haken met Staunton at the TAB at Birkenhead Point and was given $1980 and told to 'have a bet'. Staunton told Haken that the Royal Commission had seized records of his and Bill Bayeh's bookmaker (Pendlebury) and he was concerned because he had just paid $20,000 of Bayeh's account leaving a debt of $80,000.[11] This encounter was recorded covertly and Staunton was brought before the Royal Commission. He refused to answer questions and so was charged with contempt and was sent to jail. Nine months in jail changed Staunton's mind and he finally spoke to the Royal Commission.[12] Staunton admitted that in his two and a half year relationship with Bayeh he had been involved in corrupt activities with NSW police officers and specifically had acted as the middle-man in some corrupt payments between Bayeh and Haken. Staunton listened to a conversation covertly recorded the previous January in which Staunton had spoken to Haken and told how he would refuse to answer questions at the Royal Commission but that he didn't fear jail because he would make so much money from film and book rights. 'Wood can say "You're in contempt", "I'll say, mate, fuckin' beauty ... because I'll get a million dollars for the book. I'll get fuckin' two million for the fuckin' movie."'

Staunton's mate Pendlebury gave evidence to the Royal Commission stating that Bayeh had placed bets of more than $3.6 million in a nine-month period. This included the loss of $181,000 in one day. It was suggested by counsel assisting the commission that Bayeh's betting was simply a money-laundering scheme.

Bayeh's wife was a pretty blonde woman named Tanya. She once waited on tables in his cafe while studying psychology at university. For a while they enjoyed the good life together, which included a $20,000 honeymoon and regular holidays. Bayeh looked after all her family. Tanya's father was set up at a coffee shop on the Gold Coast, in Broadbeach, and a penthouse apartment.

But Bayeh had eluded all inquiries up to this point. He took precautions and thought he would be protected — after all, the commission was after corrupt police. Bayeh paid for protection and he thought he would not be touched. If some of his police associates were lost during the Commission, he knew there would be others who would take their place.

This Royal Commission was different, however. There was none of the usual police tip-offs to foil investigations and the Commission used new technology with zeal. Before it was over there would be a mountain of evidence, including telephone intercepts, photographs, video footage and taped conversations that would incriminate Bayeh and his associates. By using this evidence as leverage, the Royal Commission was able to get some of Bayeh's associates to assist the investigation. This irrefutable evidence eventually led to the dramatic arrest of Bill Bayeh in the hearing room of the Commission in 1995.

Covert technicians (or 'spooks') somehow placed a small camera in the kitchen ceiling of Bayeh's associate KX14. The footage showed two people quietly cutting drugs and placing them in caps (these numbered around 1500). What they were doing was patently obvious, but it was hard to see their faces and identification might be a problem for a jury. Suddenly the phone rang and Bayeh answered. When that unmistakable high-pitched voice of Bill Bayeh's was heard, a verdict was inevitable.

Trevor Haken played a major part in Bayeh's downfall and in getting him behind bars. His role in gathering evidence was highly dangerous. If anyone had searched Haken during one of his meetings they would have found he was wired, and he would have been dead.

In the months before he was due to appear at the Royal Commission, Bill Bayeh had taken to meeting with Haken at Birkenhead Point in Sydney's inner west. The centre shops are connected like a series of rabbit warrens, the type of place favoured by those with illicit business to discuss, and where you could easily get lost or lose someone if you wanted. Bayeh and Haken would either meet in the TAB or a coffee shop. Bayeh and Haken had agreed that if Bill was asked at the commission why they met so many times, he would say that he was an informant to Haken.

On their first meeting one Friday at the TAB at Birkenhead Point, Bayeh put $2000 into a black document bag held by Haken. Despite an extravagant lifestyle fuelled by drug money, Bayeh complained to Haken about the picture being painted of him by the Royal Commission. He protested that ever since 'Lasers' and 'Downunder' (businesses owned by Bayeh) were closed, the only place he was currently selling drugs from was his club the Penthouse Snooker Room. ('The Penthouse' was a pool hall on the upper level of 83–87 Darlinghurst Road, flanked by Pinocchio's Bar and Bistro and the Tunnel nightclub.) Bayeh protested to Haken that he had just taken over the Cosmopolitan Coffee Lounge with Peter Kay as a 'legitimate business' and was paying $3000 a week rent. (Kay had been out of jail for just two months.)

Despite the supposed defamation, there was other business to discuss. Bayeh wanted to slow down a competitor named Russell Townsend. Townsend was another individual referred to on a tape played at the Royal Commission. He was operating out of the Budget Private Hotel (aka the Budget Inn). Bayeh told Haken on tape that Townsend was selling every type of drug out of the poolroom in William Street and was making over $100,000 a week. Bayeh claimed that Townsend was looking after Lenny McPherson's interests while he was 'inside', as well as representing

Bronco Balic, another criminal identity. Townsend was selling up to 250 half caps of rock heroin per day out of the Budget Private Hotel and his other places.

Haken's role was to exchange information and to be a bagman. This meant he often acted as an intermediary between crooks and other cops. Bayeh offered Haken the $2000 to approach policemen Mal Brammer and Terry Walsh (both stationed in Kings Cross) to target Townsend. Bayeh suggested that Brammer would get $5000 for his trouble and suggested Haken tell Brammer that 'it's better the devil you know [Bayeh], than the devil you don't [Townsend]'.

Crooks need to keep looking over their shoulder and things were getting even hotter in the Cross. In a covert recording later played to the Commission, Bayeh also told Haken that Bert Kidd was moving in on the Cross and was supposedly bringing some people from Melbourne with him. Bayeh sensed the looming confrontation and wanted it to be known that he was prepared for it. He said that he had the backing of Bill Mulheron, who was in charge of the Armed Hold-up Squad. 'If Bert Kidd comes in using violence, I'll match it,' said Bayeh. He added, 'There is going to be a big bang bang, soon.'

Haken left the meeting to rendezvous with his Royal Commission minder. He would debrief and have the miniature tape removed from the recording device. It was then that the pressure would hit him. The adrenaline had pumped throughout the meeting but it was not until afterwards that sweat would pour from his body. He settled back into the darkened van hoping he had not been seen.

The next time Bayeh met Haken at Birkenhead Point, he gave Haken $3400 for the action being taken against Russell Townsend. This meeting was recorded covertly by Haken and played at the Commission. The balance was to be paid the next day. 'Make sure I'm left alone,' he told Haken. For his money he wanted to be able to operate out of the back room of the Penthouse without fear of being busted. 'I've been paying [Inspector Bob] Lysaught and [Inspector Brian] Meredith $1000 a week through Joe Sassine,' Bayeh said to Haken, 'but I don't trust Sassine no more and want you to take over.' Haken was in as deep as anyone could be with one of the state's biggest drug dealers.

This was all business. Bayeh would look after whoever he had to as long as no one got too greedy. He said that he paid Tom Domican to keep out of the Cross 'because if Domican comes into the Cross, there will be a bloodbath'. He added, 'He is my friend, he will help me in a fight.'

On one tape played to the Commission, Bayeh was heard to say that he was worried about the young Lebanese dealers and the young policemen in the Cross who were keen to take a bigger 'drink' of illicit profits. They were not being patient enough, according to Bayeh. 'They have to sit back and learn just like everybody else.' Bayeh thought that John Ibrahim had become too cocky and wanted to take over the cocaine distribution in the Cross. Meantime, Ibrahim was saying that Bayeh's old friends were not that strong anymore.

Haken met Bayeh on 30 December 1994 at the TAB at Birkenhead Point and received $2950. Bayeh was happy about the raid that had taken place on the Budget Private Hotel. 'All the doors had been knocked in by police,' Bayeh chuckled. They were temporarily replaced by chicken wire. Bayeh hoped that they would close down their business and that he could take it over. He wanted to reopen underneath the Pink Pussycat (at Lasers) the next week. Lasers was an amusement parlour at 38 Darlinghurst Road; it was also a well-supplied drug joint, taking up to $20,000 a day. To keep up the supply there were often 'drug drops' over the back fence. Doorman would carry guns and would receive police tip-offs before drug raids.

Haken would need to speak to other police about this. In a tape played to the Commission, Haken suggested that he would meet with Brian Meredith the next week at the Novotel Hotel while Bayeh sat at another table close by. Haken gave Bayeh his pager number, and Bayeh wrote it down on a business card and put it in his wallet. Bayeh was still unhappy with Sassine. He said that he had given Sassine $6000 to give to 'Bobby' (Lysaught) before he went on a course in the United States. The split was $2000 each for Lysaught, Sassine and Meredith.

Also recorded on tape, later that day, Haken called Meredith. 'G'day Lumpy, it's Kermit.' These were the call signs Haken and Meredith had while at the Joint Task Force (JTF). 'I've got a mutual friend with a problem,' said Haken. Things were busy at the Cross. Meredith complained about being ridden by Brammer. He was making things tough, even club doormen were expected to wear ID. Meredith had been instructed to give the drug sale points more attention, in particular the Budget Private Hotel.

Haken passed on Bayeh's request to lean on Russell Townsend and the Ibrahims' premises. Meredith agreed to act upon Bayeh's information but said that he wouldn't turn a blind eye to Bayeh's activities and that if he were caught he'd go down like anyone else. Haken went through the details of how Bayeh had paid money to Sassine who in turn had paid it to Lysaught and Meredith. Meredith denied any knowledge of anything like this taking place. Every time the topic was raised, he cut short the conversation.

By this stage, Graham Fowler had been served a S7 notice from the Royal Commission (a notice to appear and answer questions). Everyone comforted each other in the belief that if they held fast, things would be fine. As Fowler said to Haken, 'There's no way they'll bring us undone if we all stick tight.'

But rumours of a police officer who had rolled kept surfacing. Charlie Staunton told Haken that 'the pig' (the person who had rolled) had met with Bayeh, and that a lawyer on the inside of the Royal Commission had given him this information. Haken faced his worst fear, that of being exposed. Staunton told Haken that the Royal Commission was calling everyone into the hearings and then getting them to deny their wrongdoings. The 'pig' would then get into the box and refute the earlier evidence, 'so that even if they don't get them for the substantive offence, they will get them for lying'. Staunton had obviously worked out the game plan of exposure within the hearing room.

Haken later went to the Entrance Hotel at the Entrance, where he met Kim Thompson. Thompson told him that his current girlfriend was in the Arson Squad South Region and that she heard that Haken was drinking again — he had stopped in 1990 — and that he had rolled to the Royal Commission. Thompson reassured Haken that he didn't believe her.

Haken had a number of meetings at the Entrance with Thompson and Fowler. Thompson had a caravan up there and Fowler was negotiating to get one there as well. Danny Caines was also doing the same. Caines was a plumber who was said to be the go-between for Lenny McPherson and the police. (Caines died very shortly after the Commission broke ... from carbon monoxide poisoning in a car. Haken maintains he was killed off — and that ninety per cent of criminal suicides are really murder.) Thompson would call Haken to come up. The day the Commission first approached Fowler, Danny Caines was sent via Fowler to Haken's house to tell him what was going on, so that there was no direct link between Haken and Fowler.

There was a growing tide of suspicion surrounding Haken, including rumours that he had been seen getting into a darkened van. Another Kings Cross detective, Duncan Demol, spoke to Haken on the phone and told him that he had heard a rumour from Ray McDougall (South Region Drug Unit) that Haken had rolled. If the police had heard these rumours, then so to would have the crooks.

On 2 February 1995, Haken met with Bill Bayeh and Charlie Staunton at the Birkenhead Tavern. Bayeh gave Haken $2000. Bayeh had heard from three different sources that Haken was 'off' — that is, that he had rolled. One of those sources was John Ibrahim, who said that he heard this from Kim Thompson. Bayeh had been told, 'You must have balls to be talking to Haken'. Bayeh told Haken that he did not believe these rumours, but then added, 'I've got money now and I can cause plenty of trouble'. He looked at Haken, touched his arm and said, 'I'll get them or their wives or kids. I don't care what I have to do.'

CHAPTER 14

A FAMILY IN TROUBLE

By the time of Haken's involvement in the Royal Commission, his relationship with his wife Jane was already in difficulties. The troubles mounted through the course of the inquiry, but there was also a history of other factors.

When Haken was Detective Sergeant in charge of Kings Cross, he worked with Jim Bignell, a detective senior constable in the same office. Haken recalls Bignell as being a hard worker and totally reliable but then adds, 'Except when it comes to women'. Bignell was one of a group of four detectives who was participating in 'the laugh' at the Cross.[1] He was in a senior position for his rank and had survived the purge after the Churchill incident.

Haken befriended Bignell and would take him home for meals. At this stage, Haken supplemented his income by working on his days off building furniture with an upholsterer who lived across the road. Haken would go to work in the daytime and Bignell would be on late shift. The upholsterer said to Haken one day, 'Look, I hate to upset the applecart but that mate of yours with the green Commodore has been spending a fair bit of time at your place in the daytime.' Haken adds, 'You're always the last to know, aren't you?' Haken confronted his wife who explained that Bignell had dropped in for a cup of coffee on the way to visiting his sister at Gosford. 'This seemed to be happening about three times a week. It just deteriorated from there.'

Alcohol was a contributing factor in the deterioration of Haken's marriage. His mother comments, 'The thing that affected him the most was the heavy drinking — it wasn't any good for him. He used to go to sleep and Jane used to get very angry because he'd just nod off. It didn't matter if he was at a dinner party or not. I never knew him to become violent, though.' Haken adds, 'I was a dozy drinker. I would be asleep at a dinner party and friends would paint my face with lipstick while I was asleep and take a photo.'

On one occasion, Bignell and Haken had returned to Haken's home both quite drunk and, as usual, Haken fell asleep. He woke at one stage to see Bignell and his wife in an embrace and kissing. 'I went ballistic and told him to piss off.' Jane and Haken argued for the rest of the night. 'She didn't explain it, she never did.' For Haken and his wife, it was the accelerator towards the end of their marriage.

The relationship between Bignell and Haken's wife deepened and they secretly arranged to holiday together in Tasmania in mid 1990. 'I was trying to get things back on track. I've supposedly got a wife and four kids, and she said that the only way she could get around the problem was for her to go away and spend some time with a girlfriend of hers in Tasmania.' And so Trevor agreed to her request for a holiday but, on the same day that she left, Haken was told at work that Bignell was taking a holiday in Tasmania. 'So you didn't have to be a genius to work that one out, did you?'

Haken had some police mates in Tasmania make some inquiries and they found that a Mr and Mrs Bignell had checked into hotels together around that state for the week. Jane had made phone calls home from the hotels and Haken later received credit card charges for meals from the same hotels.

Haken couldn't get down there as he had his job and the four children to look after. Haken says, 'It was like hell visiting you. A woman in her position can just bleed you and bleed you, and not just financially.' Haken confronted her but she denied the affair. 'You say hang on a second and you even start doubting yourself. But you become armed with sufficient evidence, because finding things out was the game I was in.'

Haken confronted Bignell the day he returned from Tasmania. Bignell was totally besotted with Jane and firmly believed that she would leave Haken and marry him. Kim Thompson witnessed the confrontation and took Haken to another room and searched him to see if he had a gun on him. 'I could have quite cheerfully wrung his neck, but I wasn't going to shoot him.'

The situation grew progressively worse. In one incident, Jane had told Haken that she was going out in the family Toyota Celica when Haken, on his way to work for afternoon shift in his blue Nissan Urvan, saw Bignell driving the Celica with Jane in the passenger seat. Haken quickly did a U-turn and followed the vehicle. Desperate to confront them, he drove on the wrong side of the road trying to block their progress and pull them over. He recalls, 'It was the enraged husband trying to round-up his wife.' They didn't stop and Haken eventually let them go as Bignell and Haken's car were dodging and ducking.

Haken knew that Jane would have to pick up their youngest son from kindergarten and she was very late. She arrived without Bignell and during that initial confrontation at the kindergarten, Haken had told her to 'go home, pack your gear and piss off'. Haken and his wife returned to the family home. Bignell later arrived in his own car with the expectation that he was going to pick Jane and her gear up and take her with him.

Bignell said, 'I'm here to get Jane.' Haken replied, 'Jane's not going anywhere with you.' 'It was like a scene out of a penny dreadful, something out of one of those books you'd never want to believe. We were yelling and screaming at each other. He was so besotted that he was sure that she was going to leave and go and live with him.' Bignell eventually left without Jane.

These incidents were brought to the notice of Jim McCloskey, the inspector in charge of the police station. Haken says, 'Some things just aren't condoned. They don't mind that 'you rip, roar, tear and bust', as Rodney Harvey used to say, but not that type of thing.' Bignell was transferred out of the Cross.

Chook Fowler later told Haken that Bignell was told that if he went away quietly then when the next promotion for sergeant came up at the Cross he would be up for it. Bignell was transferred to one of the other squads in South Region and later given the promotion, but this was overturned on appeal.

Haken's relationship with Jane was still in trouble at this time but he always hoped things might improve. 'I was trying anything to keep the marriage together, and so we were going to counselling. I found it good but Jane didn't want to go.' One night they decided to go out to talk things through and so drove to a restaurant in Chinatown.

They didn't drink much that evening. The experiences with Bignell and Jane made Haken realise that alcohol had made him blind to what was happening around him. He had cut right down and would soon not drink at all. Haken believes that Jane had decided to leave the marriage at this stage. Nothing was resolved at the meal and they drove home.

On the drive home a dog darted in front of the car and Haken swerved to avoid it. The car clipped the edge of the tar and hit the culvert, breaking the suspension. 'The accident folded the wheel underneath. To look at the car from the outside, you wouldn't think it was damaged.'

Haken bumped his head but was not seriously hurt. Jane was taken to hospital. A fragment of glass, possibly from the cracked windscreen, went into her eye and she would need a new cornea. Haken took her to South Australia for an operation. It was a success, though the vision in the eye remained blurry for a year. In addition to the damage to her vision, Jane was on crutches with a broken bone in her ankle. 'Her mother insisted that I had inflicted the injuries on Jane intentionally. She suggested that I had gouged her in the eye.'

Jane took a long time to recuperate and Bignell lost interest. Haken thought everything was back on track but his wife's unhappiness deepened. Haken's mother recalls:

'She got more selfish — she'd make coffee and tell me to get my own. I wasn't aware of her infidelity but I suspected it. I think her mother thought that a policeman wasn't the best option for her daughter. Trevor obviously loved her deeply and even after some of those things turned up he still would have made it work. But it was all to no avail as it turned out. I had the house renovated but I found out she was playing up something dreadful behind my back. Like all things you always find out later, you're the last to know.

There were other people affected by Haken's actions. Haken's daughter Elizabeth (not her real name) was born on 13 February 1978. She now lives under an alias and has relocated. She has paid a high price for her father's decision to give evidence at the Royal Commission.

Elizabeth says she had a lovely childhood with her sister and two brothers. 'Dad was at work a lot, but that was just the way it was' (using an expression her father uses often). Elizabeth was always aware that her father was a policeman. The other kids at school thought that it was very cool and she was respected because of that.

She started dancing at a local dance school doing jazz and tap when she was seven. At that stage, she never had any intention of doing classical ballet. Her mother arranged for her to audition at Macdonald College (a performing arts high school). She was interviewed and during the audition was found to have aptitude for ballet. But instead of being a ballerina, Elizabeth wanted to be Kylie Minogue.

Jane Haken did some modelling from time to time and said that she would use this money to pay the school fees. And so Jane booked Elizabeth into the private school without telling Trevor. This caused a huge fight but Trevor eventually came around to the idea.

Elizabeth was in Year Seven when she came to realise the truth regarding her parents' relationship. 'I knew from an early age that Mum wasn't faithful.' She witnessed her mother's behaviour and her dad's behaviour towards her. Elizabeth would be home when her mother would make strange telephone calls. These calls didn't make sense to Elizabeth and she wondered who her mum was calling.

One birthday, Jane told Elizabeth she could have the day off from school and that she would take her out. They first saw a movie and then went to the Hard Rock Cafe.

As my dad said, my mum could spend money like water flows. I remember getting home and Dad asking whether Jim Bignell had joined us for lunch. I said no, and he didn't believe me and I was like 'He didn't, okay? And he yelled back '... I don't believe you.' So I was very aware of what was going on between them.

The more I realised that my mother was playing dad for a fool, the more distant we became. And the more involved in classical ballet I got, the more distant I got from everybody.

Elizabeth loved high school and performed very well. Trevor had told her that if she didn't achieve academically she wouldn't be allowed to dance. Around sixteen years of age, Elizabeth was taken aside by her father and told, 'Look, there's some stuff going on. I don't expect you to understand, but you've just got to be aware that if Graham Fowler or Kim Thompson comes over, or anyone from work, that you go away and that you stay away. Maybe go around to someone's house. If you have to stay home then stay inside your room.'

In addition, Elizabeth was told by her father that there was a recording device in his car. He told her that it was something to do with his work and nothing to do with her. While this sounded startling, 'All he had to say was that it was in relation to his work and I didn't question it'. Elizabeth's main concern was wondering if her conversations with her girlfriends were recorded! 'I knew Dad was involved in something that was causing him stress, but to be truthful, I was caught up in my own little ballet world.'

In Year Eleven, Elizabeth auditioned for the Australian Ballet School and was successful over hundreds of other girls from around the country. At the beginning of 1995, she moved to Melbourne to join the ballet school. It was obvious that her father was worried about something as he insisted that she move into a high-security block and that everything was to be put in another name. After only five weeks of term, while Elizabeth was on a visit home, Haken told her that there was a big investigation into police behaviour and that he would be giving evidence, adding, 'I'm in the wrong too'.

He told her that at the end of term one (eight weeks away), she should pack all her things in readiness to move. Haken told Elizabeth that he was going to give evidence against a lot of his police colleagues in front of the Wood Royal Commission. The family would have to go into witness protection and this would involve leaving the country while he stayed in Sydney to give evidence. Funnily enough, at first Elizabeth found the news almost a relief because 'I was finding the ballet school so depressing'. She laughs heartily and adds, 'The Australian Ballet School must have been bad because witness protection sounded better!'

Elizabeth's life suddenly changed dramatically. She'd only just turned seventeen and was frightened. Before she left for the secret location, she met with a witness protection agent. He sat her down and said that if she tried to contact any of her friends or any of her family that 'they', the people that her father was giving evidence against, would find her. She cannot ever forget the words he spoke: 'They will find you and they will kill you'.

'Here was the person that was supposed to advise us what was going on and what to do and he was scaring me to death.' Witness Security (WITSEC) agents usually looked after criminals, so while they were very good at keeping people 'out of harm's way', their skills in looking after a person's emotional wellbeing were not well developed. 'Most of the people in that job that we met didn't have any people skills at all. They were like bouncers.'

'He had me completely paranoid. We'd be at dinner at the hotel in our first relocation with me telling my mum not to talk. My mum would tell me not to be so paranoid and I'd say, "'Don't talk Mum, you don't know who is around us". I was beside myself. Then again, that is that world. It is a world of fear and intimidation.'

The Haken family was to be sent overseas for a 'holiday'. Six heavily armed WITSEC agents accompanied the family to the airport and checked them in. 'I don't think they'd ever tried to get so many people away on witness protection in one go. The whole thing was messed up. They went from one extreme to another. On the one hand we were not allowed to leave the sight of these armed men and then, once we were through customs, we were suddenly on our own.'

After being ushered through customs, an announcement was made over the public address system for them to return to the check-in area. Their new name had just been called across the whole airport! When they returned to the check-in area, they found that one of the boys had left his boarding pass behind. While retrieving the pass, they saw no sign of the WITSEC agents who they assumed had already left.

While on a stopover in another city they were seen by some friends of the family. Then after flying for over thirty hours to get to their destination, they were told that their hotel accommodation had not been booked. 'Here we were, some blonde-haired blue-eyed Aussies in a place where we obviously stood out, trying to find a room.' Being anonymous was not proving easy.

'The first night we were there we were broken into, and of course we thought that was associated with what was going on with Dad. We were petrified. We stayed there for a few weeks and then moved to another location for another two weeks.' Elizabeth's little sister locked herself in her bedroom for the whole time.

If the trauma of being in witness protection wasn't enough, the fractures within the family were also coming to a head. Jane Haken's mother, who also travelled with them, would tell the children that they would never see their father again. Trevor was trying to call the children but the messages were not passed on. A lot of the drama with the Commission and going away would not have existed without her behind it.' All the information given to the children by the two adults was negative. 'She would say, "Your dad's gone to court in the back of a bulletproof car". And so you felt nothing but completely alone and scared for him.'

Elizabeth returned from 'whereabouts unknown' some months later. After efforts by Royal Commission staff, she was readmitted to the ballet school. News of her father was still on the television. 'I'd wake up and it would be on the *Today* show, and then I'd come home and it would be on the nightly news. I couldn't avoid it. My friends, who were very supportive, would turn it off.' She hadn't seen the newspaper articles about her family while she was away.

I wasn't really interested in what they had written — I just wanted my life back. Most of the stuff they quoted was wrong anyway. They quoted people who didn't speak to the paper. They quoted my brother's boss as having said things, which he didn't. They quoted the director of the ballet school as having said things and she hadn't been spoken to by anyone. They literally made things up. It was easy stuff to get away with. You know, things like, 'she was at the Australian Ballet School, the director said she was very talented', and it doesn't take a great journalist to do those things. It was really sad for me to read what Dad had been through; I wasn't so much worried about us.

Elizabeth doesn't have a close relationship with her mother now.

My mum would deny until she was blue in the face that she was ever unfaithful. I used to bang my head against the wall when I was in Melbourne after speaking to my mother. My aunty explained it pretty well. She said, 'Every single time you have a conversation with your mother, what she is actually doing is mentally rearranging her underwear drawer in her mind.'

I don't believe that my mother is malicious or that she means to inflict pain on other people. There is no room for anyone else. She forgot to call me on my birthday. When does that not ever hurt? I recently popped in to see her after an absence of about six months and when she saw me she said, 'Oh damn, but I've got to go out'. And so I just turned on my heels and walked out. The next time I saw her she said, 'Are you over your little tantrum now?' She still doesn't realise. To her it's always someone else's fault.

Elizabeth sees her life as having been split into two phases: life before the Royal Commission and life after. 'Anyone in my life after the Australian Ballet doesn't know about any of this. I just have to be more careful. Sometimes I wish I could tell people, but it's not an option. I'm luckier than my little sister and brother, because they didn't have anyone to pour this out to. My little brother was eight when this happened.'

Elizabeth is an amazing survivor. In the early days of the commission, she relied on the support of her friends. By her second year at the ballet school, it got to the stage where she couldn't speak without crying. Her friend Jody, a devout Catholic would ask her to go to church with her. 'I always felt better after going to church. I felt that I was somehow okay. I was very alone. I was separated from my family and I was struggling. She'd leave me sayings like, "It's okay, God's got you in the palm of his hand. He knows exactly what's going on in your life and exactly where you are going."' They would pray together, and in her third year Elizabeth started to do volunteer work at the Sacred Heart Mission and it changed her outlook.

When you start looking at others instead of yourself all the time, then your problems pale into insignifance. You start concentrating on other people. I could see God working in my life and I could see God taking this situation that was so bad and saying, this is hard, but you will get through to the other side and it will get better.

I say to Dad that I don't think you would have ever been free of Mum if you hadn't done what you did. You didn't want to leave because you had four kids, and you didn't want to leave because you were committed, and that's great, that's an honourable thing but you would still be in a loveless marriage.

I told Dad that Jesus said that the truth will set you free. I don't think God put us here to live in sorrow.

Elizabeth hopes this will not always be her father's lot.

CHAPTER 15

THE NADIR

'It was ... like I was doing another job for the police. I never thought that I'd be dumped. There was never any suggestion that I would be an expendable item, nor did I ever give any thought that I would be exposed so widely. It was like an assassination.'

TREVOR HAKEN

If any further evidence was needed that the process of corrupt policing in New South Wales had reached its nadir, Graham Fowler provided it. He was one of the most memorable of the police officers who appeared before the Royal Commission. He was from the 'old school' and, despite having enough damning film footage and audio tape shown in the hearing room of the Royal Commission to make a reasonable documentary on the man, he steadfastly refused to admit to any corrupt behaviour at all.

Following is what the hearing room of the Royal Commission heard Fowler say to Haken privately. Fowler was talking about the Royal Commission and its enquiries into Kings Cross and whether they had evidence about Fowlers activities.

Graham Fowler: So mate, fuck, I'm 99 per cent sure mate that 'cause, because the way they open, the way they went on, they chose the Kings Cross.

Trevor Haken: Yeah.

GF: This fuckin' lynch pin.

TH: Yep.

GF: And mate if they, if they had of had anything.

TH: They would have dropped it on you.

GF: Forcing me there.

TH: Yep.

GF: Like I've beaten them.

Later in the same meeting …

GF: Mate if they'd had tapes about anything better would they have missed a fuckin' shot?

TH: They would have dropped it long ago, yeah.

GF: After half a dozen fuckin' cautions …

TH: Yeah.

GF: On and on I thought, ooh fuck, oh fuck you know.

TH: See that was, that was what worried me.

GF: They've got me; they've got me.

TH: Mate.

GF: They've just got to have something.

TH: You'd think so.

A further excerpt from a tape played in the public hearing room of the Royal Commission runs as follows:

GF: What are you worried about fucking Billy Bayeh for, you haven't fucking been wheeling and dealing Billy Bayeh have you? Billy Bayeh wouldn't fucking, well you saw it, you saw the letter, Billy won't give anybody up.

Other police officer: If he does a life sentence he will!

Fowler 'toughed it out' in the Commission hearing room because he remained confident that the Commission would never get him. If it wasn't for Haken and the recording he made, Fowler would not have been caught. He stated confidently, 'So they've got nothing. They've put a theory together, they've only been following since May or June'.

TH: So you reckon they'll call you back or is that it?

GF: Oh no, they'll call me back somewhere along but I think ... fuckin' I think I'll be surprised if I come fuckin' back somewhere along, but I think I'll be surprised if I come fuckin' back in first ... They'll get all my records back until, they're going to go hunting now and digging.

TH: Yeah.

GF: I'll be back there with my financial things because I got well ... I might have 'em fucked now with the 200 or so a week. Mmm, I've given virtually nothing. I'm not going to give 'em fuckin' nothing. I've got no record.

TH: Yeah.

GF: Let them fuckin' do it.

The Royal Commission eventually *did* do it, and the world saw the now-famous video images of Haken handing Fowler corrupt payments in the front seat of Haken's car.

Fowler eventually went to jail over a 'milkshake incident'. He faked an accident in the police centre where he slipped on a spilt milkshake and fell on the marble floor outside the lifts of the Sydney Police Station. The Royal Commission had the place under observation after a tip-off from Haken, and Fowler and Haken were recorded at the Berowra Waters Bottle Shop talking about an upcoming accident. Fowler had been chief of detectives at the City of Sydney station and was to be moved to uniform duty at Chatswood. He wanted to take the hurt-on-duty option rather than go back to uniform. He had spoken to Haken about faking a car accident (Haken and Royal Commission investigators were ready to 'assist' and record every moment of this) but Fowler changed his mind and instead decided to simplify things and have an accident at the City of Sydney station. As was reported, Fowler had forcefully denied to Gary Crooke QC, counsel assisting the Royal Commission, that the fall was pre-arranged.[1] The Royal Commission hearing room was played a tape of Fowler saying to Haken the day before the fall, 'I've got to have a fuckin' accident tomorrow, at work. I might not be down the stairs yet, I'm going to set it up'. Fowler added that he had to have 'a fucking nasty accident … I have to go for a payout, stress isn't good enough.'

Sure enough, the next day (30 November 1994) Fowler took 'the milkshake option' and 'slipped' on the marble floor. He was taken away by ambulance to hospital but was sent home a few days later following a number of incidents involving alcohol in the hospital. The Royal Commission recorded conversations with Fowler talking about the evidence against him.

Graham Fowler: But if they just, I almost panicked when I fuckin' saw 'em start attacking Quinnie about the fuckin' milkshake.

Trevor Haken: Well, what's he going to say anyway? Fuckin' what's he going to say?

GF: Exactly as I say if they haven't got us fuckin' with him mate they haven't fuckin' got us have they and we have seen him for fuckin' months.

TH: Sweet as a nut.

GF: I know. We've got 'em fucked.

Fowler was eventually tried and convicted for attempting to defraud the medical insurance unit and for lying to the Royal Commission. He has not been tried for his Kings Cross activities and the world famous footage of accepting bribes, which Haken belives is something the DPP should be asked to explain.

Haken's assessment of Fowler was forged in the Cross when 'Chook' was returned to take charge of the detectives.

> He was nice enough when you were on a par with him but he was a standover man both to his staff and to the people in the street. He was called the GOC (Grumpy Old Cunt) or GOP (Grumpy Old Prick). I didn't mind the guy but he was a horrendous 'dudder', that is, he would rip you off. If there was a quid around he'd take 75 cents in the dollar. I didn't worry because there was plenty around in the Cross. If you knew you were being dudded you didn't worry because there was so much out there. Perhaps that's why I survived so well. I played the odds; the other side of the coin was that I worked hard, the harder you worked the more people wanted to put dollars in your pocket! Lazy men were never bribed, why would a crook bribe you if you did nothing?

When former Police Commissioner Tony Lauer took the Fairfax organisation to court for comments that were made about him in the *Sydney Morning Herald*, Lauer argued at the hearing that the Police Service had done what it could within the limits of its resources and ability to address the problem of corruption. At one stage, Fowler had been identified in an internal inquiry as engaging in corrupt activity but Lauer and the police board did not prevent his promotion. Lauer agreed that he suspected Fowler of corruption but that the offenders were the 'tip of the iceberg'. Lauer didn't oppose Fowler's promotion 'because the view was that he was entitled to the benefit of the doubt as accorded by the judge'.

Graham Fowler has now served his time in jail and is once again a free man. He has not been prosecuted for many of the matters raised at the Royal Commission.

Contrast this with Haken's predicament, as described by the criminal intelligence analyst attached to work with him at the Royal Commission. Haken's contribution was vital:

Everybody we called knew we had something on them, it was all on tape. They knew that as soon as John [Agius] said, 'Do you want to see the tape?' They were done! Then we got [undisclosed corrupt informant]. We wouldn't have got him unless we had Trevor.

When you are interviewing someone and you have a lot of information, you know they'll eventually tell you. Most often, unless they're really hard like Fowler, they'll tell you what you want to know.

In contrast, what would the Royal Commission have been like without Haken?

I imagine we would have done very little. I can't imagine that we would have got the vast amount of information that we did. We knew so much, mainly about Kings Cross ... and that was generated by Trevor. The team I was attached to looked at Kings Cross and the Joint Task Force. The ability to use the technical stuff was pretty amazing, that was part of the success as well.

CHAPTER 16

DEAD MAN WALKING

'He would have done less time if he'd killed somebody'

TREVOR HAKEN'S DAUGHTER

Trevor Haken and the analyst assigned to him to assist in collating the vast amount of information he was giving, developed a good rapport, although their time together was intense. The investigators would not tell Trevor anything about what was going on at the Royal Commission even though he felt a part of the team. It was policy at the Commission to keep all information to a need-to-know basis. To protect the integrity of each investigative team, each team guarded their information and tactics.

At the affidavit meetings Haken would appear hyperactive, continuously drinking strong coffee with sugar. The analyst found Haken an interesting person both in and out of the hearing room. 'He's very smart, very focused, an actor, and can be very manipulative.' Haken was intense about everything he did, focusing his energies on going over and over the details of his statements. Despite all the pressure he felt for his safety, his biggest concern was what he had done to his family. The analyst saw his human side and came to feel sorry for Haken. The analyst found that other agents were less sympathetic to his predicament. The analyst recalls:

He was very lonely and the cops were not interested. Even though he had done the wrong thing in the past, he was in a sad situation. One thing I've learnt is that people aren't all that bad and he's not all that bad. He finally did the right thing and he did it at great sacrifice and we might not have caught him. If we had, he might have gone away for a couple of years and then come back.

The day Haken was announced publicly as an informant, the analyst went into the witness room secreted somewhere in the building that housed the Royal Commission. The television broadcast of the afternoon news was speaking about Haken and his undercover work. 'I walked in with [name of another agent] and we both sat down near him. Haken was quite upset, concerned about what he had done, that he had taken the point of no return.'

He watched the six o'clock news and said, 'This is really hard to do to my mates. I feel really bad.' The analyst tried to make him feel better by telling him, 'They've done the wrong thing and you've done the right thing'. Haken replied, 'Yes, that's easy to say but I feel like I've betrayed them.' 'I remember him talking about betraying his friends, particularly Chook Fowler. Some he felt responsible for getting into the situation, and with some others he was quite happy to do it.'

The weekend after his initial exposition to the public, the analyst and another agent flew to an undisclosed location to go through Haken's affadavit. 'To make sure it was accurate we ended up going chronological as his interviews were all over the place.' Haken was able to work undisturbed on the affidavit: 'He has an incredible mind in that respect'.

As the star witness for the Royal Commission, security for Haken was tight. There were reminders about the seriousness of the situation. Before Haken and the witness protection team flew to another location, they drove around the city for two hours with witness protection to 'dry clean' (lose) anyone who might be following them. If investigators caught a plane, they would all sit in different areas and would not acknowledge each other. When they got off the plane, they would walk on their own. The analyst says, 'One of the witness protection guys would then slip a piece of paper in your hand and there would be an address. You would then take a taxi to that place and Haken would be there.'

The analyst was struck by the poor conditions in which Haken was housed. 'He was stuck in this rotten motel in the outskirts of an industrial area in [undisclosed location] and they were pretty ordinary rooms and very hot. They picked places like that on purpose — places where nobody wanted to be seen and nobody looked.' Similar to the viewpoint held by Haken's daughter Elizabeth, the analyst was not impressed by witness protection.

They treated him really badly, in terms of that he was our ace witness. Perhaps it was because they're cops as well. They were Feds and they had no interest in anything beyond his physical safety. They were more interested in racking up all of the overtime and meal allowances they could. They fed him crap. He couldn't go and find food so they would cook to save money from their meal allowances and they would cook cheap and nasty food and Trevor would have to eat it. They did their own exercise because they were all into body building but they never took Trevor for a walk or anything.

They also drove him around and around for security purposes.

It has been suggested that if law enforcement agencies were serious about protecting witnesses then you'd hire people who really don't look like cops or from the military. It seemed that at the Australian Federal Police and in most police forces the guys who want to work VIP protection are always the beefy, bodyguard types.

The analyst and investigation team from the Royal Commission would only see Haken once a week, and so he was very happy to see them. He worked until midnight or one a clock in the morning and found the loneliness tough. He kept in touch a little with his wife who had been sent off on her 'holiday'. The analyst paints a troubled picture.

> She [Haken's wife] was ringing and complaining because things were all going wrong. When we were in [secret location], he was in this lousy motel, he had just publicly rolled and his wife was ringing him constantly saying that their accommodation wasn't up to scratch and that they'd been robbed and that he'd better pull his finger out and do something about it and that he was a bastard.

Another former Commission investigator recalls, 'He was concerned that he would lose her. He was besotted with her, even though the relationship was at an end.' The analyst says that Jane Haken had enjoyed the benefits of what Haken could provide.

> His wife is quite beautiful. She would spend a lot of the money that he would make illegally on things — cosmetics or clothes. And she had a ball on all of this money, but she claimed that she never knew anything about what he was doing. There was just all of this money coming to her! She slept with a colleague of Trevor's and he caught them at it. He went a bit crazy about this and then gave up the drink.

There were no end of dramas for the Royal Commission. The mother-in-law would often threaten to go to the press, which threatened the security of the whole thing.

On how pivotal Haken's contribution was to the success of the Royal Commission, the analyst states pointedly:

> Totally, absolutely totally. His role was so important in getting all the others to tell us what they knew. The tactics, putting him up there and Trevor saying, 'I have told the Royal Commission all the bad things I have done, I have been working undercover for the past eight months and I am prepared to tell you everything.' Then they left it at that and brought in Fowler and showed him that tape.

Life since the Royal Commission has not been good for Trevor Haken. It has been many years since he first rolled. Surprisingly, Haken himself did not fully comprehend the decision he was making. He thought that by deciding to assist the Royal Commission he became a part of that team. He saw his contribution as a chance to do real policing again, to reveal the truth. Haken recalls:

> I envisaged that I was part of the team, that I'd swapped sides and was a part of the Royal Commission, but that was a mistaken view. I was still part of the small group within the Commission that were working as tight as can be. The first time I ever really knew that I wasn't going back into the cops was when [Justice] Wood said, 'You've got no future in the police'.
>
> I was the one person who had clarified things for the Commission and yet others who had covered themselves in

a shroud of lies have benefited. I hadn't really given any thoughts to leaving. It was ... like I was doing another job for the police. I never thought that I'd be dumped. There was never any suggestion that I would be an expendable item. Nor did I ever give any thought that I would be exposed so widely. It was like an assassination.

I can't do anything. I've been told by minders, 'Oh you can pack shelves or mow lawns'. It leaves you a little bit cold when everybody else who 'maintained the integrity of the police department' was given a medical pension and have been given the benefit of presumed innocence by silence or deceit.

Haken was told by one of the most senior people at the Police Integrity Commission that the only reason he helped the Royal Commission was that he wanted indemnity from prosecution. Haken says, 'He didn't or couldn't consider any alternative. The stupidity of that was that prior to going on side to the Commission, they or anybody else had no proof of the vast majority of matters that I got them proof of.'

The analyst has not had contact with Haken for many years but her reflections are still relevant:

He's very angry with the Royal Commission. They seem to have abandoned him. He was so intense, he demanded a lot of support and concern. I couldn't help but see him as a person that was suffering. It was such an intense working team and he felt a part of it, and he developed a rapport with people and he gave everything he had to it at the time, and at the end it just disappeared completely.

Perhaps he should know that's how it has got to be. Of course, he's not able to make a proper living. He always

knew that he was in for a pretty hard time. He didn't know
where he'd end up. He didn't have many expectations.

Most people wonder what Haken was doing when he rolled and
became an informant. She says, 'He was focused ... but not
anything to do with retaliation. He had to make a decision and
once he chose that path, like with his drinking ... he was totally
devoted.'

The methodology of the Royal Commission and the example of
Trevor Haken's undercover work provided a template for enquiries
that would follow. Mates would again be used against mates and
the star witness would again be 'milked dry'.

Trevor Haken was a detective sergeant and so was a detective
codenamed M5 (the code name given to the Police Integrity's
Commission's star witness of Operation Florida). A detective
sergeant is a high enough rank in the police to be in a position
where you can act corruptly and get away with it (as you are
generally the one doing the supervising). Most police leave behind
corrupt activities once they reach the rank of an Inspector or
above. You are getting paid more, you are generally not out there
on the street and in a position to take money from a search
warrant (though some did) or to get your hands dirty.

M5 was part of the North Region Major Crime Squad. He was
one of a group of detectives who had been suspected of being
corrupt over a number of years. There was never enough evidence
forthcoming in relation to these allegations and they were all
finalised without action, or in police terms, 'written off'.

In the process of investigating a murder, the New South Wales
Crime Commission had a number of telephones intercepted. It
was through these interceptions that they stumbled across proof
and corroboration of M5's and others corrupt activities.

NSW Police Internal Affairs and the Crime Commission confronted M5 with the evidence they had on him. This is what is described in legal terms as a 'Star Chamber'. The subject of an enquiry is seated in the middle of a room and is compelled to answer all questions without the normal protection of the right to silence.

The evidence presented to M5 was 'water tight'. It included M5 and others admitting their involvement in criminal activities and corruption. This included responses to current internal affairs enquiries and exactly the same corrupt activities of Haken and the detectives of his era (loading of evidence, verballing suspects, scrum downs, stealing money, etc). The Royal Commission had come and gone but there where many who had escaped investigation who continued 'business as usual'.

M5 was given the option of assisting the Crime Commission and Police Internal Affairs or facing the consequences of charges arising out of the damning evidence of the telephone evidence and other corroborative evidence which they had. In simple terms, it was spelt out to M5 that he could take his chances with the legal system but that it seemed likely that he would serve several years in prison.

M5's agreement to assist was the beginning of 'Operation Florida', a joint task force between the Police Integrity Commission, the Crime Commission and New South Wales Internal Affairs. M5 did worked undercover this for over two and a half years.

M5 initially agreed to assist investigators by wearing listening devices and providing information about other corrupt police, somewhat similar to Haken's role. He engaged in Integrity tests and other strategies to obtain evidence of corruption.

One integrity test was where a search warrant was conducted by M5 and other police. M5 was provided with cash (several hundred dollars) which he later divided amongst other officers included in the warranted. He told the other officers that the money was stolen from the premesis, the officers kept the money.

M5 approached a senior officer (an Acting Inspector) in a neighboring area and requested information on the brief of evidence against a drug dealer who had just been arrested in that area. M5 told the senior officer that he was approaching him on behalf of the drug dealer to see the strength of the case against him. The senior officer provided M5 with copies of paperwork from the brief and in return was given $500. (The ABC program *Four Corners* showed film of this meeting taken by Internal Affairs Police.)

The senior officer was approached by investigators from Operation Florida who requested his assistance in their enquiries. In the same way that M5 had been given a choice, 'either jump on board or take your chances with the legal system.' He declined the offer and preferred to roll the dice. He was sentenced to several years prison for receiving a corrupt commission and other crimes.

M5 was tasked by Investigators to get evidence on his police colleagues who were his long term mates. He was wired and engaged them in conversations and activities which incriminated the participants. He was a great asset and invaluable to the success of Operation Florida. As one source has said, 'He was Operation Florida'.

Investigators debriefed M5 at an early stage and heard the story of his life as a corrupt officer spanning his whole life as a detective. One incident came about when the Royal Commission was in full swing. North Region Major Crime Office had a cupboard filled with firearms which were specifically for the purpose of 'loading' suspects. It is alleged that a senior officer (now a Superintendent) instructed other members of the squad to dispose of the firearms in case the Royal Commission was to search the office (the Royal

Commission had, without warning, searched a number of Crime Squad offices and police stations).

As a result, M5 and other officers gathered all the firearms and took them out on a boat to the middle of the Hawkesbury River and dumped them into the water. Years later, M5 directed the task force investigators to the location and the guns were retrieved.

M5 was put in stations and situations to target certain individuals (long time friends and associates) and either obtain evidence or test their integrity. M5 knew that he was indemnified from prosecution and so he wrestled with the reality that he was assisting the prosecution of his mates for the same crimes that he had himself committed.

The stress of these activities, the pressure and conflict of 'betraying' on your mates and the always threat of discovery took a toll on M5. At one stage he entered a psychiatric clinic suffering from stress, anxiety and depression related to his undercover work. He was hastily removed from this facility and told that his work was not finished and he had to keep working undercover. It is alleged that he was told that by being in the psychiatric facility he wasn't cooperating fully with the investigation and as such his indemnity against prosecution was now in question. He had no real choice, he had to continue his undercover work. This in incident is said to be the subject of a law suit brought against the task force by M5.

So what happened to M5 after his efforts of nearly three years of undercover work with the task force? During his giving of evidence, M5 confessed to accepting substantial amounts of corrupt money. The Australian Tax Office promptly hit him with a bill for this undeclared income. His wife and family were plucked out of their jobs, schools and communities and were relocated under the witness protection to an undisclosed location. He is at the mercy of bureaucrats who now look at him as a liability and a dead weight. M5 no longer has friends as they were all police and he has informed on most of them. A number of those who he informed against and who had committed the same crimes as M5 later escaped charges and conviction and either resigned, retired, were pensioned out or what is more of a concern, are still in the job. M5 must look at this situation and asks similar questions and say similar things as Trevor Haken; 'Was it worth it, no. I'd do the five or however many years in jail and at least have some sort of life and have my friends when I got out.'

M5 and Trevor Haken are the most recent and most effective undercover police informants of modern times. Alongside the Fitzgerald Inquiry in Queensland, The Royal Commission into the NSW Police Service was arguably the most successful police enquiry ever undertaken. Operation Florida was the largest internal police enquiry in Australian history and successfully exposed a corrupt core of police who had escaped the attention of the Royal Commission.

The star witnesses of both the Royal Commission and Operation Florida have shared a similar fate and it seems now share a similar viewpoint. Haken does not hesitate to reply when asked what he would say to a police officer who is considering the same path as himself at any future enquiry.

'Tell them to fuck off'.

Trevor Haken's story is a great example of how 'whistleblowers' are left high and dry. It is ironic that a government willingly spent tens of millions of dollars on a Royal Commission yet baulks at spending the money to look after Haken who was pivotal in the success of that very commission.

Haken's life after giving evidence has been a long struggle for security. He lives like a ghost. Though Haken has now disappeared, there are still signs of his existence. Years after the Royal

Commission handed down its report, Haken would appear out of nowhere and give evidence against former associates in trials emanating from his evidence. For a long time, his name still appeared on rosters at City Central Police Station in Sydney. He was listed as being on long-term sick leave, a legacy of never having officially resigned or terminated from the New South Wales Police Service. It's a fitting tribute to police bureaucracy, or to their black sense of humour, that one of the most highly publicised protected witnesses was still officially expected to turn up for work.

Within the walls of Central Police Station there was a small secure room. It stored accountable books such as police notebooks and duty books. In a back corner of this room were past briefs of evidence sitting in boxes marked 'Haken Briefs, Do Not Touch'. The briefs were, however, regularly looked at by the curious who viewed Haken with a mixture of contempt, awe and fascination.

When Haken was first approached by the Royal Commission, he was told that no matter what might happen in the future, his welfare and security would be guaranteed by the Royal Commission and the state of NSW. At no point in time was Haken paid in any way for his months of undercover work. He received some expenses for actual costs incurred and for vehicle expenses (as it was being used as a mobile recording studio). Haken was forced to use all of his sick leave and accrued leave and to use his savings to survive as the Royal Commission did not want him to return to active service in order to carry on the undercover role.

At the end of nine months of undercover work, his finances were in ruins. After he was exposed as an undercover operative for the Royal Commission, Haken's bank accounts with the Police Credit Union were frozen. The reason given to Haken as to the refusal of the Royal Commission to compensate him for his loss of salary was that they could not be seen to be buying evidence. Haken was advised to sell his house and promised that he would be assisted in relocating somewhere else. This promise was not kept. Haken kept his end of the bargain. He fulfilled every promise he made, he has attended every matter in court. His struggle to survive over the years since he was first approached in September 1994 has been on many levels. It has taken him nearly ten years to come to some sort of arrangement about which he is not able to speak, but it is clear that he had no other options.

Haken was once called a few days before Christmas to be told that there was a civil action being brought in the courts against him from matters that were raised at the Royal Commission. The Plaintiff in this case, a drug dealer, wanted access to Haken and any of his assets. The Police Integrity Commission (P.I.C) seemed to be assisting the plaintiff in this case by serving documents on Haken but would not assist Haken in defending this action. The P.I.C. has stated to Haken that he would not be assisted in any matter arising from the Royal Commission. It was very clear to Haken that he had no rights and nowhere to go.

Haken gave evidence at the Royal Commission that showed senior police had made it known within the force that any serving member, who held the line, denied corrupt practice and was not prosecuted or convicted as a result of the Royal Commissions enquiries would be looked after by the service. The offer was that those police who held the line would be either given the posting of their choice or would be assisted into a medical pension. Many of Haken's old associates were given medical pensions after being named at the Wood Royal Commission. He wonders, 'How can a man too sick to work as a police officer today be well enough tomorrow to be a security officer with a major firm or an airline or even other government authorities'.

Haken states, 'What is cruel really, is that those people I had a huge degree of trust with and those who I formed an association with have just shut the doors.'

Haken lives by himself. 'I'm trying to ease myself back into society but when you live like a hermit, it's very difficult.'

He does not socialize with anyone. He cannot work. Most things he does have a risk attached to them. Social activities are reduced to shopping for supplies and even this is kept to a minimum. 'When you go into a supermarket the first thing you do is check all the aisles to see who's there.'

As every good 'dog' (surveillance operative) knows, we are all creatures of habit. Accordingly, Trevor Haken's patterns of behaviour are constantly changed to minimise risk. He cannot develop new relationships.

The demands for Haken to continue to give evidence while trying to resolve his own security have been a nightmare.

'I'm living under a package of about four different names. You are living with the scythe over your head saying 'if you don't do what we tell you to do we'll cut you off with nothing'.

His daughter remains upset with those who were meant to look after him.

My dad doesn't have any support, there is no support network. Every time I get to see him he is so unhappy and so angry but he has good reason. He has these people who just piss him off. So for a long time I was the only one he could speak to. There is no one to throw things around to; he is completely out of society. He doesn't have any confidence anymore. They say they'll do something and it doesn't happen. It's all been so sordid; it seems like the biggest waste of someone's life. He could have done less time if he'd killed someone.

Haken has experienced many confronting moments. He recalls one incident in an emotional voice, 'imagine, if you can, driving in a car with two WITSEC (witness security) officers when for no apparent reason they turn off onto a dirt road in a country area. One FEDPOL (Federal Police) officer takes out his Glock (police issue automatic pistol) and racks the slide, then turns and says, 'What information did you give to the Royal Commission about (Federal Police officer named), he's a mate of mine.' The officer handed Haken the pistol who quickly handed it back to him.

When questioned about this, Haken tells me that the officer was suggesting none too subtly that he should 'top himself'. He continues, 'anything could happen to me and who would know and who would care? This is the sort of filthy behaviour by people purporting to look after me. It's an absolute disgrace.'

One of the great promises of faith is that people can change, that there is redemption. Trevor Haken has never done anything by the book, he has walked on both the sunny and dark side of the street, both enforcing the law and breaking it. As far as contributing to the policing of New South Wales and the prevention of future corruption, Haken's decision to tell the truth and become an undercover informant was a momentous decision and a leap of faith. He decided to take a stand and change his life, never imagining ten years down the track the dark place he would find himself.

APPENDIX A

ALL THEIR OWN WORK

A 'notebook confession' was one of many insider terms. Just as detectives had their own rules, they also had their own language and expressions to describe their world:

'A graders' were those who were perceived as being the elite of both the law enforcement (detectives) and criminal fraternity (for example, Neddy Smith). Once you were part of either these elite groups you were 'playing A grade'.

A 'cockatoo' was a lookout at places such as an illegal gambling venue or shooting gallery.

'The Darlo Drop' was where four police officers swung someone they had arrested by the arms and legs, then let go to see if the victim would hit the ceiling. They would then watch as the person fell to the floor. This was a pasttime popularised by Darlinghurst Detectives.

'Goldenhurst' was the name given to Kings Cross by detectives as it was an area where you could make a lot of corrupt money.

A 'rat' or 'dog' is a fellow police officer who breaks the code of silence and reports other officers.

A 'gig' was a police informant.

To 'fit someone up' was to construct false evidence against them. A common practice was to give people 'the trifecta' — charging them with offensive language, assault and resisting arrest, regardless of whether they had committed a crime.

To 'jam somebody' is to ensure by the facts (whether legitimately or not) that bail will be refused or given under such conditions that they could not meet it.

To 'load up' was to plant evidence, such as a weapon or drugs, in order to gain a conviction. For decades there was little, if any, procedure in place for security of drug evidence. It is widely acknowledged that at one stage (for over fifteen months), Central Police Station drug rooms had no security. This was where up to $200 million worth of seized drugs were stored and it was 'wide open'. The room could be accessed with a pocket knife. There was no purity testing and the opportunity to 'recycle drugs' was immense.

'Holding the line' was sticking to an agreed version of events that might not necessarily be the truth.

'Letter of comfort/assistance' was a letter written by police and given to the court before sentencing to show that a criminal had been of assistance. The intention was that the judge would take this into consideration when sentencing.

To 'turn over' a suspect was to search and interrogate someone.

A 'shakedown' was to extort money via the abuse of police powers from licensed and unlicensed premises, drug dealers and crooks.

The 'green light' was when police allowed crooks to carry out crimes in return for money or information.

'The barbecue set' was a social get-together for senior and/or corrupt police in the 1980s. Some of these occasions would include criminals who had been given the 'green light'.

'A cup of tea' was the surreptitious way detectives would drink alcohol by having it served in a teapot. This often took place when receiving a corrupt payment.

A 'drink' was a corrupt payment. A 'gorilla' was $1000, a 'document' was $1000, and a 'monkey' was $500.

When police fabricated evidence during pre-trial meetings, these meetings were called 'scrum downs'. To strengthen a prosecution case they would agree what to say during the trials at the 'scrum downs'. If they were questioned about these meetings in court, they would say that their purpose was to 'refresh each others' memories'. There were times when scrum downs took place while a trial was in progress to counter defence tactics. Police would not admit these meetings to the court.

To 'fillet' or 'gut' a brief was to remove vital evidence from a legal brief.

'Salting of exhibits' was where police interfered with exhibits to assist the prosecution (normally by adding something extra).

'Pulling a brief' was withdrawing a brief in evidence to prevent prosecution.

'Running interference' was doing what one could to interfere with an investigation so that a prosecution might fail.

A 'big girl' or a 'lady' was an ounce of a prohibited drug.

'Whippy' was the name given to money found by police while carrying out a search warrant. When dividing up money taken from a crime scene, police would often say to each other, 'that'll pay for shoe leather'. This would refer to the effort that went into making the bust and was seen as due compensation.

'The whack up' was the division of the money taken while carrying out a search warrant.

'The laugh', 'the giggle' and 'the joke' were the terms given to corrupt payments made to police in return for protection from prosecution.

A 'shooting gallery' was a place where drug users could rent a room, 'shoot up' the dope and rest for a short time. The gallery was often the same place the user could buy the drug from.

'Whistleblowers' (also viewed as a 'rat' or 'dog') were individuals who reported misconduct or corruption within an organisation. Justice Wood noted that whistleblowers faced ostracism, alienation and retribution. A female police officer who gave evidence to the Royal Commission was taken aside by a Kings Cross sergeant and told that she was going to learn her lesson 'the hard way'. She was called a 'dog' by the same sergeant.

'There's a whale in the bay' was code for an internal investigation. A Kings Cross Detective phoned through this cryptic message to another detective who was being investigated.

'THE BETTER OF TWO EVILS' — PHIL GIOVANNI

There were further revelations to come at the Royal Commission regarding other individuals. Also captured on tapes shown at the Commission were meetings between Trevor Haken and Phil Giovanni. Giovanni ran the Penthouse snooker room, which was used as a distribution point for cocaine. Haken regularly met with Giovanni and their association was mutually beneficial. Giovanni got protection and gave Haken information and was part of the 'laugh'.

The Royal Commission was able to tap into an active crooked cell, with tapes providing up-to-the minute information about the ever-changing crime scene they sought to investigate. Haken was away from the street for only a few weeks, but in that time things had changed dramatically. It's an important lesson for any operation based on intelligence — things can change very quickly and the differences can be enormous. Someone who might be a doorman one day is now a street dealer or street heavy. Someone who was considered a pariah might now be back in the fold. Things weren't always what they appeared.

Haken and Giovanni had agreed to meet at the Heart Hotel in Essex Street in The Rocks. The Royal Commission wasn't taking any chances and before Haken left for the meeting investigators insisted he take off his shoes and socks to see that he had nothing concealed. His pants were then searched and his shirt removed to check that he was totally clean. Although Haken was their star informant, his every move would be monitored. He is not sure about other methods they used to check his integrity but is certain these took place. Haken was given his instructions and told that if he varied his movements in any way that he was to report it to tape as he moved along.

Giovanni was suffering from a hangover and so only drank a coke. Haken had his usual soda, lime and bitters. Haken noticed that Giovanni's hands were wounded.

TH: Trevor Haken

PG: Phil Giovanni

UI: Unintelligible conversation

TH: 'Mate, what have you been doing with your hands? Don't tell me, I don't want to know.'

PG: 'You wouldn't believe me if I told you.'

TH: 'What was it?'

PG: 'My missus done that.'

TH: 'Oh yeah, shit. Ta mate. Is she right?'

PG: 'She flipped out on me. I was holdin' her down and she grabbed me finger.'

Giovanni then demonstrates to Haken how his fingers were pushed back.

TH: 'Broke it?'

PG: 'The doctor thinks it's chipped.'

Giovanni then hands Haken a cigarette box with money inside. This was the normal method he used to pay Haken. There was no conversation to indicate what took place. This was also normal procedure.

PG: 'I went to the Eastern Suburbs Leagues Club last night but I was so fuckin' drunk.'

TH: 'With your woman?'

PG: 'Yeah.'

TH: 'After she broke your finger?'

PG: 'Yeah, that was last week; the trouble is we're together too much. Like she got to give me a bit of space, you know what I mean? She sees too much of me you know, doesn't trust me.'

TH: 'Why should she?'

PG: 'Why should she?'

TH: (Laughs) 'This is a nice little place, isn't it?'

PG: 'I've been here two or three times after you.'

(Haken had arranged to meet Giovanni there a number of times but had failed to appear.)

TH: 'Mate, I'm sorry but things just got a bit fuckin' out of hand.'

PG: 'Yeah, I reckon.'

TH: 'Fuck. What have you heard?'

PG: 'Well I heard that ... ah, Louis Bayeh has put you in.'

TH: 'Yeah.'

PG: 'You were suspended for a while.'

TH: 'No, no I fuckin' I went off fuckin' let you know so you know exactly where we're at. Fuckin' I think Louis got a finger in the pie somewhere but … ah no, I just took some time off. 'Cause I had that other business of my own coming up. You know that motor car thing.'

PG: 'Mmm.'

TH: 'And ah, it wouldn't surprise me if Louis' having another slice, 'cause Louis you know, I never got on with him at all. He's just a … um, he's just an arsehole so I can't understand it 'cause I got on all right with the others and …'

PG: 'I wouldn't touch them with a fuckin' forty foot pole, mate.'

TH: '… anyway I just decided to take some time off and wait and see.'

PG: 'Oh yeah, I think mate, I think everything's quietened down a bit. I haven't done anything out of place at all … um, I know what's going on, they're just fuckin' all the premises and apparently they …'

TH: 'Did they hit you at all?'

PG: 'No the boss up there he's [UI] been told to clean up and [UI] no drugs.'

TH: 'That's Brammer.'

PG: 'I don't know who he is.'

TH: 'Yeah, I used to work with him.'

PG: 'Big bloke … and ah, he doesn't mind a bit of gambling and all that but he's cracking down on the drugs.'

TH: 'Yeah.'

PG: 'I don't know, I see, I don't know if I can do anything. But I've got … ah, I've got Rocky (explanation needed from Haken) on the street.'

TH: 'Who?'

PG: 'Rocky. When he came back to me and said … ah Phil, I've made a clean break of things I, I did the wrong thing by you but I apologise and I just got into a habit with the gear and I've given up now … I'm fit, I've been working out in jail and I don't want to touch the stuff.'

Haken and Giovanni then speak about a trotter Giovanni is racing in Gosford. The conversation then returns to Haken's situation.

TH: 'I don't know what to do. It's only been three weeks since I had that court matter and … ah, that was a shit of a week, I tell you. So I just fuck, take a few weeks off to get over that and then I'll think about what I'm going to do. If I go back.'

PG: 'Yeah.'

TH: 'Well it'll be a different kettle of fish completely, but if I don't, well I might.'

PG: 'Might as well.'

TH: 'It just depends on what they want to do with me, 'cause I'm not going to cop some of the shit like fuckin' Kim [Thompson] copped, you know. They've cut his legs off.'

PG: 'It's a fact of life they don't fuckin' seem to understand.'

TH: 'Yeah.'

PG: 'Which is the better of two evils, controlled crime or uncontrolled crime?'

TH: 'I've tried to explain that to people, mate but they just won't listen to you.'

PG: 'With controlled crime you've got … um, you've got … um, everything in hand.'

TH: 'Yep.'

PG: 'And then you put your finger on any fuckin' person. You know who everyone is all the time.'

TH: 'That's what I tried to say when I was up there, there wasn't a murder and there was no bloody gun play, there was nothing went wrong.'

PG: 'Yeah.'

TH: 'And I'm not blowing my bags about it Phil, but when I went, the fuckin' they let that bloody [Russell] Townsend and fuckin' [Danny] Karam in and the bloody street went berserk.'

PG: 'Mm.'

TH: 'It's crazy see, the fuckin', you got those other two lunatics that run the tunnel.'

PG: 'Yeah … ah fuckin' nasty business mate, fuckin' nasty business, that lot.'

TH: 'Very fuckin' nasty's right.'

PG: 'Yeah greedy, evil.'

TH: 'See even your mate, fuckin' your mate Shifty, he's been …'

PG: 'He's not my mate.'

TH: (Laughs) 'I'll use that term loosely, hey?'

PG: 'Apparently he's got charged with someone over an ounce.'

TH: 'I heard that.

PG: 'And ah ... he's out on bail. And ... he's got all the others and they fuckin', they fuckin' start picking on us, good luck to them. Oh they've been um ... threatening Rocky.'

TH: 'Who they have? ... ah John and his brother Sam from Illusions.'

PG: 'Yeah Sam, yeah Abrahams.'

TH: 'What are they fuckin' doin', what are they running slip shod over everybody again now, are they?'

PG: 'Yeah they teamed up with Russell.'

TH: 'Have they? But I thought Russell and Danny had the ... ah, Budget Hotel?'

PG: 'Danny's inside, Danny's inside.'

TH: 'He's gone back in, oh well I'm a week behind the fuckin' times then. It's bloody hard you see because I was, I was in court for a week and then I've been off for a few weeks so it's, you sort of fall behind a bit.'

PG: 'I've got a couple of boys helpin' Ah, they're not fuckin' street smart as Rocky yet, they don't know the ropes, so you know.'

TH: 'Yeah.'

PG: '... 'cause they're checkin' twenty dollar bills and they're markin' twenty dollar bills, you know.'

TH: 'Is that what they're doing?'

PG: 'Yeah.'

TH: 'Fuck.'

PG: 'Poor Rocky, poor cunt, he goes for a feed up at the Thai ah … last week, he takes caps out of his fuckin' mouth, puts them in his shirt pocket and in walks a couple of detectives. Oops, shit — caught. And ah … I didn't hear from him for days and then I, little Billy told me. Told a mate of mine to tell me, and I'm ringing up his girlfriend. Fuckin' stupid little girl wouldn't answer the phone and then she finally told me he was in Long Bay and this fuckin' gook name.'

TH: 'What's that "Who Sang Why" or something?' (Laughs)

PG: 'They said no, he's not here. I tried to track him down and he turns up in jail. He said, "Oh a Chinese mate of mine told me the judge put a thousand dollars bail on me", he admitted to possession and he had no money on him. I said you stupid cunt. Fuck it. But my mate, he's pretty good, he's … ah they won't get "boo" out of him.'

TH: 'Yeah, no, well he … he amazed me when he got carved up.'

PG: 'He didn't want to dob, did he?'

TH: 'No never told me a word. I couldn't believe it, I thought he was so, I thought he was deadset going to Chinese heaven, mate.'

PG: 'He wanted to get the guy himself … They threatened him, they threatened to kill him now.'

TH: 'Did they? Who threatened him, John and that?'

PG: 'No, Russell's boys.'

TH: 'Mate, where does fuckin' Russell [Townsend] come from? He's fuckin' he come out of the fuckin' woodwork.'

PG: 'Just a big dumbo, that's Russell.'

TH: 'Yeah but he was workin' on the bloody ...'

PG: '... on the doors, you know.'

TH: 'Mate the only time I remember him, he was working at the top of the stairs for Con. But then all of a sudden he came out fuckin' like Lord Muck, mate, I can't work him out, it's got me fucked. Like he never pays me any ...'

PG: 'The rumour is that the Lebs [Lebanese] are going to fuckin' get him.'

TH: 'Bad luck for him.'

PG: 'For Rocky.'

TH: 'No don't worry about Rocky, you keep him under wraps, no I don't care if the Lebs take Russell out [UI] but that's with John and Sam [Ibrahim].'

PG: 'Yeah.'

TH: 'John and Sam aren't with Billy [Bayeh] though, are they?'

PG: 'They're with Billy, yeah.'

TH: 'They're with Billy too? Has Billy moved back with 'em? 'Cause I was told that they were at loggerheads.'

PG: 'Um ... [UI] they're all the, they're behind the tunnel talkin' every day, fuckin'.'

TH: 'What about your mate bald-headed Tony?'

PG: 'I believe they knifed a guy recently in the Cross.'

TH: 'I read about um ... one got knifed last week. But I didn't see who.'

283

PG: 'Mate everytime Rocky walks past him, he gets on the phone straightaway ... ring the nick, cunt.'

There is talk about an arrest of a friend of Giovanni's and how Giovanni's restaurant is going.

TH: 'If Rocky's goin' the same as he used to, he had a pretty good bloody set-up.'

PG: 'Mmm, oh he's a good. But ... ah the Lebs. [UI] Caught up in last week punched him in the mouth and bashed him.'

TH: 'Who's bloody, who's doin' that for 'em?'

PG: 'Um ... one of the Lebs.'

TH: 'One of the Lebs themselves?'

PG: 'Yeah. So you know they probably don't know who he's workin' or what. You know they [UI] they don't want him ... they don't cut it.'

TH: 'They don't like competition.'

PG: 'Yeah, you got something pretty good and even marketable you know, it's clean, no chemicals in it and they prefer that, whereas [UI] Cocaine [UI] cocktail.'

TH: 'Mixing?'

PG: 'Yeah, they're mixing cocktails [UI].'

TH: 'Yeah, Speed. That's a fuckin' dangerous combination when they put that speed with the bloody ...'

PG: 'Yeah it gives them a quick instant rush and five minutes later he's ... it doesn't last long.'

TH: 'Yeah but that's what they want.'

PG: 'They're backing up again.'

TH: 'That's what they want, mate. Hey that's why I prefer him to have a leg in town. You'd be all right you know. [UI] doesn't it?'

PG: '[UI] killing off your customers, they don't live as long. You've got to keep 'em alive.'

TH: 'They're no good to you dead.'

PG: (Laughs)

TH: 'Like Grace Bros, isn't it? Keep the accounts comin' mate. Oh dear. But it's right what you said mate, if you, if it'd been allowed to continue there weren't any fuckin' killings, there weren't any fuckin' shootings or bashings until these pricks fuckin' got an open hand. It gives me the shits.'

PG: 'Can't you talk to someone?'

TH: 'Well that's what I'm thinking about getting back. Because if I can get back up there, I know the bloke who's in charge, he's a bit of a squarehead [straight] but at least he understands the rules. Mate, I thought I was going to get the sack, if it went down on that matter they would have just given me the arse.'

PG: 'But it worked out all right?'

TH: 'Yeah ... got acquitted on all matters. Oh fuck, it was only a stink with the insurance company in the first place.'

PG: 'Mm.'

TH: 'You know, so anyway I've got two lives, either they let me go back and I get promotion or I'm going to tell them to jam it. See if [UI] you know 'cause I'm not going to stick this fuckin' business of sitting there punching machines all day.'

PG: 'You ought to be fuckin' Chief Inspector by now with everything I've given you.' (Laughs)

TH: 'Well mate fuckin' hey that's all you need is a few good jobs and you're fuckin' you should get promoted but that's not the way the silly pricks work.'

They talk more about some past associates and then the discussion turns to the Bayehs.

PG: 'Stupidest fuckin' thing I ever did was give up to the fuckin' Bayehs. Billy, I should have chased him out of town. Fuckin' stupidest thing I ever done in my life.'

TH: 'Yeah well you're not on your own there mate. That's the trouble with Billy, he comes across as being bloody all right, till he gets the upper hand and then he fuckin' just drops you like a hot potato. And he does worse than that, doesn't he? Hey, what he did to you was unforgivable.'

PG: 'Yeah he's been tryin' to crawl up me arse ever since. I don't want to know him. He said to me one night, Phil, "I'm a cunt [laughs] but I'm not a dog." I fuckin' walked away laughing.'

TH: 'Yeah.'

PG: 'There's plenty worse than him, you know. If I can get hold of that Lebanese Tony [baldy Tony, the "Inspector"] ... He's fuckin' dangerous, you know. He's always in somebody's ear. He's got a brother or something in Redfern.'

TH: 'No, no, no, no it's his cousin, yeah.'

PG: 'They're all cousins.'

TH: 'Yeah, I think they must be all one family. They all got one pair of parents over in fuckin' Lebanon.'

PG: 'Yeah, I'll tell you the go. You know that tunnel there, where the road swings around?'

TH: 'Comes up from Victoria Street.'

PG: 'Yeah, they do their talking out back there. If you can get a listening device around there one afternoon or something. They don't talk inside the club.'

TH: 'They all talk just outside the back.'

PG: 'Yes.'

TH: 'Who's that, Billy and Tony?'

PG: 'Yeah, they all talk away there with their cousins.'

TH: 'Yeah.'

PG: 'Get a listening device and hang the lot of them. Um, will you get a bit of cover for Rocky?'

TH: 'Yeah, well that's what I was just thinkin' about ... um.'

PG: 'Cause they're fuckin' hassling the fuck out of him. They take him in every day.'

TH: 'Yeah. Let me go and have a yarn to somebody up there. Keep off the main street to the back and fuckin' he should be all right. All right mate, I'll see you. I'll give you a ring, if I don't give you a ring later this week.'

ENDNOTES

Prologue

1. The television program, *A Current Affair*, had proposed that something strange and sinister had taken place and that police were obviously covering up.
2. *Accountability, Decentralisation of Power and Government, Sweden and Canada*, Churchill Report, John Hatton.
3. *Sun-Herald*, 15 May 1994
4. *Sun-Herald*, 15 May 1994, p. 29
5. *Daily Telegraph*, 3 October 1995, p. 1
6. *Daily Telegraph*, 3 October 1995, p. 1
7. *Sydney Morning Herald*, 29 July 1994
8. *Canberra Times*, 29 July 1994
9. *Sydney Morning Herald*, 29 July 1994
10. *Sun-Herald*, 24 May 1994
11. *Sun-Herald*, 15 May 1994, p. 1
12. *Sydney Morning Herald*, 1 May 1997

Chapter 1

1. *Sydney Morning Herald*, 4 September 2004, News Review, p. 33
2. See Appendix A
3. 'Bumper' Farrell was a legendary figure in Sydney policing in the mid-twentieth century, noted for his brutal methods.
4. *Daily Telegraph*, 'The Shame of Bayeh's Lawyer'
5. Statutory Declaration — Trevor Haken, p. 148
6. *Character and Cops: Ethics in Policing*, AEI Press, Washington DC, p. 37

Chapter 3

1. *Sun-Herald*, 27 June 1971
2. *Sydney Morning Herald*, 5 July 1971

3. *Sydney Morning Herald,* 11 July 1971
4. Statutory Declaration, p. 2

Chapter 4

1. Statutory Declaration, p. 2
2. *Sydney Morning Herald,* 7 November 1995, p. 5
3. *Daily Telegraph,* 7 November 1995, p. 7
4. *Sydney Morning Herald,* 7 November 1995, p. 5

Chapter 5

1. Statutory Declaration, p. 3
2. Statutory Declaration, p. 3
3. Statutory Declaration, p. 4
4. Statutory Declaration, p. 4
5. Statutory Declaration, p. 4
6. Statutory Declaration, p. 4
7. Statutory Declaration, p. 4
8. Statutory Declaration, p. 5
9. The Royal Commission (Final Report Volume 2. May 1977, p. xvi) reported that 'A graders' was an expression used by police to describe the perceived elite members of the Police Service, usually referring to senior detectives in the specialist squads and task forces.
10. Statutory Declaration, p. 5
11. Statutory Declaration, p. 5

Chapter 6

1. Statutory Declaration, p. 6
2. *Telegraph,* 22 August 1995, p. 4
3. *Sydney Morning Herald,* 22 August 1995, p. 5
4. *Sydney Morning Herald,* 18 August 1995, p. 6
5. Statutory Declaration p. 6
6. Statutory Declaration p. 6
7. Statutory Declaration p. 7
8. Statutory Declaration p. 7

9. *Line of Fire*, Allen and Unwin, 2nd edition, 1995
10. Statutory Declaration p. 9
11. Statutory Declaration p. 10
12. Statutory Declaration p. 11
13. Statutory Declaration p. 11
14. Statutory Declaration p. 11
15. Statutory Declaration p. 11
16. Statutory Declaration p. 12
17. *Telegraph*, 'Motoring Towards the Truth', 28 September 1995

Chapter 7

1. Evidence to the Royal Commission on the Joint Federal and State Task Force into Drug Trafficking. Royal Commission into the NSW Police Service. Final Report Volume 1. Corruption. May 1997, p. 186
2. Final Report into the Royal Commission into the NSW Police Service, p. 184
3. *Sun-Herald*, 24 September 1995, p. 35
4. *Sydney Morning Herald*, 10 February 1995, p. 4
5. Statutory Declaration p. 13
6. Statutory Declaration p. 13
7. *Sydney Morning*, 28 September 1995, p. 8
8. *Daily Telegraph*, 21 September 1995
9. *Daily Telegraph*, 21 September 1995
10. Statutory Declaration p. 13
11. Statutory Declaration p. 13
12. Royal Commission into the New South Wales Police Service. Final Report Volume 2: Reform May 1997, p. xvi
13. *Sydney Morning Herald*, 26 September 1995, p. 6
14. *Daily Telegraph*, 5 October 1995, p. 17
15. Statutory Declaration p. 16
16. Statutory Declaration, p. 16
17. *Sydney Morning Herald*, 4 October 1995, p. 6
18. *Daily Telegraph*, 4 October 1995, quoting evidence at the Royal Commission from the Fed JTF14

19. *Daily Telegraph*, 4 October 1995
20. *Sydney Morning Herald*, 26 September 1995, p. 6
21. *Sydney Morning Herald*, 4 October 1995
22. *Daily Telegraph*, 5 October 1995, p. 17
23. Statutory Declaration p. 16
24. Statutory Declaration p. 18
25. *Daily Telegraph*, 19 September 1995, 'Officer attacks inquiry on tape', p. 4
26. *Daily Telegraph*, 19 September 1995, p. 4
27. *Sun-Herald*, 24 September 1995, p. 35
28. *Sydney Morning Herald*, 28 September 1995, p. 8
29. *Daily Telegraph*, 13 February 1996, p. 15
30. *The Australian*, 18 September 1995, 'Police Chief faces grilling over secret inquiry tapes', p. 4
31. *Daily Telegraph*, 19 September 1995, 'Corrupt link' between chiefs,' p. 1
32. *Daily Telegraph*, 21 September 1995, p. 1
33. Statutory Declaration, p. 19

Chapter 9
1. Statutory Declaration, p. 22
2. Statutory Declaration, p. 23
3. Statutory Declaration, p. 23
4. Statutory Declaration, p. 22
5. Statutory Declaration, p. 22
6. Statutory Declaration, p. 22
7. Statutory Declaration, p. 23
8. Statutory Declaration, p. 23
9. Statutory Declaration, p. 24
10. Statutory Declaration, p. 26
11. Statutory Declaration, p. 28

Chapter 10
1. Statutory Declaration, p. 38
2. Statutory Declaration, p. 38

3. Statutory Declaration, p. 38
4. Harry Blackburn was a scientific officer in the police force. The inquiry, led by Carl Spain and Phil Minkely, set out to investigate allegations against Blackburn of sexual assault, for political purposes they paraded him before the media when they arrested him. Subsequently, after a further inquiry led by Clive Small, the charges were withdrawn and he was compensated.
5. Statutory Declaration, p. 31
6. *Sydney Morning Herald*, 23 September 1995, 'On a Roll: Policemen Singing at the Royal Commission', p. 6
7. Statutory Declaration, p. 31
8. Statutory Declaration, p. 32
9. Termed thus by Sydney's *Daily Telegraph*, 21 June 1995
10. *Sydney Morning Herald*, 13 October 1995, p. 7
11. *Daily Telegraph*, 4 July 1995, p. 4
12. Statutory Declaration, p. 29
13. Statutory Declaration, p. 30
14. Statutory Declaration, p. 30
15. Statutory Declaration, pp. 30–31
16. Statutory Declaration, p. 46
17. Statutory Declaration, p. 32

Chapter 11

1. *Sydney Morning Herald*, 2 December 1995
2. *Sun-Herald*, 22 October 1995, p. 33
3. Tom Domican was known as an enforcer and a violent standover man, who had connections with the Labor Party. Bill Bayeh told Haken that he paid Domican $1000 a week to stay out of the Cross, while Louis paid him to act as his bodyguard and enforcer. He had been charged with murder a number of times but was always acquitted. Domican's house was fired at by Christopher Dale Flannery. Flannery later disappeared in mysterious circumstances; his body has never been found.
4. Statutory Declaration, p. 56

5. Statutory Declaration, p. 40–41
6. *Daily Telegraph*, 14 July 1995, 'Tactics forced me out', p. 4
7. *Sydney Morning Herald*, 15 July 1995, p. 10
8. Statutory Declaration, p. 43
9. Statutory Declaration, p. 43
10. Statutory Declaration, p. 56
11. Statutory Declaration, p. 64
12. Statutory Declaration, p. 76
13. Statutory Declaration, p. 69
14. Statutory Declaration, p. 76
15. Statutory Declaration, p. 64
16. Statutory Declaration, p. 75
17. Statutory Declaration, p. 75
18. Statutory Declaration, p. 77
19. Statutory Declaration, p. 82
20. Statutory Declaration, p. 77
21. Statutory Declaration, p. 79
22. Statutory Declaration, p. 79
23. Statutory Declaration, p. 82
24. Statutory Declaration, p. 83
25. Statutory Declaration, p. 83
26. Statutory Declaration, p. 42
27. Statutory Declaration, p. 83
28. Statutory Declaration, p. 83
29. Statutory Declaration, p. 92
30. Statutory Declaration, p. 96

Chapter 12

1. Drury was a police officer set up by other police and shot in his own home by Christopher Flannery.
2. Connie had a cottage industry that supplied urine samples for heroine-using addicts to present at the methadone clinic. Connie was the link between the Pergers and the Salviettis.

Chapter 13

1. Statutory Declaration, p. 39
2. *Daily Telegraph*, 6 October 1995, p. 2
3. Statutory Declaration, p. 39
4. Statutory Declaration, p. 39
5. Statutory Declaration, p. 39
6. *Daily Telegraph*, 6 October 1995, p. 2
7. Statutory Declaration, p. 34
8. When tapes from listening devices planted in Haken's car were played at the Royal Commission, one outstanding feature was the foul language used by police. Associate Professor Brian Taylor, the Director of the University of Sydney's Language Centre, told a Sydney newspaper that the 'language of the police served a solitary function — to show that you belonged to a group'.
9. Statutory Declaration, p. 42
10. Statutory Declaration, p. 13
11. Statutory Declaration, p. 156
12. *Daily Telegraph* 14 March 1996, 'Jailed witness decides to come clean'

Chapter 14

1. Statutory Declaration, pp. 31–32

Chapter 15

1. *Daily Telegraph*, 7 June 1995

www.ingramcontent.com/pod-product-compliance
Lightning Source LLC
Chambersburg PA
CBHW032117020426
42334CB00016B/989